HOOKED ON A
PHOENIX

ASHLYN CHASE

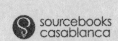
sourcebooks
casablanca

Published by Sourcebooks Casablanca, an imprint of Sourcebooks, Inc.
P.O. Box 4410, Naperville, Illinois 60567-4410
(630) 961-3900
Fax: (630) 961-2168
sourcebooks.com

Printed and bound in United States of America.
OPM 10 9 8 7 6 5 4 3 2 1

To Peggy and Dave, my favorite Canadian couple.

(Hey, what do you want? I've run out of family and American friends to dedicate books to.)

Also, Peggy is my fabulous beta reader who has kept my series bible up to date, so I don't forget the details of past characters. It may be six hours between books for a reader, but it's six months between writing one to the next. I can barely remember what I ate for breakfast yesterday, never mind what color Drake's eyes were five books ago! According to Peggy, his eyes are green, and I had a muffin yesterday morning.

Chapter 1

"DO YOU WANT EVERYONE TO HEAR US? KEEP YOUR VOICE down," Gabe whispered to Parker Carlisle, his best friend since childhood. He scanned the celebrants at his brother Jayce's Christmas Eve wedding reception. No one was paying any attention to them—until his mother looked up. She didn't have paranormal hearing like her sons and husband, but that never stopped her from knowing exactly what was going on. Her smile faded as she took in Gabe's serious expression.

Gabriella Fierro wandered over to the son named in her honor.

Gabe muttered, "Oh, shit. My mother is coming. Look at the cake or something. Act like nothing is wrong."

"Nothing *is* wrong, except you're being an idiot." Parker was wearing his dress uniform, probably for the first time. The guy was fresh out of basic training but looked like a national hero standing there beside the dance floor.

"We'll talk later…"

Mrs. Fierro looked radiant in her teal-blue mother-of-the-groom evening gown. Her short, freshly colored auburn hair made her appear years younger than fifty-five. "Is everything all right over here?"

"Hi, Mom. We're fine."

"It's nice to see you again, Parker. Don't you look handsome and grown-up in your uniform. It's been, what, five or six years since you moved from the neighborhood?"

"Ten, but who's counting?" Parker smiled.

"Really? Ten years since your parents… I'm sorry. I shouldn't bring up such a sad event at a happy occasion like this." She touched his arm gently.

"Don't worry. It's been a long time, and Misty and I have adjusted."

Gabe snorted. *He wants me to spy on his sister while he's gone. He calls that adjusting?*

Mrs. Fierro frowned at her son. "Gabriel?"

Damn. His mother never had to say more than her children's names, and they'd fess up to anything. She just kept her gaze on him and waited. It never failed. But this time, he wouldn't give up any information. No. Matter. What.

She glanced back and forth between her son and his best friend. "What's going on here?"

After another uncomfortable moment of silence, Parker caved. "It's nothing to worry about, Mrs. Fierro. I just asked Gabe to keep an eye on my little sister while I'm overseas."

Gabe clenched his jaw. That was enough to get his mother involved.

"Overseas? You're being deployed?"

"Yes, ma'am. Not yet, though. I have to go through some specialty training before going to Afghanistan."

"Oh my goodness! Gabe, did you know about this?"

He sighed. "Yes, Mom. I did. I just don't want to be responsible, you know, all the time." *I also don't like the idea of spying.*

Gabriella jammed her hands on her hips. "Gabriel Peter Fierro. How dare you? You're a firefighter. You're responsible for people every single day. Are you telling me you can't be there for Misty? She's practically one of the family."

Gabe looked away.

When he didn't answer, his mother bristled. "Don't think you can pull that *strong silent type* thing with me. I'm going to get to the bottom of this." She turned to Parker and took his hands in hers. "Of course he'll keep an eye on Misty. We'll *all* be there for her, if she needs anything. Anything at all."

Parker let out a sigh of relief. "Thank you, Mrs. Fierro. I'll rest easier knowing she has someone here in the city who cares about her—and your whole family to turn to." He glanced at Gabe. "She shouldn't need anything, anyway. She wants to be independent. She's not here tonight because she's volunteering at a homeless shelter. She insists she's old enough to take care of herself, but she's only twenty-two. I know she's technically an adult, but…"

Mrs. Fierro smiled. "I understand. We were all twenty-two once. At that age, kids think and act like they're immortal. But as firefighters know, that's not the case." She gave Gabe a stern look. As if reminding him that he and his brothers were nearly immortal but their friends were not.

"Ma. It's not just that."

She stared at her son and waited. When he didn't continue, she crossed her arms. "Then elaborate!"

Gabe was saved by his older brother—the groom— excusing himself from a dance with their aunt to come over and drape his arms around Gabe and Parker. "Why the serious expressions? This is a celebration. You're all supposed to be happy…for me!"

Mrs. Fierro broke into a grin and cupped Jayce's cheek. "We're very happy for you, darling. I was just telling Gabe he should be next. I want grandchildren!"

"Oh, Christ." Jayce rolled his eyes. "Why don't you wait until one son is on his honeymoon before you start hounding the others?"

"You're right, darling. Now get back to that beautiful wife of yours and give her a hug for me."

Jayce looked over his shoulder and spotted Kristine talking with her mother and new stepfather. He grinned. "I think I'll do that."

Gabriella narrowed her gaze at her younger son. "I gave you an out, but I want more detail," she demanded. "Not that I don't want you to have a wife and children, but that's not what this is about. We'll have that discussion another day."

Gabe groaned.

"Will you excuse us for a moment, Parker?"

"Of course."

"Come, Gabriel. Dance with your mother. And smile!"

Gabe muttered under his breath. He knew he was in for it now. At least on the dance floor, she wouldn't smack him upside the head. She took one look at the Joker grin he had plastered on his face and said, "Dear God. That smile is frightening. Never mind. Just wear a neutral expression."

When he obliged, her voice took on a sympathetic quality. "Talk to me, honey. What's really bothering you?"

When she used that tone of voice, he had to open up. She was nothing if not the most understanding woman on earth. She might not like whatever he told her, but she'd put herself in his shoes before reacting.

He sighed. "You're right that I'm a firefighter and I can be responsible for strangers for a few minutes. But this is different. I can't handle taking care of someone long-term—especially someone special to us, like Misty."

"Why not?"

He hung his head. "You know. I'm just not good at taking care of…things."

"Is this about the dog?"

Gabe bit his lip and nodded.

"Oh, honey. That was years ago. You were a kid. Don't tell me you've been holding on to that all these years."

"Mom. That dog was my responsibility, and while you guys went skiing, I made up an excuse to stay home and lose my virginity."

She rolled her eyes. "I remember. You were fifteen, and you paid the price long ago. As I recall, we grounded you for a month, and you grounded yourself for another one."

"Nothing you and Dad could have done to me would have been worse than my own guilt over leaving Buddy outside where anyone could untie him." He felt a burning behind his eyes. Before tears could leak out, he straightened and took a deep breath, steeling himself against the emotional threat.

His mother squeezed the hand she held. "I recognize that reaction. Your father would do that occasionally when he told me about some horrific thing that happened on the job."

He couldn't speak. He just let his throat close up, staring off into the distance over the happy crowd. Fortunately, his mother didn't press him. This *wasn't* a stranger they were talking about. It would devastate him if he let something happen to Misty.

His mother was right. She was almost part of their family. She'd followed Parker everywhere after their parents died. When she wasn't occupied with dance class or school, she wanted to be part of whatever he was doing.

Parker had never treated her like a tagalong kid. She wasn't underfoot, so Gabe hadn't really noticed. The elderly Carlisle grandparents tried to keep everything as normal as they could, but eventually, they couldn't pay the taxes on a pricey South End town house and support all of them on a fixed income. So they moved to the suburbs.

Recently, Parker and Misty had lost their grandparents. Now Parker was trusting Gabe to take care of the only Carlisle family member left—while he was halfway around the world serving their country. Gabe was screwed. They both were.

Gabe had tried to come up with a plan that wouldn't look suspicious. Nothing like opening a new bank account at a branch about as far away from his place of work as he could get...

Misty worked in the financial district as a bank teller. He understood why she'd moved from Saugus back to Boston. Once this city was in your blood, it almost never left. The suburbs must've been pretty dull for a fun-loving twenty-two-year-old. According to Parker, she'd spent the last few years taking care of their elderly grandparents. The girl deserved some fun.

Parker had given him her address before he returned to Camp Lejeune for additional training. She couldn't afford the pricey financial district, so she had found an apartment in an old building in the North End. Gabe worried about her living there. He had heard about some rapes in that neighborhood, and as much as she claimed to be an adult, from Parker's description she was still an idealistic kid.

Gabe had taken the subway to North Station. Before continuing on, he surfaced and tromped around the old Italian neighborhood, looking for her address. Sandwiched between other old buildings, it wasn't the worst place on the block, but it wasn't the best either. He hoped there was a way to figure out which floor she was on. She'd be safer on an upper floor.

He quietly crept up the stairs to the small porch and saw two mailboxes. One said *Carlisle*. At least she was smart enough not to use her first name, indicating a female living alone.

Gabe was in the mood for a walk. It wasn't that far to the financial district, and he needed to clear his head. He had racked his brain trying to think of some other way to casually keep an eye on her. He came up empty, so he walked to the bank to open a new checking account.

He'd just tell her he was being transferred to the nearby fire station soon and wanted to have a handy place to do his banking. If that didn't tip her off, his coming in person to deposit his paycheck probably would. He'd just have to worry about that later.

When he finally made it to the bank, he tried to look casual as he scanned the tellers, looking for a little girl with long brown braids. Naturally, she'd look a little different by now, but that's how he remembered her.

When he didn't see anyone who could have been that

girl, he was afraid he might have come on her day off. He checked the tellers' nameplates and was shocked to realize the gorgeous brunette with long wavy tresses and a slammin' body was in fact Misty.

Whoa. His dick twitched. *This can't be happening.* His best friend's little sister was a grown *woman.* The first woman in a long time to rev up his libido. *Shit. Now what?*

He got in her line, despite it being the longest, and waited his turn. He could probably have approached one of the offices and asked for the manager, but doing it this way would give him a chance to "accidentally" discover she was there.

Oh my. What a surprise. Who knew you were working here? It sounded stupid, but it was all he had.

When it was finally his turn, he did his best acting job—not that it was very good. "Hello, miss. I'm here to… Wait a minute. I know you…" Then he made it look like he was staring at her name tag, but he was actually staring at her full breasts. His breath caught, and he had to get ahold of himself in order to speak without squeaking like his fourteen-year-old self. "Misty? Misty Carlisle?"

Recognition lit up her hazel-brown eyes. "Gabe? Oh my God. What are you doing here?" Then she laughed. "Well, obviously, you're doing your banking, but I didn't realize you lived around here."

"Oh, I don't. I was just…thinking of moving to the area, because it looks like I'm going to be transferred to your local firehouse."

"I guess you're following in the family tradition, then?"

"Absolutely. I wouldn't want to do anything else," he said proudly.

"Well, now I feel even safer, knowing you're on the job." Her grin could melt the polar ice cap, or whatever was left of it after global warming and his inner heat had done its work.

The fact that she always felt safe in a city this size and volunteered at a homeless shelter suggested that she might still be a little idealistic or naive. The guys in the shelter were sometimes hardened criminals. Some of his cop buddies had told him stories that raised the hair on the back of his neck.

Dammit. No wonder Parker wanted someone to keep an eye on her. And yet she wanted to be independent. This was no easy assignment.

"That's sweet. I take it you live around here?"

"Not really. I live in the North End. It's a short walk, and I enjoy it on pleasant days."

"There aren't many of those at this time of year."

"If anyone would know that, it's you firefighters. I can't imagine working in some of the conditions you have to go out in."

He shrugged. "Yeah, there are times I kind of wish I could sit behind a desk, but most of the time, I love my job."

She smiled shyly. "I like what you do too."

Someone behind him cleared his throat.

Gabe realized he'd better get down to business. "So, how do I go about setting up an account here?"

"I'll get the manager for you." She left her window and exited through a side door, coming around to the customer area. "Just follow me."

Her black pencil skirt hugged her perfectly formed bottom, and her hips swished as she walked. He could almost feel himself salivating. *Good God. I hate you, Parker.*

Misty poked her head into an office marked ADAM FORSYTH, MANAGER. "Hi, Adam. My friend here would like to open a new account."

The manager frowned at Gabe. That didn't seem like a very friendly reaction to a new customer.

"Friend?"

"Yes," Misty said. "This is Gabe Fierro. I've known him forever." She smiled at Gabe, and he couldn't help smiling back.

The manager sat up straight and said, "Well, come in."

During their chitchat, when Gabe revealed the fact that he was a firefighter, the man's demeanor softened. *Yup*, Gabe thought. *Everyone loves a firefighter.* And yet his youngest brother, Luca, wanted to be a cop. He knew of at least fifteen cops who had become firefighters just because they were tired of being hated.

It only took about twenty minutes and his most recent paycheck before he was all set and ready to be on his way. He glanced back at Misty before leaving and saw a terrified expression on her face.

"What the hell is happening?" he asked the manager.

"Huh?" He followed Gabe's nod in Misty's direction. "Oh my God. We're being robbed!"

Gabe had learned through his firefighting career to assess a situation before charging in. The security guard had been disarmed by a tall, heavyset man. Hands raised, the other tellers had backed away from their windows by about three feet.

Misty was the only one frozen in place, and a bald, wiry guy in front of her seemed to be holding a weapon. He was left-handed, so Gabe couldn't see it, but Misty probably had.

Gabe turned to the manager and said, "Shit, dude. You're the manager. Help her." The manager was hesitating, so Gabe stepped in. He strode over toward the guy threatening Misty. "What's going on here?"

"Like I said, hands in the air!" As soon as Misty raised her hands, the criminal gave Gabe an evil smile and turned the gun on him. "You sound like the manager, except that you're dressed too casually for that. Don't be a heroic customer."

Beyond Gabe, the manager was just disappearing back into his office until the guy yelled to his accomplice, "Go get him, dumb-ass, before he calls the cops."

The manager tried to slam the door closed before the big guy got there. But the guy stuck his foot in the door and pushed it open. Grabbing the manager, he hauled him out to the customer area.

"What do you want me to do with him, boss?"

"Make him lock the front door, then bring him here. Get the other two on the ground with their hands behind their heads first."

"You heard him," he said to Gabe and the security guard.

The security guard lay down, but Gabe didn't.

"I told you not to be a hero," the robber said through gritted teeth.

Gabe didn't move.

"What's the matter? Do you want proof that the gun is loaded?" The guy fired a shot into the air, and everyone jumped. The noise reverberated around the high ceilings.

Gabe was filled with a cold chill, but this was no time to lose his head. "If you let the employees go, I'll cooperate."

The guy laughed. "Nobody's going anywhere, except you. You're going to meet your maker if you don't lie down, *now*."

Gabe reluctantly kneeled and put his hands behind his head.

"What are you, stupid? I said *lie down*."

Gabe had hoped that if he distracted the robbers, Misty would be able to hit whatever emergency button would call the cops. So far, she hadn't lowered her hands, so he doubted his plan had worked.

He sighed and lay down with his head to one side so he could keep an eye on Misty's window. If this guy went after her...

"Now, Mr. Manager, lock the door, then come back here and tell me how to open the vault."

"It's on a timer. I can't open it unless it's eight a.m. or four p.m."

"Yup. We already knew that, so it's a good thing you didn't lie. It's almost four o'clock now. Lock the damn door!"

The manager scurried off to do as the guy demanded.

The scrawny, bald robber waved his gun toward the other employees. "All of you get on the floor too. I'd say get comfortable, folks, but I doubt that's possible on the cold, hard floor. Oh well, too bad for you."

When Misty didn't move, he pointed the gun at her again. "What's your problem, sweetheart? Are you deaf?"

"Can't you see she's frozen in fear?" Gabe shouted.

He hoped he hadn't just put Misty in danger. Visions of his dead dog, bloody, broken, and lying against the curb, crossed his mind at that moment. *Oh God, if this guy hurts her...I couldn't live with myself.*

"Okay, sweetheart. You're going to be the one opening the vault. Back away."

Misty's voice shook as she answered, "B-but I don't know the combination."

"That's okay. Your manager does. Now get over to it and wait there." The guy muttered under his breath, but Gabe heard him say, "I want to see that spectacular ass," and then he licked his lips.

Misty was finally able to move, but Gabe couldn't see her. He started to get up.

"Where do you think you're going?" the heavyset one asked.

"I'm an EMT. I want to keep an eye on the tellers to make sure everyone's all right."

"Sometimes you don't get what you want."

Then the boss criminal looked as if he were thinking something over. "You know what? It's your lucky day, hero. I changed my mind. In case anyone comes to the door, I want it to look like the bank is closed. Mr. Manager, turn out the lights. I want everyone behind the counter on the floor, facing the back wall. Don't even think about getting near an emergency button. As you saw, the gun is loaded."

Chapter 2

MISTY HAD HOPED SHE COULD FIND A MOMENT TO HIT THE emergency button under the counter. The gunman didn't ask the tellers to empty their drawers, during which time one of them could have tripped the silent alarm or at least slipped a dye pack in with the money.

They were going after the bigger haul. The vault. And it sounded as if they knew what they were doing.

As the manager, security guard, and Gabe were marched into the teller area, Misty hoped a customer would come up the steps, see what was going on, and call the cops. She listened carefully, but all she heard were the sounds of traffic and her coworker's sniffles. She glanced over at Betsy, a young mother of two, and hoped nothing would happen to her. To any of them. Even her slimy manager, Adam.

Gabe caught her eye and gave her a pointed look. She gave him a slight headshake. She didn't want him trying to be a hero. She couldn't believe her lousy luck. After all this time, finally moving back to the city as an independent woman, the last thing she needed was for her childhood crush to feel like he had to rescue her—like a surrogate big brother.

If he lived through this, he'd tell Parker. If he didn't live through this, she'd die. She'd adored Gabe during their years growing up in the South End. Their brownstone was three doors down from the Fierros, and when they were young, it wasn't easy to find kids in the neighborhood to play with. But the Fierros' door was always open to her, and Gabe had always treated her kindly. Of course, it was probably just because she was Parker's little sister, but she had hoped there was more to it. To say she liked him would be tantamount to saying bears liked picnic baskets.

She had hoped they'd run into each other at some point and was secretly thrilled to see him here today. Although she would have preferred they'd met at a different time and place.

"On the floor!"

The robber's harsh voice jolted her out of her musing.

The security guard and manager lay face down, but Gabe walked around them and went down on his knees in front of Misty. She was the only one standing, and to be honest, she was leaning against the vault to keep her knees from shaking. She was dizzy and felt like she might faint.

Gabe's reassuring presence calmed her somewhat. He gave her a quick smile then lay down with his hands braced on the floor next to his shoulders.

"Okay, lady. Face the lock."

As soon as she turned around, the criminal whistled. "Ha. I knew she'd have a spectacular ass. That's why I asked you to do this, sweetheart."

She wanted to argue with the guy, tell him she wasn't his sweetheart and refuse to cooperate, but he'd probably call it "being mouthy," and that wouldn't help right now.

Adam was giving directions to her, but she barely heard him.

"What?" she said with a tremor.

"Tell her again." The gunman kicked the manager's leg.

"I said turn the lock to the left four times all the way

around. Then stop at zero, and turn it to the right three times. Stop at twenty-one."

Misty did as he said, spinning the dial left four times.

"Not like that. It's very sensitive—and old. Turn it slowly and carefully."

Misty took a deep breath and let it out, trying to relax. She had already forgotten if she had gone around three times or four. Her hand shook. "I don't think I can do this. Can my manager take over, please?"

The gunman placed his foot on the manager's ass. "You'd like that, wouldn't you?" He chuckled. "Sometimes there's a code the manager can dial in, but I'm betting you don't know that either, sweetheart. So you're my choice for doing this. Pull yourself together."

"I'll do it," Gabe said.

The gunman rolled his eyes. "The customer wants to be a hero again. Fine. I don't like the way you look like you're ready to spring, anyway. But understand, I have my gun trained on your girlfriend."

"Shit," Gabe muttered.

"I can do it," Misty said. "Seriously. I was just nervous, but I can do this."

"Awww… Isn't that sweet? They're both trying to protect each other. Well, forget it. There are two of us and two of you. And we have weapons. We win." He scanned the others across the floor and asked, "Does anyone else want to be a hero?"

The other tellers either shook their heads or murmured, "No, sir."

"Good." He waved his partner over. "Keep an eye on this one." He nodded toward Gabe. Then with a nasty smirk on his face, he said, "I'll keep my eye on his girlfriend."

Gabe narrowed his eyes, and his lips compressed into a thin line, but he got up and moved to the lock.

The robber kicked the manager again. "Start over."

"Turn the dial carefully four times to the left. When you get to zero, begin turning right," Adam said.

Gabe did as he was told, and when he was slowly approaching the third revolution, he confirmed, "Stop on twenty-one?"

"Yes."

He reached the mark. "Now what?"

"Two revolutions to the left, and stop on forty-four."

Gabe did that, then asked, "And now?"

"One revolution to the right. Stop on thirty-five. That should unlock the mechanism, then turn the wheel to the right to open the door. It's heavy."

Misty wasn't worried about a heavy door. With Gabe's muscles, he could probably lift a safe over his head…not this one, though. In height, it spanned from floor to ceiling, and its width took up most of the side wall. It was like a room in itself. Gabe continued to follow all the manager's directions, but when he turned the wheel, it didn't open.

The gunman kicked the manager hard and said, "Don't fuck around with me. Did you give him the right combination or not?"

"Yes. Sometimes it takes a second."

At that moment, something clicked, and the gunman pushed Gabe out of the way. He yanked on the handle and grunted as the door opened. "That's better." He grinned and grabbed something out of his jacket's deep front pocket…two backpacks that folded up small and flat.

His partner had taken out identical packs from his own jacket pockets. "Should I empty the drawers, boss?"

"Depends. Are there any dye packs in there?" he asked Misty.

"Yes," she said.

"Brownie points for honesty." He handed Misty his backpacks and said, "Go in there and fill these up."

She took the backpacks and pushed open the heavy door enough to enter the vault.

"Hey, numb nuts. Toss me yours, so I can give her more to fill."

A second later, she was shoved in the back. As she stumbled forward, the door slammed shut, encasing her in complete blackness. "What the hell?" she cried. For a moment, she didn't know if she was alone or not.

"It's me, Gabe. Relax. They can't get you in here."

She spun toward his voice. "Gabe? I can't see a thing in here. Where are you?"

A warm hand found her arm and gently caressed it on his way up to cup her face. "I'm right here. We're safe."

She lurched into his strong arms and grasped him around his waist. He held her for a moment, then extricated himself gently.

"Wh-why did you do that?" she whispered.

"Misty, I couldn't let anything happen to you. The minute he didn't have his weapon pointed at you, I took the opportunity to keep you out of harm's way."

"What about everyone else out there?" she cried.

"You didn't see the way he looked at you. Plus, I wouldn't be surprised if they took you with them, for insurance for their getaway."

She hesitated, not knowing how to feel about that. "You realize we're stuck in here until morning."

"I'm sure the criminals won't wait that long to be

caught. As soon as they leave, someone will call the cops, and the fire department will come too. They'll be able to cut through the door and get us out in no time."

She huffed. "You watch too much TV. This vault was created in the 1920s, back when bank robberies were a lot more common. This thing is made of steel-reinforced concrete. Not the kind of concrete used in construction. Something much stronger. The walls are over a foot thick. The door, as you saw, is even stronger. I was told the bank was actually built around the vault."

"Are you saying the FBI couldn't even get us out? This is a federal crime, so the feds will take over from the local police. TV doesn't lie about that."

"The feds have no more access to this vault than I do." She swayed, then caught herself and laid her head on his chest. He didn't hug her. In fact, he stiffened.

What's that about?

"Gabe, do you still see me as a little girl? Is that the problem?"

Jesus. Gabe backed away a step. "What problem? There's no problem. Well, other than being stuck in a safe."

"I was just looking for a little comfort, and you backed away. All I can figure is that you still see me as Parker's little sister."

"I can't see you at all." Gabe hoped sidestepping the question with humor would kill the topic. How could this woman think he perceived her as a little girl? She was a full-grown, gorgeous, well-developed female. "Let's try to find a light switch. I'll take the right side of the vault. You take the left."

"My left or your left? I think I'm facing the door, and you're facing the back wall. Wait. Actually, I don't know where I am."

"Just slide your hands along any wall, and we can play Marco Polo until we find each other again."

"Fine." She didn't laugh.

Parker hadn't mentioned anything about *not* hooking up with his sister, but Gabe couldn't imagine that he'd condone that.

Patting the wall next to him, working his way toward the back, he figured they could just talk and keep track of each other that way. "Look, Misty. I don't think of you as that little girl. Not anymore. I'll admit, until I saw you today, the picture of you I had in my head was more like a cute twelve-year-old kid. But you've obviously…changed."

"So have you."

"Not as much as you have."

"Well, I guess…" She sighed. "Never mind."

"No. What?"

"I guess I'll just have to hug myself."

Gabe slapped his forehead. "Misty, I…" He didn't know how to finish that sentence. *I'm afraid to? You turn me on, and you're not ready for what I might want?*

"You what?"

"Where are you?" Gabe reached out a hand and grabbed something soft and round. "Oops. I was looking for your arm, not your… Sorry."

Misty giggled.

"Okay. You reach for my arm, and I'll find yours," he said.

"What for?"

"I want to give you that hug." *I'd be an ass not to.*

"Okay." He felt a soft touch on his upper arm and slid his hand along it until he found her shoulder. Then he enveloped her in a warm hug. Holding her close, he tried to visualize the little girl she once was. Maybe that way, he could keep a lid on his libido.

She grasped him tight and leaned against his chest. He felt protective of her, and in some ways, he liked it. *Shit. This is not good.* He still didn't want her dependent upon him, long term, but this was one of those temporary circumstances in which his first responder traits wouldn't rebel.

"Don't worry, Misty. I'm sure they'll have us out of here before long."

"I still doubt that." After a long silence, she added, "I hope we have enough air to survive in here until morning. Do firefighters have any idea how much oxygen a person needs?"

There was an exact formula for that, and it took him a minute to remember it. "How big is this vault?" he asked.

"I'm not sure. Maybe twelve by twelve? Something like that?"

"I'm pretty sure we'll be okay." People used up more oxygen if they panicked and hyperventilated, so the best thing he could think of to do was keep her calm. "If worse comes to worst, we can always share some oxygen, like underwater divers." Did he really say that?

She was quiet.

"I was kidding," Gabe said. *What a dumb joke. Get your head out of the gutter, Fierro.*

"Oh." She sounded somewhat disappointed.

He stroked her back and said softly, "I'm sure the fire department must be here by now. Relax. Firefighters can get into anything." *Including a lot of trouble*.

"I hope you're right." After another long silence, she said, "I doubt we'd hear gunshots through this door."

"Shit. Don't even think that way. Your coworkers were cooperating, and the gunmen probably decided to leave before getting caught."

"Linda is pregnant. Again. She has three little kids at home. Betsy is a mom of two. I can't help worrying about them."

Maybe talking about her coworkers would distract Misty from their predicament, but it would use up more oxygen too. Now Gabe had to decide whether he believed his own words.

"Worrying won't help your coworkers. It will just get you worked up. You need to stay calm."

"Don't you worry about your fellow firefighters?"

He thought about that for a moment. They were all well trained to handle themselves in any emergency. Usually, he was too focused on the fire or whatever situation required his full attention. But yeah, there were times when somebody was in danger and he worried, especially if he couldn't help...or it was one of his brothers.

"I guess so."

Gabe wanted to lean over and kiss the top of her head, but that might open the door to a precedent he didn't want to deal with later. If she expected more, he could probably blame it on the moment, but he didn't want to mess with her head...or his.

—•—

Baldy was pacing back and forth, waving his gun. "Now what, Mr. Manager?"

Adam shrugged. "Once the safe is closed and it locks, it won't open again for eight hours."

The antsy bank robber stopped pacing in front of him and placed the barrel of his gun against Adam's forehead. "There has to be an override code or something."

Adam was shaking so badly inside, he thought his knees would turn to jelly and he might fall or faint. "Th-there's some kind of emergency code, but only the bank president has it. He's on a cruise right now."

"Can you call him?"

"He goes on cruises specifically because there's no internet or phone. Even if I could get ahold of him, he'd probably realize something was wrong and call the cops."

The "boss" stomped his foot.

"Well, we tried," the heavyset one mumbled.

The bald guy's jaw was clenched, and his face was growing redder. At last, he looked at the ceiling, threw his arms in the air, and yelled, "Fuck!"

Everyone stared at him silently for a few moments.

"Uh, boss?"

"What?" he shouted.

"I think we should probably go." He nodded toward the front door where a customer was pulling on it frantically, then leaning against the glass, cupping the area around his eyes, and trying to see in.

The smaller guy slumped. "Christ. I'm not leaving

with nothing. Everyone empty your pockets into this backpack." He tossed the flat bag at the manager.

Adam caught it and reached into his own back pocket first. Then he carried the bag to Betsy, one of the female tellers.

"Our wallets are in our purses," she said.

Baldy ripped the bag out of Adam's hand. "Open the drawers and don't touch the contents. My partner will load up the cash." Then he looked at the remaining tellers. "Next stop, purse city, ladies."

Misty wanted to cry. She was trying to be brave, but she really, really wanted to cry. She felt tears burn behind her eyes and tipped her face up, hoping to keep them from running down her cheeks. Gabe leaned away. Maybe he thought she was looking for a kiss.

Then she swayed and bumped against him. *Was that bulge... Oh my!*

"Misty, I guess we might as well sit down, since we're going to be waiting for a while," Gabe said.

Sitting against a solid wall before her legs gave out sounded like a great idea. The place was filled with shelving, but there was a flat surface beside the door. She felt behind her, found the smooth wall, and slid down to a sitting position. She hadn't told anyone about her legs failing to cooperate lately, even in the best of circumstances. She hoped it was just a weird muscle spasm or something that would go away.

Gabe found her shoulder and scooted down beside her. She couldn't see an inch in front of her face, but she pictured their legs straight out in front of them like little kids as they sat side by side. Gabe took Misty's hand in his and gave it a squeeze.

It was comforting and familiar, yet not enough. Her thoughts traveled back to her childhood…

She'd been in love with Gabe as long as she could remember. The first fairy tales she'd heard replayed in her mind when she was little and daydreaming, with Gabe as the handsome prince. Her favorite story was "Sleeping Beauty." Her favorite daydream was being awakened with Gabe's kiss.

She had been sheltered. At least, compared to her suburban friends. In the city, she'd had to be watched at all times. That made sense. Cities could be tough places for kids. So many people became hardened or downright toxic. Gabe and Parker watched over her. She didn't know if Parker had been told to do so, but Gabe certainly hadn't. Yet when Parker had to go inside to use the bathroom or answer a phone call, she knew she was just as safe with Gabe.

Then, even though her grandparents had taken them to a small town where she was safer, they still watched her like a hawk. She'd rebelled. Breaking curfew. Not telling them where she was going…and now, looking back, she felt terrible about it. She and her brother were all they had left of their daughter. Her uncle was useless, only showing up to borrow money. Now he had all of it. Private studio lessons weren't cheap. Whatever hope she'd had of a professional dance career couldn't be afforded anymore, so she had to change her goal. But to what?

After a long silence, she asked, "Gabe, do you have any regrets?"

She thought she was in for another long silence when

he finally said, "The past is the past. There's nothing we can do about it."

"I wasn't talking about the past, necessarily. I mean hypothetically, if you died today, is there anything you would wish you had done that you haven't?"

"Hypothetically? Not really. At least I don't think so. You?"

"Yeah. But if we get out of here, there's still a chance." She wasn't about to tell him that the chance she wanted was with him.

"A chance to what? Dance professionally? I remember how you loved to dance."

"Well, maybe. That, or I would have liked to open my own dance studio."

"That sounds nice. There's no reason you can't do that, because we *are* going to get out of here. I promise."

Feeling hopeless, she said, "Don't make promises you can't keep."

"Misty, let's talk about something else. So, tell me about the suburbs."

"Gee, do you have five seconds?"

Gabe laughed. "We might have five hours."

Misty took a deep breath, then regretted it, knowing that air might be at a premium soon.

Gabe was speaking again. She had to bring herself back to the present when he asked, "What about school? I imagine you finished high school. Was it public or private?"

"Yes, I finished Saugus High School. It was public, but nice. Fairly new. The kids weren't too bad, either."

"Really? Sounds like you lucked out. Some of the kids at Boston Latin were assholes."

"But I thought that was a good school?"

"Sure. The teachers were good. The classes were good. The kids were assholes."

"Oh well. You can't win 'em all," she said. Kids could be jerks when they were jealous. She imagined a lot of guys would be jealous of the handsome teenager Gabe must have been. He probably attracted plenty of female attention, but she didn't want to think about that now...or ever.

"So, do you like being a bank teller and want to make a career of it, or is this just a step to something else?"

Misty snorted. "Does anyone want to be a bank teller when they grow up?"

Gabe was quiet, so she forged on. "Yeah, I guess it's a step. I wanted to dance professionally, maybe doing music videos or live tours, but there really isn't much call for that around this area. I could save up and go to Hollywood—eventually. But by then, I'd be too old."

He laughed. "Old? You're only twenty-two!"

"Almost twenty-three. My birthday is in a couple of weeks. I should have gone to Hollywood or Vegas right out of high school, but I needed to be close to my grandparents until..." A lump formed in her throat, so she just stopped talking.

"Until they left you," Gabe said.

She sighed. "Yeah. Sometimes it feels that way." *Freakin' abandonment issues...*

He squeezed her hand again. "Well, you have me. I may be a sorry excuse for a relative, but I can be a good friend."

A friend. Well, she knew where she stood. Or sat, at the moment—thank goodness. Fatigue swamped her, and her posture slumped.

She felt Gabe slide his arm around her back. She

didn't know how he'd react to her leaning her head on his shoulder, but she did it anyway. He didn't pull away. The two of them sat in a cocoon of silence for a few minutes.

"So, how about you? Did you always want to be a firefighter?"

"Doesn't every little boy? Especially if the whole frigging family is in the fire service?"

"I wouldn't know," she said. "I was a little girl with girly-girl dreams when we lived near you. But I can imagine the pressure you must've been under to carry on the family tradition."

"I don't mind. I love the job. Right now, my parents are struggling with my youngest brother, Luca. He wants to be a cop."

"In a family of firefighters? Doesn't that make him the black sheep?"

He chuckled. "You know it. My mother is usually so calm about our jobs, but with Luca... Well, he's the baby. And she doesn't want her baby getting shot."

"But she's not worried about the rest of you in a fire?"

He was quiet for a moment, then said, "She knows we can take care of ourselves."

"The last time I saw Luca, he was about six or seven years old. I have a hard time seeing him as a cop."

"Just like I had a hard time seeing you as a mature woman, until... Well, there you were. All grown-up and beautiful to boot."

Misty smiled, not that he could see it. She kept her head on his shoulder. Leaning on him felt good, natural, like coming home. She basked in his warmth, very glad he didn't pull away.

Chapter 3

"Do you really think we'll get out of here before...
you know," Misty asked.

"Of course we will! I bet we'll be free within the hour."

"What do you bet?"

"Huh?" It sounded as if Misty was willing to name
stakes. *Intriguing.* "What do you want if you win? I mean
besides an escort home. That's a given," Gabe said.

"Hmmm... Let me see. How about a kiss?"

What could he say to that? He wanted to. God, did he
want to! But Parker would kill him...and Misty would
too, eventually. He was never going to get serious about
a woman and didn't want to mislead her.

"Uh, Gabe?"

"Misty, this isn't seven minutes in a closet."

"No, it's a helluva lot longer." She was quiet for
a moment, then asked, "Do you have a girlfriend or
something?"

"No. Not at the moment."

"Then are you still hung up on someone?"

"I've never been in a serious relationship."

"Really?" Misty seemed shocked. "Aren't you, like,
twenty-six?"

"I made up my mind long ago. I'll never get married, be
a family man and all that. It has nothing to do with you."

"Then what?"

He sighed. "You mentioned regrets... There's one

thing I don't think I'll ever get over. Do you remember our dog, Buddy?"

"Yeah. He was a good dog."

"Yes, he was. Do you know how he died?"

"I heard he got off his leash and was hit by a car. I cried when I heard about it. Is that not true?"

"Oh, it's true, all right. And it happened because of me. My girlfriend at the time was allergic, so I tied him to the railing beside the front door. As you must remember, we had no backyard. I was supposed to be taking care of him while my family was away. Instead of acting responsibly, I put him out front where anyone could hurt him, just so I could make out with a girl. Later, I found his collar unbuckled, still tied to the railing. Some asshole purposely let him go free. And then he got run over. I've never felt more terrible in my life. I can never put myself in that position again."

"Gabe, I know it was horrible—believe me, I understand—but that's not something you can change. All you can do is learn from it. And you'll make different decisions. I took care of my grandparents, and my grandpa fell while I was out. After that, I had to get someone to take over for me, even if I just had to run to the pharmacy or go grocery shopping. And you can teach kids about the dangers of running into the street—looking both ways and so on. You can't teach dogs that."

"I know it's not exactly the same thing, but pets depend on people to take care of them. You can't just learn from mistakes. Frankly, you can't make mistakes. I found Buddy as a puppy, rummaging around in the garbage behind a restaurant. I took him home, and after much begging, I was allowed to keep him. He became everybody's dog, though. We all loved his adorable goofy grin, and he loved every one of us. When I went looking for him, I found him in the gutter. Just pushed aside like trash."

"Oh, Gabe. I'm so sorry." She moved enough to hug him, and he let her.

Finally, he took a deep breath and let go. "Yeah, well, the worst wasn't over. I had to tell everyone else what had happened. The whole family cried and mourned like they'd lost a child." Gabe had let everyone down. He was still angry with himself for being so stupid.

"That must have been awful. Absolutely horrible! And I can understand that maybe you don't want to have another dog, but why—"

"Because every woman I've ever dated wants kids. If I couldn't even look after a dog, how could I trust myself with a baby? A child is even more clueless than a dog."

"Are you saying you'd leave a baby tied to the front door?"

"Probably not."

"Probably? Oh, come on. You'd never do that, Gabe. There's even a thing I've heard of where overwhelmed mothers can drop off their babies at a fire station, no questions asked. Sheesh!"

"Yeah. It's called Safe Haven. Look, there are any number of ways a child can die. I've seen some horrible examples. Kids accidentally drowning in a bathtub, for instance. It only takes one distraction, and there are so many distractions these days."

"You're right, of course. It *could* happen. Does that mean you're never going to take a risk? Even if it could lead to great happiness?"

Gabe sighed again. "I think it's time to change the subject. What else have you got?"

As they were trying to think of something else to talk about, he heard a noise. It sounded far away, but it was some kind of rasping sound. It had to be an electric saw.

"Oh, thank God! The cavalry is here," he exclaimed.

"You mean, the fire department is trying to get us out?"

"Yeah. I told you they would."

"I guess you're going to win that bet."

To say he had mixed feelings was an understatement. He and Misty were just getting to know each other again. With all the ways to do online banking, who knew if he'd ever come up with another excuse to see her?

She had pushed him out of his comfort zone. He wanted to keep things superficial, so why didn't she let him? He could call in a few days to see how she was doing, but after that?

After what seemed like hours of the same rasping noise plus a few other additional noises, Gabe had pretty much identified what they were trying to do. It sounded like cement saws were concentrating on the ceiling. They had probably checked the building plans and discovered the weakest spot.

Misty had said the door was the strongest, and he had seen how thick it was when it was open, so he doubted they were even attempting to take off hinges or cut a hole in it. The walls might be as thick as the door.

At last, something broke through the ceiling toward the back of the vault. A tiny sliver of light appeared.

Gabe stood and helped Misty up. Holding her hand, he pulled her back against the door. Unfortunately, dust was starting to fill up the little room. He yanked a handkerchief out of his pocket and handed it to her. "Here, put this over your nose and mouth. It's clean."

"What about you?" she asked.

"I'll use my sleeve."

As the rasping became louder, they were aware of voices also coming from the ceiling. It was impossible to understand what they were saying, but man, what a comfort to hear the rumbling of humans giving orders and acknowledging them.

"Gabe?" Misty asked.

"Yeah?"

"Thank you for keeping me calm and safe during all this, I guess."

"You guess?"

"Well, I haven't seen my coworkers yet. I know you couldn't have stuffed all of us in this vault, but you did what you thought was right."

If Gabe wasn't holding her hand and using his other one to block the dust, he would've slapped himself upside the head. He already felt like a jerk, but was she serious? She wished he'd pushed all her coworkers into the vault, knowing the air wouldn't last a fraction of the time?

"Well, I did what I did. I hope your coworkers are okay, but at least I know you are. If you'd been taken and raped and Parker found out I was right there... Shit. Never mind." As light began to invade the room from above, he was finally able to see Misty's outline. "You are okay, aren't you?"

"Yeah, I'm fine. Are you?"

"Other than feeling like an idiot, I'm perfectly fine." Gabe laughed, then coughed. "Don't try to talk. Just breathe through your nose. Keep your eyes closed so the dust doesn't get in them."

"They're already closed."

She bumped up against him, let go of his hand, and slipped her arm around his waist. He had no choice but to put his arm around her shoulder. Any lower would give her and anyone who entered the vault the wrong idea.

Parker had painted a different picture of Misty than the one he was discovering. Naturally, Parker would see her as his little sister forever, someone naive who needed to be looked after. But the woman standing next to him seemed pretty capable.

"Gabe? When this is all over, can we go out for coffee or something? I don't want you to just walk out of my life after this. I'm betting that as soon as your firefighter buddies show up, you're going to drop me like a hot potato and saunter off with them."

He tried to muffle his laugh in his sleeve. She didn't know he was supposed to be keeping an eye on her, but even if he weren't, he wouldn't just walk off with his buddies and leave her there.

"Sure. Coffee sounds great."

He opened his eyes briefly to check the progress of the hole in the ceiling. More light shone through now, and he could see they were working on two sections at the same time. More voices were rumbling. He wondered how many guys were up there. Probably a dozen or more. It wouldn't be much longer.

Gabe suddenly became aware of the fact that he was stroking Misty's arm from her elbow up to her shoulder and down. She sighed and sagged against him. The impulse to enclose her in his arms and hold her close was something he had been battling since this all started.

The dust was almost overwhelming. Misty's voice was muffled when she asked, "Are you sure you're okay? You're trying to breathe through a leather jacket. I have the only handkerchief. Maybe we could share it."

He almost snorted. "Yeah, right."

"Gabe!" She kicked him.

"Oww."

"Am I that hideous that you don't want to look at my face up close?"

"Of course not. It's just that... Well, it's the opposite."

She seemed to take a deeper breath and relax into him a little more "Oh. Well then, here." She slapped her hand behind his head and pulled him down to her face, then dragged the handkerchief over their eyes, noses, and mouths. They were not only sharing a cloth; their mouths were inches from each other. Not even inches. He suddenly felt her lip touch his, and without even thinking, he leaned in and increased the pressure.

It started as a chaste kiss, but soon grew in intensity. She opened her mouth, and their tongues found each other. She cupped the nape of his neck. This girl could kiss! Before he realized it, his hands were pulling her closer and wandering over the dip in her lower back. Trying to stop at her hip was killing him. He wanted to squeeze her delectable buttocks.

He didn't know how long they stood there kissing, because his brain had left the building. At one point, he realized what he was doing and knew he should pull away. But another big part of him—growing bigger by the second—thought, *that ship has sailed, and it won't be turning around.*

A loud crash startled him out of his altered state.

Pulling away a few inches, he lowered the handkerchief enough to squint and see what was going on. A huge chunk of cement had hit the floor. Light flooded the small chamber.

"Hey, Captain, we're in!" were the first words Gabe heard clearly. If he wasn't mistaken, that was his brother Noah's voice.

Relief swept over him. He turned to Misty and cupped her jaw. "We're almost out, babe."

She sighed. It was hard to tell if that was a sigh of relief or resignation. He'd just assume it had to be relief. Now that he could see her, her dark hair was almost white with cement dust. He grinned, realizing he must look similar.

She smiled up at him. "Now I know what you'll look like when you're old."

He laughed out loud. The dust didn't choke him this time. It was beginning to dissipate. A few more chunks of concrete fell, and Gabe quickly pulled the handkerchief over both their faces again as a new wave of cement dust hit them.

"Let me go in, Cap'n. That's my brother down there."

Yup. Noah's voice.

Gabe heard the captain give his okay, and moments later, a ladder was lowered into the hole. The long legs and wiry frame that descended the ladder did indeed belong to his brother Noah. When he turned around, he found them with his flashlight.

"Nice of you to drop in," Gabe said casually.

Noah laughed. "Are you sure about that? You two look pretty cozy. Am I interrupting something?"

Gabe sprang a few inches away from Misty but kept a hand on her shoulder. "This is Misty Carlisle, Noah." As if that would explain everything. He hoped it would at least justify his reason for having his arms around her.

"The little girl from down the street?"

"I'm not a little girl anymore."

Noah aimed the flashlight on her, sliding the beam down slowly and then back up. "No, you are not. Hey, there's a light switch behind you." He shone the flashlight on a spot on the wall next to the door.

Shit. Talk about feeling like a complete idiot… Gabe flipped the switch, and both he and Misty blinked away the blinding light that invaded their cozy darkness.

Noah looked her up and down again, and a slow smile spread across his face. "Yup. You are *not* a little girl anymore."

Gabe wanted to punch his younger brother, because he looked like he was salivating. That wouldn't give away his feelings at all.

An authoritative voice called down, "Fierro. Are they all right?"

"Oh, yeah. They're just fine and dandy." Noah snickered.

"Well, get them up here."

"I guess I can't tease you right now, Bro. It'll have to wait until Sunday dinner. Don't worry. That'll give me and Dante plenty of time to come up with some zingers."

Gabe put his hand on the small of Misty's back and gently led her toward safety. "You go first, Misty. I'll be right behind you." He shot his brother a glare, daring him to challenge his elder authority.

Misty gingerly stepped over pieces of concrete in her high heels. At last, she had safely made it to the ladder. As she climbed up, her tight ass hugged by her pencil skirt was all too apparent. Gabe glanced over at his brother. Noah was grinning but quickly shifted his gaze back to Gabe's and waggled his eyebrows.

Gabe stared at the bottom of the ladder and shook his head.

As soon as she'd made it up and out, Noah lowered his voice and asked, "How the hell did you get stuck in a bank vault in the first place?"

"I promised Parker I'd look after Misty. I'd just opened an account here when the bank was robbed."

"And you dove into the safe to protect your money?" Noah asked with a smirk.

"Of course not. They were making Misty do their dirty work. Opening the safe, going in and filling the bags... They had guns and fired one to prove it was loaded. I waited for a distraction and reacted."

"And you thought locking the two of you in the vault would keep her safe."

"I never said I was thinking straight at the time, but yeah."

Noah scratched his head. "I guess it worked. Not what I would have done, but it was...effective." He leered again.

"Knock it off, Noah. Or I'll knock it off for you."

"Oh, tough guy." He slapped Gabe on the shoulder and said, "Don't worry. I won't say a word...until Sunday dinner when I have the whole family to protect me."

A cheer went up when Misty emerged.

"Thanks, guys."

Someone helped her off the ladder, and someone else handed her a bottle of water. Before she opened it, she asked, "Are my coworkers all right?"

A few firefighters glanced at each other, and one of them said, "Yeah. I think so. The cops took their statements, and they all went home a couple of hours ago."

Her eyebrows shot up. "All of them? Even the manager?"

A familiar-looking guy shrugged. "Yeah. He said he had an appointment or something."

One of the other firefighters grinned. "I think he shit his pants and had an appointment with his closet, Dante."

"Dante?" she said to the first guy. "Dante Fierro? Is that you?"

He stared at her a moment. Then his eyes widened in recognition. "Misty?"

She nodded. "I think you're the only one who's recognized me since I returned to Boston."

He crossed his arms. "I'll be damned. You look… different."

She grinned. "I got rid of the braces. And, well, I'm covered in cement dust."

"Yeah, there's that."

"You look about three feet taller."

He grinned and kicked at the floor. "Yeah, I was a little runt for a while there. You were a couple years younger than me but about a foot taller. All the girls were."

One of the firefighters came over with a blanket and draped it around her shoulders.

"Thanks." She glanced over at the hole in the floor and asked, "Where's Gabe?"

"Good question…" Dante wandered over to the hole with the ladder sticking out of it. "Hey, Noah. Is Gabe alive, or did he die of starvation? He probably hasn't eaten for at least three hours."

"He's fine. We're just having a little chat," Noah called up.

The captain huffed. "Stop cramming cash in your pockets and get up here."

Seconds later, the ladder vibrated with heavy footsteps, and Gabe emerged. Dante grabbed his hand and helped haul him up and out.

Firefighters who apparently knew him were slapping him on the back, and clouds of dust rose from his jacket. He grinned and greeted them, then walked right over to Misty.

"Are you all right?"

"Yeah. I guess all my coworkers have deserted the place, but at least they're okay. If they're all okay, then I'm all right."

"They're just a little poorer," the captain said. "The criminals didn't want to leave with nothing for their trouble, so they made the employees empty their purses and pockets. Plus, the manager had to give them the cash from the drawers without slipping a dye pack in."

"Oh no." Misty excused herself and ran down the stairs as fast as she could in high heels, straight to where she'd left her purse in the back room. All the cubbies were empty—and so was her purse. "Oh, shi…shoot."

"What's wrong?" Gabe must have followed close on her heels.

"They emptied my wallet too. That had my CharlieCard in it." Her shoulders slumped. "Damn. Now I'll have to walk home."

"We'll take you home in the truck," Dante said. Apparently, he had followed Gabe. "That is, if you don't live far from here. We've got room for one more, but if we get another call, you'll have to wait until we've handled it."

More firefighters filed down the stairs, carrying the equipment they'd brought in.

"No need to drive her home," Gabe said. "I was going to take her out for a drink after this anyway." Gabe gazed at her with some kind of intense expression on his face.

"Yes," she said. "But thank you, Dante, for the offer."

Dante clapped his brother on the back. "Okay, Bro. You win. Just don't forget to call your station. We went on duty a couple hours ago, and since you're on the same rotation, your captain must be wondering where the hell you are."

"Actually, I switched with someone. He needed tomorrow off. But thanks for worrying about me, Mom."

"Yeah, yeah. I was just trying to save your job. Next time, I'll let you get fired."

Gabe chuckled. "Nah. You're right. Thanks."

"You're welcome."

Misty had always enjoyed the insults and banter the Fierro boys heaped on each other. Gabe had been the quietest, but it looked as if he could dish it out when he wanted to.

The captain joined them. "So, another Fierro. Gabe, is it?"

"Yes, sir."

They shook hands, and the older man smiled pleasantly.

"You and the young lady will have to give statements to the police. They're waiting outside."

"Oh joy," Gabe muttered.

Chapter 4

IT WAS ABOUT TEN O'CLOCK WHEN THEY FINALLY FINISHED talking to the police. The clear, crisp night air and stars twinkling overhead would have been romantic, if not for the bank robbery. Misty walked next to Gabe with her hands in her coat pockets.

Something made him want to put his arm around her shoulder and pull her closer. He told himself it was just his protective instincts, but another part of him was calling bullshit. The kiss they'd shared in the vault was more than just a reaction to being in danger. It wasn't impulsive. And it sure as hell wasn't protective. He had been thinking about it long before they were stuck in there.

He looked up the street and spotted a club. "Maybe we could get a drink there." He tipped up his chin in the bar's direction.

Misty wrinkled her nose. "I don't really like that place. I've only been in it once, but it was really loud. To be honest, I just feel like going home."

"Sure. Of course. You've probably had enough excitement for one night." She looked tired, or maybe it was just what was left of the cement dust making her look like she'd aged about a decade.

"Yeah. I feel like I've had enough excitement for a month, at least. If you want a drink, you don't have to walk me all the way home."

"I want to," he said without hesitation.

"More than you want a drink right now?"

"Yeah." He surprised himself, but being with her really was nice. Of course, he wanted to be sure she got home okay too. Naturally.

She smiled up at him. "Thanks."

They walked on in silence for a few minutes. "So, you live in the North End?" Gabe asked, feeling like a lame conversationalist.

"Yeah. It's a decent one-bedroom apartment. Nothing fancy. You can come up and see it, if you'd like. I can even offer you that drink."

Was she inviting him up for a nightcap? Gabe wasn't sure what that meant. Maybe nothing. He really would like to see her place and make sure everything was secure.

"I'll come up for a minute."

"If you like wine, I can offer you a glass of red before you go."

"I don't know an Italian who doesn't like wine—especially red."

She smiled at him, and those pretty lips sent a message straight to his groin. He mentally chastised himself for reacting like a randy teenager. *She's my friend's little sister, for God's sake! Stick to the mission, Fierro.* He had thought of this "favor" as Operation Protect Misty, but he was no longer sure from whom he was protecting her.

Soon they were walking up her driveway to a side door. She slipped a key in the lock, and after opening that one, she used a different key in a different lock to open the door.

Good. A dead bolt.

Once inside, there was a stairway next to a door. Misty walked up the stairs, and Gabe was relieved again.

She was on the second floor behind a double-locked outside door and probably another dead-bolted inside door. Smart girl.

She opened the upstairs door with one key, which made him slightly nervous. If someone who lived here wanted in, a credit card would probably open that door.

"Do the landlords live downstairs?" he asked as he followed her inside. The layout was that of a traditional older home. They stood in a short hallway, but he could see a living room. No kitchen or dining area shared the space. They must be separated by the yellowed, wallpapered walls.

"Just one landlord. She's an older lady and lives alone. She likes having someone else in the house."

"That's probably a good idea. It might even be better if she rented to a male."

Misty removed her coat and was about to hang it in the closet when she stopped. "What are you saying?"

Had he blown it? "Nothing. I just mean, you know... I've seen a lot of crap go down in the city. Two women alone are only slightly less vulnerable than one woman alone."

Misty laughed. "You might not feel that way if you met her. She likes being a badass. She has tattoos and a bunch of piercings. Three days after I moved in, I heard a downstairs window fly open, and she was yelling her head off. When I looked out my window, I saw her shaking a baseball bat at some young guy who was running down the street. He looked like he was running for his life."

Misty reached for his coat.

"Did she ever tell you what that was about?"

"Yeah. Some high school kid was looking for contributions for school uniforms or something. She said it sounded suspicious, so she ran him off."

"With a baseball bat?"

"I'm just glad Massachusetts has tough gun laws. Otherwise, the kid would probably be full of buckshot."

Gabe felt slightly better about her situation, despite her landlord sounding somewhat unhinged. Maybe she just had something against guys. That might keep Misty single.

As soon as both coats had been put away in the closet, Misty gestured to the living room. "Have a seat. I'll be right back with our wine."

A comfortable grouping of furniture surrounded a giant ottoman. He wondered how she had gotten something that big up those stairs. Oh, right. Parker could have carried that thing. There was a wood-burning fireplace between two small chairs. Even though snow hadn't fallen yet, a nice roaring fire sounded comforting.

"Hey, Misty," Gabe called out. "Would you like me to build a fire?"

A moment later, she returned with two glasses and a bottle of red wine on a tray. "You don't get enough fire on the job?"

He rolled his eyes. "I know some guys who don't allow fires in their homes unless it's for cooking and want it watched constantly. But I grew up differently. Maybe because we always had plenty of people around to keep an eye on things, a nice crackling fire limited to a safe chimney wasn't something to be afraid of."

"I'll bet you had a fire extinguisher handy, though."

"Of course. Several of them."

"Why does that not surprise me?" She took a deep

breath and sighed. "I'd love to build a nice warm fire sometime, but I'm afraid the dragon lady doesn't allow it." She poured a glass of wine and handed it to him.

The term *dragon lady* startled him at first. She couldn't know about his sisters-in-law. *Nah, it's just an expression.* The no-fire rule was probably a good idea, considering the landlord couldn't keep an eye on what a tenant did.

"Okay." He extended an arm. "I'll just have to keep you warm myself." *Holy shit. Where did that come from?*

She smiled as she poured some wine for herself and then snuggled into the space beside him. "Mmmm... This *is* nice and warm."

He took a sip and wondered how to approach the subject of her safety without coming off like a bossy boyfriend or big brother. "So, do you have a fire extinguisher?"

"Yes. There's one in the closet. And she put sprinklers in. See?"

Gabe had already noticed the devices in the ceiling, but they might not be operable. People had been known to install the apparatus without hooking it up to any plumbing. It looked good enough to pass inspection, and that was all they wanted. Without making a hole in her ceiling or starting a fire, he couldn't gauge their effectiveness. It was time to move on to the next part of her safety assessment.

Her working in a bank.

"Have you thought about trying some other type of job?"

"I have to admit, I was kind of wishing I worked somewhere else a few hours ago."

"I think that's an excellent idea." He took a sip

of his wine. It was rich, without a hint of bitterness. Unlike himself.

She leaned away from him and studied his face. "I didn't mean I was actually going to quit. It took about six months to get comfortable doing this teller thing. I can't imagine starting all over again in some other job that requires training. Besides, I could be held up anywhere. Stores are robbed all the time."

"You could waitress."

She made a sound of disgust.

"What?" He set down his wine glass on the ottoman. With the tray on top, he figured it could function as a coffee table, which is where he assumed a glass should go.

"Is that all you think I'm good for? Waitressing?"

"Not at all. I was just thinking..." After a brief hesitation, he realized he'd insulted her but didn't know how or why. "There's nothing wrong with serving the public. I do it myself, every day."

She snorted. "It's hardly the same thing. I like to get dressed up and feel like a professional, not come home smelling like French fries."

"I wasn't talking about fast food. There are some high-end..."

She was scowling at him.

"Never mind. It doesn't matter what you do, as long as you're safe. I know it's hard to get professional jobs with just a high school diploma. At least, I never heard about your going to college. Did you?"

She seemed to stiffen, then set her wine next to his and crossed her arms. "No. I was taking care of my grandparents so they could die at home."

He felt terrible but didn't know how to make it better.

"You know, I had you pegged differently. When we were growing up, you didn't treat me like a dumb girl. If you guys were playing a game, you treated me equally. It didn't matter what the game was. Hide-and-seek. Battleship. Cards. Whatever. But now it seems like you'd be worried that I'd hide in the wrong place or sink my own battleship."

He laughed. "I don't think that. You're smart and plenty brave. But I also know you're beautiful, and—" He didn't know how to finish that sentence. He really didn't. Was he being chauvinistic? He didn't mean to be. He scratched his head. "I just don't want anything bad to happen to you."

"Why? Before this afternoon you didn't even know I worked in a bank. Or... Wait. Did Parker put you up to this?"

"Parker?"

"Yeah, Parker. My brother. Your good friend. Remember him?"

Gabe tried for a casual chuckle, but it came out more like a nervous laugh.

"Oh, shit. He did!"

"No. I heard you moved back to Boston. He did tell me that." He thought about how he could tell the truth without giving anything away. He didn't want to outright lie to her, but pretending that he just happened to walk into her bank was pretty suspicious.

She was staring at him like she wouldn't believe whatever came out of his mouth next. He had to admit he wouldn't believe it was a coincidence either. "I'm sorry, Misty. You're too smart to believe anything but the truth. Yes, I promised your brother I'd be there for you if you needed anything. But he also asked me to keep it quiet."

"Why?"

"He knows you want to rely on yourself. I admire you for wanting to be independent. For the record, I thought the secrecy thing was a terrible idea. I couldn't think of a way to casually bump into you so you wouldn't know I was keeping tabs on you. I should have realized you wouldn't fall for it."

It was time to change the subject. Quickly. "You know, Noah suggested I invite you to Sunday dinner at our parents' house."

"Noah, huh?"

"Well, yeah. He mentioned it while we were down in the vault. But I wouldn't have asked you if I didn't agree with him."

"So apparently, you're asking me?"

This felt like a trap. He had the feeling there was some kind of right answer, something he wasn't saying, but what exactly could it be? "Yeah, I think it's a good idea. You could catch up with the rest of the family, and they'd love to see you."

"Just them? Not you?"

Okay. He knew where this was going. "Sure. Me too."

She let out a long sigh.

"Misty—"

She held up one hand to stop him from saying any more. "Fine."

Uh-oh. He got the "fine" response. That usually meant something *wasn't* fine. He didn't understand woman-speak very well, but that one he knew. It was probably best to sidestep the trap at this point.

"So, would you like to come?"

She looked at him with a smirk and raised an eyebrow. He thought about what he had just said. *Oh, shit… Is she coming on to me? Little Misty?*

"I'd love to come."

"When?"

Another sparkle in her eye. He imagined she was thinking "right now." *Fuck.* Little Misty was a femme fatale. And he'd do well to remember it.

Alone in his studio apartment near the theater district, Gabe called Parker on his computer. They had set up Skype so they could talk in case Misty was in trouble.

"Parker, you're an ass."

"What? I'm a million miles away in a dusty shithole, defending your freedom. What could I have possibly done?"

"I thought you were still in some kind of specialty training stateside."

"Yeah, yeah. So what did I do?"

"It's what you didn't do. You didn't tell me your sister grew up to be a knockout." Gabe leaned back in his desk chair, not caring if his buddy was being shot at. He'd like to shoot at him too right now.

"She is?"

"Oh, come on, man. Don't pretend you don't know it."

Parker shrugged his camo-uniformed shoulders. "Okay. I guess she's pretty. But that's why I wanted someone looking out for her. She doesn't even realize it, and I see the way guys look at her."

"So you thought she'd be safe with me?"

"Of course." He leaned forward, and his brows contracted. "Why wouldn't she be?"

Gabe closed his eyes and rubbed his forehead. "Christ, man, I'm only human." He wasn't, but Parker didn't know that. Sometimes he wished he had paranormal libido control, but that wasn't one of his powers.

"Wait a minute." Parker bristled. "Are you telling me you might…come on to my sister?"

Gabe didn't answer.

Parker's expression changed from confused to stormy. "Gabe?"

"Look, something happened, but it's not what you think."

"What do you mean? What happened?" When Gabe didn't respond right away, Parker demanded, "What the hell happened, asshole?"

"Nothing! I don't want to worry you." Gabe swore under his breath.

"Too late, shithead. What did you do?"

"I didn't do anything."

Parker leaned back and crossed his arms. "So you're saying *she* did something."

Gabe scratched the back of his neck. "Well, um…she did come on to me, but there were extenuating circumstances."

"Whoa. Be very careful, my friend. That's my little sister you're talking about. I know she's a man magnet, but she's not a slut."

"Of course not! That's not what I was saying."

"Then what the fuck are you saying?"

Gabe sighed. "I shouldn't have said anything."

"Well, you've achieved that!" Parker glared at him for several seconds.

Finally, Gabe gave in. "Look, I didn't want to worry you, but your little sister's bank was robbed. I happened to be there at the time. You asked me to look out for her, and that's what I did. She was grateful, and she kissed me."

Parker relaxed a bit, then he stiffened. "On the mouth?"

Gabe laughed. "You're not worried about the bank robbery, but you're concerned that I kissed your sister on the mouth."

"Of course I'm worried about the bank robbery, but you said you were there and you kept her safe. She's okay, isn't she?"

"Yeah, she's fine. You're welcome."

"Fuck." Parker closed his eyes and shook his head. "I messed up. I should've thanked you first."

Gabe let out a sigh of relief. "That's okay. It must be frustrating to be so far away. I think I understand now why you wanted someone nearby. Someone she could turn to in an emergency. She's your little sister. But she's not helpless."

"I didn't expect her to need your help at all, never mind so soon."

"But she did. I don't know about you, but I'd feel better if she wasn't working in a bank."

"To be honest, I never thought a bank robbery would happen. It seemed like a pretty tame job to me. I guess now I have more to worry about." He raised his eyes and seemed to gaze at the sky—or ceiling. It was hard to tell where he was.

"Worrying won't help anyone. I promised I'd look after her, and I will. I'll do whatever I can to keep her safe and sound until you get back. Maybe even help her find a new job."

Parker inhaled deeply and let out a long breath. "I know you will. That's why I asked you."

"She's coming over for dinner Sunday at my parents' house. Everybody will be happy to see her. She'll have a lot of people to turn to besides me."

"That doesn't let you off the hook, you know. I still want you to keep tabs on her—from a distance."

Gabe didn't know how to tell his friend he'd blown the secret part of the mission. He yawned. "Sorry, it's late over here. I should get some sleep. I go on duty at six tomorrow morning."

"Sure. Hey, listen, thanks for telling me what happened. I want to know everything, and I doubt Misty would've told me about it."

"Well, if she does, act surprised. I already feel like a snitch."

"And your country thanks you for your service."

"Don't be an asshole."

Parker laughed. "No guarantees. Call me soon, okay?"

"Yeah, whatever." Gabe hung up with a smile on his face. At least they were still friends.

For now.

Chapter 5

"MISTY! IT'S SO GOOD TO SEE YOU." MRS. FIERRO ran to the open front door and clasped Misty in a tight hug, then she stepped back and held her by her arms, looking up at her. "My, how you've grown up. When you left, you were about my size."

Misty giggled. "It's nice to see you too, Mrs. Fierro."

"Oh, sweetheart. You can call me Gabriella now."

"Okay, Mrs. Fier—I mean Gabriella."

Gabe hoped his mother wouldn't take his inviting Misty to dinner the wrong way. He hoped Misty wasn't taking it the wrong way either. He had offered to borrow Dante's car and come get her, but she said she'd be fine taking public transportation. Maybe she got the "just friends" message.

But did his libido listen?

She looked gorgeous. Even prettier than she had at work the other day. For one thing, she wasn't wearing a suit. Her dress wasn't exactly conservative but not trashy either. It hugged her curves and left little to the imagination. He supposed it would be called a little black dress. The neckline looked like the top of a heart and revealed a peek at what promised to be generous cleavage. A white pearl necklace lay across her glowing skin.

He grabbed her coat and hung it next to his in the closet while his mother took her into the living room. Then he joined the rest of the family.

Everybody was already there. Everyone who was still in town, that is. Jayce and Kristine were on their honeymoon in the eastern Caribbean. St. Thomas, or St. Martin, or some other sainted island. No one had heard from them since they called to say they'd arrived safely. On a honeymoon, no news was good news.

Ryan and Chloe were living in Ireland, in a freakin' castle, and working for the local volunteer fire department. So that left Miguel and Sandra, holding hands on one side of the couch, and their father, Antonio, next to them. Gabe's three younger brothers were lounging beside the fireplace. His father rose with everyone else and welcomed Misty with open arms.

As Noah and Dante hugged her, each of them glanced over her shoulder and gave Gabe a knowing smirk. Luca was the only one who seemed unaware of Gabe's interest in her.

He sighed. There had to be a way to explain his relationship to her without making it sound like he was her boyfriend or her babysitter.

When she had been properly greeted, Dante gave up a comfortable armchair for her.

"Can we get you a beer or glass of wine?" Antonio asked.

"I'd love a glass of wine."

Antonio glanced at Gabe. "Go get the girl a glass of wine, Gabriel." His father flopped back onto the couch.

Uh-oh. His dad sounded annoyed. He must have thought Gabe was supposed to offer. But this wasn't his house, so why should he? He wanted to make sure everyone knew he was just her friend. Not her date. But how could he do that right in front of her without insulting her?

"So, what have you been up to?" Gabriella asked Misty as Gabe left the room to get two glasses of wine. One a little fuller than the other—for his nerves.

He didn't hear all of her answer. Mostly because Dante had followed him into the kitchen.

"Do you think I need help to pour two glasses of Chablis?" Gabe offered him the corkscrew.

"Nah." Dante lowered his voice to a whisper. "I was wondering if you'd mind if I ask her out."

Gabe leaned away, shocked. "What the hell kind of question is that? First of all, she's not my property, so you don't need my permission. And second of all, if you do ask her, I'll have to pound your bony ass into the pavement."

Dante burst out laughing. "I knew it."

Noah leaned around the corner of the kitchen. "He is, isn't he?"

"Oh yeah. You win."

Gabe glanced between his grinning brothers. "Did you two have some kind of bet?"

They just smirked at him.

"Un-fucking-believable." Gabe finished pouring two glasses of wine and ignored his brothers as he brought them into the living room.

He handed Misty her glass, and she looked up at him with a smile.

His cock hardened.

Quickly taking a seat, Gabe tried to hide the evidence of his arousal. He no sooner got comfortable than his mother said she had to check on dinner and asked Gabe for help in the kitchen.

He almost groaned aloud. That was never good. She

liked to be alone in the kitchen when she was cooking, so she was probably cooking up something else altogether.

"Misty was telling us about the bank robbery."

Gabe scratched his head. "Yeah. That was pretty frightening for her."

His mother smiled up at him with her usual empathy. "It must have been pretty frightening for you too, darling."

"Yeah, but only because I was worried about her. Thanks for that, by the way." He crossed his arms.

"Excuse me?"

"You were the one who insisted I look after her."

"And I'm glad I did." Gabriella stirred the simmering pasta sauce. "She would've been all alone after that horrible experience if you hadn't been there. She was just saying you got her through it."

Gabe looked at the ceiling and took a deep breath. "I wasn't thinking straight. I feel like an idiot for pushing her into that vault and locking us in. She was concerned about her coworkers, and I was only concerned about her."

Gabe's mother smiled at him and put her arm around his waist. She had to look up at her six-foot son. "Someday, my darling, we'll have to sit down so I can introduce you to yourself."

His eyebrows shot up. "What do you mean by that?"

She stroked the side of his face. "Only that you are probably the most sensitive of my sons and the least aware of it."

Gabe burst out laughing. "Someday, Ma, we'll have to sit down so I can introduce you to myself. I think you've got me all wrong."

"Oh, no. I've got you pegged exactly right." She pulled his face down and kissed his cheek. "Now, we'd better get this food on the table."

Gabe couldn't help thinking about what his mother had said, even though it was ridiculous. *Me, sensitive? That's a laugh and a half.*

As the family gathered around the table, Gabe's mother directed the seating. Naturally, Misty landed right next to Gabe. That was completely unnecessary. He was acutely aware of her every move, every inflection in her voice. But now he had to smell her perfume too. She smelled like gardenias, in the middle of winter no less.

He tried to think of her as the same little girl he knew growing up. But he could no longer see her that way. She was someone he barely knew, but at the same time, he knew her too well. His mind was all jumbled up. With his mother pushing him toward her and Parker insisting he keep his hands off, he was doomed to make a mistake, one way or the other.

Shit. Dante was flirting with her. And he was glancing at Gabe for his reaction. He wished he could kick Dante under the table. But with his luck, he'd get the wrong set of legs.

He heard his name from her lips and pulled himself back to what Misty was saying.

"Gabe thinks I should find a new job." She turned her face toward him, but her expression was impossible to read.

"That might not be a bad idea. What would you like to do instead?" Antonio asked.

"That's just it. I don't know what kind of job I can get

that I'd like any better. I've found I'm pretty good with finances. I wanted to teach dance when I first moved back to the city, but when I checked out the dance studios, none I'd like to work for had an opening."

"You could try again," Gabriella suggested. "Maybe something has opened up."

"Actually, I called around again and only found one with a possible opening. It's in Roxbury."

Gabe sucked in a breath. "No fucking way are you working in Roxbury."

"Gabriel!" Gabriella exclaimed. "Watch your language."

Noah, who was sitting on his other side, snickered.

Gabe turned on him. "You think that's funny? I suppose you think her working in Roxbury is a great idea?"

Noah leaned back and put his hands up in surrender. "I didn't say anything, Bro."

"Misty, pay no attention to my sons," Gabriella said. "Of course you can work wherever you want, but remember your safety is important to *all* of us. I'm sure Gabe has responded to many emergencies in Roxbury, and it *is* a rough neighborhood."

"I think it was named the neighborhood with the most drive-by shootings," Luca said. "You could get caught in the cross fire in a gang war there."

Misty's eyes betrayed a deep sadness. "I never said I was going to take the job. I mean, it's tempting. They have a new Center for the Arts, and I've heard there are some wonderful things going on there. The pay is good, and I have rent—"

"Gabe will cover your rent," Gabriella quickly interjected.

Gabe's jaw dropped. "Ma? Can I see you in the kitchen?"

"No, you may not. If you can't afford it, we'll all chip in."

Misty straightened her spine. "No! I can't let you do that. It's very kind of you, but I'll be fine."

Gabe stood. "In that case, Misty, may I see *you* in the kitchen?"

"Uh-oh. Misty's in trouble," Luca chanted.

"Shut up, squirt," Gabe fired back.

But Misty *did* feel like she was in trouble. Parker had asked her to go to Gabe for advice or anything else she needed and, moreover, to listen to him. It was for Parker's sake that she followed Gabe into the kitchen.

When Gabe turned around, Misty folded her arms. "I wasn't really going to take a job in Roxbury, you know."

Gabe let out a deep breath. "Well, thank God. I had hoped you'd have more sense than that. Why did you even bring it up if you weren't considering it?"

Misty shrugged. "Your mom asked if I had looked around."

Gabe was quiet for a moment, then he strolled up to her and whispered in her ear, "I'll gladly pay your rent so you can look for another job, but I'd rather my family not know about it."

Startled, she gazed at him. "I can't let you—"

He put his finger to his lips. "Shhh. You have to whisper. They have very sensitive hearing, and I'm sure they're eavesdropping."

She narrowed her eyes and whispered, "I don't need

you to take care of me. I'll have to give two weeks' notice anyway. I'd rather not quit until I have another job to go to."

"But that may take several months."

"Then it takes several months."

"I've made money with investments and can afford to help," he said.

The two of them just stared at each other, unmoving and unrelenting. Challenging each other. Daring each other.

At last, Gabe grabbed her upper arms and pulled her to him. Then he bent down and kissed her, fervently. She grabbed onto his shirt and gave as good as she got.

He didn't know how long they'd been in their desperate lip-lock when someone cleared his throat. It barely registered in Gabe's mind, until he remembered his family was probably waiting for them.

He let go and whirled around. He was barely aware of Misty stumbling into him and righting herself.

Gabe's father stood there with his arms crossed. A smile started at the corner of his mouth, but he quickly schooled his expression.

"We're waiting for you. Are you through…um, telling Misty what to do with her life? Or whatever it was I just witnessed."

Gabe rolled his eyes. "Let's eat." He strode back to the dining room, followed by Misty and his father.

When everyone was seated again, Gabriella said, "Gabe, would you please say grace?"

Gabe's eyebrows shot up. "Grace? Is it

Thanksgiving?" Since when did they say grace on an ordinary day?

His mother just stared at him.

"Okay, fine." He folded his hands and bowed his head. The rest of the dinner guests followed suit. "Good food. Good meat. Good God, let's eat."

Gabriella let out a long sigh. "I apologize for my son, Misty. What can I say? I did my best."

His brothers chuckled.

"Hey, you did a good job raising us, Mom," Gabe said.

Antonio reached over and squeezed his wife's hand. "She certainly did. Any five-foot-two woman who can have seven grown boys quaking in their boots is a pretty remarkable mother."

Gabriella laughed. "Since when do my sons quake in their boots?"

"Never," three voices said at once.

"Right. So, getting back to you, Misty," Gabriella said. "How is Parker? Have you heard from him?"

"Yes. We've been able to talk several times. He's still stateside right now."

Gabe wondered why he had to keep an eye on Misty if Parker was so available. As if she sensed his question, Misty continued, "It all depends on our schedules and whether he's out on training maneuvers."

"Oh, good. I imagine he worries about you while he's away," Gabriella said.

Gabe realized Parker probably didn't know how often he'd be allowed to speak to his sister after he deployed. Maybe because they were the only family each other had, the military would let them stay in close contact. It didn't excuse Gabe from his responsibilities, but it eased the tension a little bit.

"Yeah, I know he worries about me, but I'm more worried for him."

Gabe concentrated on his mother's pasta primavera and let the others carry the conversation. Noah talked about a fire he had responded to in Dorchester. Luca was asked about his classes. He had learned not to say much about his criminal justice major, but he was able to elaborate on his general studies at Northeastern University.

Miguel and Sandra talked about a vacation they were planning. The two of them were going to St. Kitts for their anniversary in February. Ten years. Everyone seemed to latch onto that topic with excitement.

Gabe hadn't gone away on vacation in a long time. And now that he had Misty to take care of, he doubted he'd be going anywhere real soon. Just another reason why commitments and responsibilities were not for him. He didn't like being tied down.

The only upside to staying home was that his bank account had grown exponentially. He'd made a few investments in the stock market, just to test the waters, and had been able to pick good stocks with growth potential. He liked knowing where his money went, so he didn't go in for those money markets that some unknown management company looked after.

Gabe did have the money to support someone else, but that was the last thing he wanted to do.

"You'll have to tell us how you like St. Kitts," his father was saying. "I've heard it's a great place to retire." He glanced at his wife, and she rolled her eyes.

It was already looking suspicious that his father had

retired twenty years ago and barely looked the part. Thirty-two years of service would have made him fifty years old when he retired. In truth, he was much older than eighteen when he'd started. Now, he should be over seventy, but he didn't look a day over fifty.

He flew on occasion just to age his human body. In bird form, a phoenix aged like a normal bird—sort of like a hawk. About two months equaled birth to maturity. He did not allow his sons the same luxury. He was so worried they'd get caught, he'd forbidden them to shift.

Antonio was getting antsy. He wanted to move to the Caribbean and retire there, like, tomorrow. Gabriella was human and getting on in years, but she refused to leave until all her sons were happily married. It was a stalemate, and Gabe guessed a third option didn't exist.

His mother could die before all her sons had found the kind of mates who would accept their paranormal identities. But she would die trying. And she wanted grandchildren—a lot of them. Her two oldest sons had married dragons, and dragons could only reproduce with other dragons. So they were out. And Miguel, third in line, was now out of the running too.

Miguel and Sandra had met in high school and had stayed together through thick and thin. Sandra had been shocked but quickly accepted his alternate form when he revealed it to her. Recently, they had lost a child. Sandra had miscarried in her second trimester. She'd had to have a hysterectomy, so more children were not in the cards.

That put the pressure on Gabe. And he'd bet his mother was already picturing Misty in a long white gown. Then a maternity dress. Gabriella was a notorious matchmaker. Well, she was going to be disappointed again.

He looked over at Dante and Noah. They were twenty-four and twenty-two, still kicking up their heels and having all the fun that young single guys have. They both gazed at Misty with rapt attention as she talked about the islands she had visited on a cruise.

"Jamaica and the Dominican Republic were considered dicey, and we were told not to leave the port areas without a guide. But the other islands seemed plenty safe."

"I've heard all kinds of things about crime in the Caribbean," Luca said. "Especially if tourists go off on their own."

Sandra nodded. "Some of those countries are pretty poor, making those who can afford a cruise or a vacation natural targets."

Miguel put his arm around Sandra's shoulder. "Don't worry, babe. I won't let anything happen to you."

"I know you won't." They smiled at each other and exchanged a quick kiss.

How the heck did people do it? Invest so much in another person who at some point was going to let you down or leave you? Even if their "till death do you part" vows did hold out, his human mother and sister-in-law would eventually break the hearts of everyone around this table.

Phoenixes could live as long as five hundred years. They could die as humans, but if bathed in fire right away, they would reincarnate. About a dozen reincarnations is the max, but he hadn't known anyone to try it more than three or four times.

When an elder needed to disappear before local humans became suspicious of their longevity, they'd take the opportunity to start over in a younger body.

The phoenix physiology was similar to a hawk's when in bird form or human when in that form. As shifters with a choice, they usually stayed human to prolong their longevity.

They didn't have any formal ceremony around reincarnations, but their families would generally help them with a controlled fire and let them go. The exception was when it happened as an accident while they were still in their prime. Then families would have a home base to fly to. The brownstone in Boston's South End had been his family's headquarters since his great-grandparents bought the place new in the 1800s.

Now, Gabe's great-grandparents headed a phoenix shifter clan in Arizona. Great-Grandad had become sick of New England winters—much like his father was now. With no female phoenixes born in nearly two hundred years, his grand- and great-grandfathers had married humans. Gabe tried not to think about the heartbreak they must have gone through when they lost their spouses.

His father and brother Miguel had to know this would happen to them. How did they expect to live two, three, or four hundred years as widowers? The concept just boggled Gabe's mind. They say to love and lose is better than not loving at all.

He disagreed.

Misty hadn't seen Gabe in a week. She wouldn't have minded his company as she waited in the doctor's office, trying to read a magazine. She'd read the same paragraph in the same article three times.

"Miss Carlisle?" The nurse standing at the doorway with a chart in her hands smiled at her. Was that a smile? It looked more like a grimace. Maybe she was having one of those days.

Misty gathered up her purse and left the magazine on the side table, then followed the nurse down the corridor until she stopped at a scale.

"Oh," she groaned. "Do we have to do this?"

The nurse looked her up and down. "What are you? A size six?"

She was a four but said, "I haven't been getting much exercise lately."

After a chilly silence, she stepped on the scale and then followed the nurse into an exam room. Some high-tech equipment on a rolling stand nearby produced a little clip that went on her finger. Then the nurse waved some kind of wand near her forehead without touching it. Boy, the city had some crazy medical toys they didn't use in the suburbs.

"Well, your vital signs look okay."

"That's good, I guess."

"Change into the gown, and have a seat on the exam table. Dr. Warren will be with you shortly."

The nurse shut the door behind her and left Misty alone.

She knew the drill. Put on the unfashionable garment with the gaping opening in back and climb up on the cold exam table where a sheet of white paper would protect her from the last patient's germs. Now she didn't even have a magazine.

After she'd read all the signs stuck to bulletin boards and decided she had at least half of the illnesses they were describing, the doctor finally walked in.

"Good morning. I'm Dr. Warren." He extended his hand for a handshake. It was cold, just like everything else in this place. "What seems to be bothering you today"—he glanced at the chart in his hand—"Misty?"

"I'm having some weird symptoms. It's probably nothing, but they're not going away."

"What kind of symptoms?"

"I seem to be a klutz. This is new for me. I was a dancer and always had a good sense of where my feet were. But lately, I'm stumbling or losing my balance for no reason."

The doctor smiled. "Anything else besides a little klutziness? Any tingling or numbness?"

"Yes. Occasionally in my feet. I just thought it was because it was cold outside."

"Dizziness?"

"Sometimes."

"Hmmm… Any problems with your vision?"

"Yeah, now that you mention it. I was thinking about seeing an eye doctor. My vision went kind of spotty once."

"Hmmm. Floaters?"

This guy's *hmmms* were starting to cause her concern. "Is anything wrong, Doctor?"

"I need to finish the exam before I come to any conclusions." He rechecked her blood pressure the old-fashioned way, with the stethoscope and cuff, then used the other items on the wall and looked in her eyes and ears. He checked her reflexes with his little rubber hammer, then listened to her lungs with his stethoscope.

"Hop down. I want to see you walk down the hall," he said.

As he was opening the door, she stopped. "You want me to go out there with my butt hanging out of this gown?"

"Sorry." He chuckled. "No, you can get dressed now. Come out when you're ready." He closed the door behind him.

Seriously? That's it?

A few minutes later, she had sashayed down the hall with this man undoubtedly checking out her bum. Then she had to do the heel-to-toe walk. Naturally, she didn't lose her balance. Why was it that whenever she went to the doctor, the symptom she was going for disappeared by the time she got there?

She had to walk the hall again, and when she reached the end, she turned a little too fast. Suddenly, everything shifted to the left. A nearby nurse grabbed her arm and steadied her.

The doctor's facial expression immediately changed. A slight Mona Lisa smile turned into a suspicious frown.

When she made it back to him, he ushered her into the exam room again.

"What is it, Doctor?"

"It's too early to say definitively. I still need to rule out a few possibilities." He asked her a few more questions about her general health, looked over her thin record, and scratched his chin.

"C'mon. Tell me *something*. Am I dying?"

He smiled briefly and said, "No. You're not dying. Well, no faster than the rest of us, anyway. But I am concerned. It could be a number of things. Blood tests will tell us if it's something like Lyme disease, a group of diseases known as collagen vascular diseases, certain rare hereditary disorders. You're on the young side for MS, but its onset can start as early as age twenty-two."

"I'm going to be twenty-three next week."

"Really?" He glanced at her chart. "So you are. Happy birthday!"

I might have MS, Lyme disease, or half a dozen other things? Yeah, a big fat happy birthday to me.

"We need to do some neurological tests to narrow it down. I'm ordering blood tests, an MRI with contrast, and a spinal tap. I want to see you soon after I get those results. We'll use these tests to rule out some possibilities and go from there."

He placed a hand on her shoulder and gave it a squeeze. "Don't worry. We'll get to the bottom of this."

She sure hoped so.

He scribbled on a form and said, "Take these to the secretary on your way out. She'll schedule the tests and follow-up appointment. You can get your labs done today, if you like. Nothing requires fasting."

"Oh, goody."

Eventually, she went home a few vials of blood lighter and several dollars poorer.

She sighed. *Now what?* The whole thing made her want to run screaming, but she had to get these tests while she had insurance. If she quit the bank, that would end. And there was no way Gabe could cover her health insurance and her rent, as much as he might like to.

She still didn't know what to do about his recommending she find another job. Parker was backing him up. She hadn't talked to either of them in a few days, but the one thing she knew was that she couldn't quit the bank. Not now.

She had to find out what she was dealing with before she made any kind of changes. If Gabe and Parker didn't like it, that was just too bad. Parker would be on the other side of the world. And Gabe… What could he do? Spank her? The visual made her shiver—but not in an entirely bad way.

She huffed and marched home in the chilly air, watching her steps carefully.

Chapter 6

GABE HADN'T FORGOTTEN MISTY'S BIRTHDAY. HE JUST wasn't sure what to do about it. He had to work the day before, but he'd be off at six that night. He should call her. At least he could take her out to dinner—or something.

Instead, he pulled his cell phone out of his pocket and called Jayce. The wind was bracing, so he ducked into one of the nicer hotel lobbies. Looking around, he felt like he should dress up just to stand by the window.

"Hey, buddy, what can I do for you?"

Sometimes, when someone called him "buddy," he thought of his long-lost, floppy-eared, mixed breed puppy. A little knife would jab his heart, and he'd have to push it away until the next time.

"I need to know what restaurant to take someone to. It should be nice but not impressive."

Jayce was quiet for a moment, then asked, "You mean like a chain? Like Applebee's?"

"No. Something, you know, different."

"No, I don't know. What's it for?"

"A birthday."

"Just any old birthday? Or something special, like thirty or forty?"

"It's nothing special. Twenty-three."

"So why are you calling me?"

"Because you know all the restaurants around. Before you met Kristine, you dated half of Boston."

Jayce laughed. "You're exaggerating."

"Not by much. How is she, by the way?"

"She's doing good, trying to keep her honeymoon tan with that bottled stuff."

"How's that working out?"

Jayce chuckled. "Not great. She looks a little like a tiger."

Gabe grinned. "I guess it's a good thing we have olive skin and kind of a permanent tan."

"Yeah. That's what I've been thinking. So, you need a restaurant for someone's twenty-third birthday."

"I know there must be a thousand of them, but I was hoping you could help me narrow it down."

"Do you know what she likes?"

"You mean, like Italian food? Or Chinese? And by the way, what makes you think it's a woman?"

"Because if it were a guy, you'd just ask him where he wanted to go."

Gabe had hoped this wouldn't turn into an interrogation, but it looked like it might. Glancing around, he found a comfortable armchair that wouldn't show a stain if his uniform was a bit dirty.

"So," Jayce was saying, "is this young woman about five foot five, with long dark hair and big blue eyes?"

"Shit."

A handsome couple stepped off the elevator at that moment and cast him a look that said, *You don't belong here, heathen.*

He rose and moved through the revolving door back onto the sidewalk while his brother laughed.

"Look, it wasn't my idea to look after Misty, but now that I have the job and it's her birthday the day after tomorrow, I figure I'd better do something about it. I can't think of anything except taking her out to dinner."

"Geez, Gabe. I knew you didn't have much game, but I thought with someone you've known this long, you might be less clueless."

"Thanks a lot. Now can you help me or not?" He waited for the light to change and then crossed the street near the public library.

"You can go online to a place called OpenTable. Check out a few places in the North End and make reservations."

"But she lives in the North End. Shouldn't I take her somewhere else?"

"Sure. But I still don't know exactly what you're looking for. Do you want a quiet atmosphere where you can talk? Or a loud, lively place with dancing?"

"Hell, I don't know. That's what I was hoping you could help me with."

"Well, since you're such a scintillating conversationalist, I'd probably suggest you take her dancing. We know she likes to dance."

"But I don't want her to get the wrong idea. This isn't a date."

"You're really not giving me much to work with here, Gabe. How about taking her to the ballet?"

"Ugh. Not if I have to be there too."

Jayce gave a long-suffering sigh on the other end of the phone. "I don't know what to tell you, buddy. I think there's a comedy club in Quincy Market. Maybe you can make reservations for the show and grab dinner at the Union Oyster House after."

"I guess. Seems a little touristy, but at least I wouldn't hate it."

"This isn't about you. This is for her. And by the way, don't forget to buy her a present."

"A present?" he nearly shouted.

A couple of passersby looked up at him but kept going.

"Shit, yeah. You need to buy her a birthday present. She has no one else but us, right? She might not get anything."

"Like what kind of present?"

"I don't know. Something nice like a cashmere scarf or leather gloves. Can you think of something she needs?"

"She had her wallet stolen. That was a week ago. She probably has a new one by now."

"You know what?"

"What?"

"It shouldn't be this hard. Why don't you just ask her what she'd like to do and where she'd like to go? Then maybe take her shopping and let her pick out something she wants for her birthday. If she's just a pal, you don't have to surprise her."

Oh brother... Why didn't I think of that earlier?

"Yeah. That works. Well, Jayce, I'm almost home. Thanks for the advice."

"Let me know how it goes."

"Yeah. I'll do that."

Jayce laughed. "Don't screw it up, or I'll hear about it anyway. I have eyes and ears all over the city."

"Whatever." Gabe didn't much care anymore. There sat Misty on his doorstep, shivering and looking miserable.

"Misty, what's wrong?"

She glanced up at him. How could she tell him what

she was going through and not sound needy? She rose
and tried to smile.

"I, um, have to tell you something. And please don't
tell Parker."

Gabe hesitated. At last, he said, "Let's go inside.
It doesn't sound like a discussion to be having on the
doorstep."

Misty followed him through the front door as soon
as he unlocked it. She had never been to his place. The
building was massive and plain. It was like a big brick
block with windows. Many of the buildings around it
had embellishments on the doors and windows. Not
this one. Maybe it used to be a factory or warehouse, or
because it was built more recently, they hadn't bothered.
Older buildings had the pretty frills.

As she entered the elevator, her shivering stopped.
She wasn't sure if it was the warmth of the lobby or
being with Gabe that helped. At any rate, she felt a little
more relaxed…safer, if that made sense.

When they reached the top floor, the elevator door
opened, and he blocked it with his arm, then followed
her out. Turning right, he strode down the hall to the end.

"You have a corner unit?" Misty asked.

"Yeah, more windows. The place gets plenty of
light." He opened the door, and she stepped inside. It
was a loft apartment. Exposed ductwork on the ceilings
and brick walls gave it an industrial feel. A stainless-
steel prep island and appliances added to that look.

"Very masculine."

"That's good, since I'm very manly." He gave her a
smile to show he was joking around.

The furnishings were minimalist. He didn't even have

any window treatments. She wondered if he didn't want any artwork on the walls or if he just hadn't bought any.

Misty rubbed her arms absently.

"Are you still cold?" Gabe asked.

"Oh, no. Not really. I'm just…a little stressed."

"Have a seat. What can I get you? Coffee? Water? Wine?"

She chuckled. "I need the wine, but it's only eleven o'clock in the morning. It's supposed to be at least noon for that, right?"

"I won't tell if you won't."

She let out a deep breath. "Okay, I'll take that wine and your silence too."

As he strode to the open kitchen, he glanced over his shoulder and frowned. She must have looked like she was staring at him, but she was really staring into space. She quickly pulled her attention back to her lap, then it automatically returned to what he was doing. He grabbed a bottle of wine out of the refrigerator and poured her a glass. Correction, it wasn't a glass. It was a Solo cup. Well, she'd know what to get him if she ever needed to give him a present. Wine glasses and artwork.

When he returned and handed her the cup, she took a large gulp. She figured if he wasn't going to be fancy, she didn't have to trot out her best manners either. He sat on the cushion next to hers and stretched his arm across the back of the sofa. He could easily put his arm around her shoulder. In fact, she wished he would.

"So, what has you stressed?"

"Gabe, you have to promise me that you won't tell Parker. I don't want him to worry."

"I'm starting to worry for him. Spill it."

She took a deep breath and said, "I went to the doctor for dizziness. He seemed to think it could be something awful."

Gabe's eyebrows shot up. He leaned back and gawked at her. "What makes him think that?"

"I've been having some balance problems. Stumbling, almost falling, and sometimes I feel dizzy, and I've seen spots in front of my eyes." She took another good gulp of wine.

Gabe hesitated, then said, "I thought you just wanted me to catch you."

She snorted. "Well, it happens even when you're not around. You just happen to catch me when you are."

"That sucks. Not my having to catch you—I don't mind that—but your balance thing. Is that what made you go to the doctor?"

"Yeah. I didn't want to start a job at a dance school if I couldn't stay upright. A dance teacher falling over all the time wouldn't inspire confidence."

"Christ. So you might have something wrong, but you might not? How will you know?"

"They're doing some tests, even though there isn't a specific test for some of the stuff he mentioned. They're ruling out some of those things first."

"Like what kinds of things?"

"Oh, please, don't make me go through the list. I've never even heard of some of the diseases he mentioned."

"Would you like me to go with you? You know...for those tests."

She was surprised at his offer. Or was it an offer? "Do you mean you'd go with me because you want to or because I need you to?"

"Either. As long as it's during my time off."

"I'm scheduled for an MRI next Thursday. I've never had one. Are you free then?"

Gabe strode to the kitchen, opened a drawer, and withdrew a single sheet of paper. After consulting it, he said, "I'm free Thursday. And to answer your other question, I *want* to go with you."

A sense of mild relief washed over her. She had hoped he'd go with her. At least she wouldn't be facing this alone.

He returned to his seat beside her. She must have looked pathetic, because he put his arm around her and stroked her shoulder.

He seemed uncomfortable. She didn't blame him. She had just dropped a bomb on him. Would Gabe understand her need to stay at the bank? Insurance was a must right now.

"Gabe, I'm keeping my job. I need the benefits."

He nodded slowly. "I get that. I may have overreacted about the job. It's not like the bank gets robbed every day, right?"

She chuckled. "Nah. Just every other day."

They faced each other and smiled, albeit sadly. Humor usually helped lighten her mood, but not when it was followed by pity.

After a short hesitation, Gabe said, "Friday is your birthday. I was hoping to surprise you, but I didn't know what you'd want to do. Why don't you come up with something?"

"You mean you'd like to spend my birthday with me?" She was a little surprised but genuinely pleased. This guy was either taking his responsibilities seriously or maybe he really enjoyed her company. She hoped it was the latter.

"Of course. The evening, at least. I'd never let you spend your birthday alone."

She deflated slightly. That meant he felt sorry for her. "I, um… I have plans with some girlfriends."

"Oh! I didn't realize you had…" Trailing off, he looked uncomfortable.

Her jaw dropped. "You didn't know I had friends? How pathetic do you think I am?"

"I didn't mean that! No, really. I don't think you're pathetic at all."

She took a couple of deep breaths. At last, she came out with the truth. "Actually, I have plans the weekend after next with some friends, but not tomorrow or the next night. I just…well, I didn't want you to feel obligated to look after me."

"Misty, I don't feel obligated to spend time with you. If I didn't enjoy your company, I would probably just text the occasional 'Hey, how are ya?'"

She smothered a snort. "Well, *that* makes me feel better."

"So, what would you like to do Friday night? I asked Jayce for suggestions, but all he and I could come up with was either the ballet or a comedy club."

"Wow. Two ends of the spectrum. I can guess who came up with each one of those options."

"Yeah, you probably can. But I really want you to decide. Pick anything. What would you like to do on your birthday?"

"I…I don't know. I hadn't thought much about it." That was a lie. She had thought long and hard about how to spend her birthday. She just hadn't thought she'd have company. Now her plan didn't fit. Gabe at a spa? That would be a hoot.

"We could just go shopping for a present and then go out to dinner," he was saying. "What kind of food do you like?"

Shopping for a present? She didn't need anything but his companionship—and maybe more… She could start with the restaurant. "I know we both like Italian food. I like Indian and Chinese food too. What do you like?"

"All of those." She could see him struggling. "It doesn't matter what I like. It's *your* birthday. So, what would you do, ideally? Forget about me for a second."

She chuckled. "Actually, I'd go to a day spa, get a facial and a massage, then grab Chinese takeout and eat at home. After that, I'd probably watch a movie."

At last, he smiled. "Sure. Let's do that."

Her eyes widened, and she burst out laughing. "So you'd go to a spa with me?"

He shrugged. "Why not? I'm secure in my masculinity. A massage after work actually sounds pretty good."

"I'm picturing you wearing green goop on your face and cucumbers covering your eyes."

He groaned. "You wouldn't make me do that, would you?"

Oh, she was tempted. "Probably not."

"If I can get you to change that to *definitely not*, I'll take you. And Chinese food after sounds perfect. The movie depends on what you pick."

"Let me guess, you like action-adventure, something with lots of violence."

"Yeah, but it's your day. What do you like?"

"Actually, I like lots of different movies, including action-adventure. I can do without the violence, though."

"Fine. Action-adventure, with no violence. Is there such a thing?"

"I sure hope so."

They spent a few seconds staring at each other in silence. At last, Gabe gathered her into his arms and held her close.

He could almost hear his mother giggling.

He didn't see himself as the most sensitive of his family. That questionable honor fell to Luca. The youngest. Didn't it? He was the one their mother babied.

Gabe's mind wandered back to his childhood. His brother Ryan had been raised as his twin. The eldest son had met with a deadly accident at age seven. With a quick explanation to Jayce and Miguel, his parents set Ryan on fire, and he reincarnated out of the ashes. But apparently he didn't stay in phoenix form long enough to mature to his former age. He shifted into human form right away. Their parents couldn't stand the idea of burning a baby, so Ryan stayed as he was.

Gabe was just an infant. Suddenly he had a "twin." He didn't remember any of it, but the story was well known among family members. A neighbor saw the two babies, so the Fierros decided to raise their eldest and middle child as twins. He and Ryan should have been close. They had a good relationship, but not like real twins.

His first memories were of Jayce teasing his younger brother Miguel and of Ryan trying to join in. Gabe used the distraction to crawl up into his mother's lap and get some prime cuddle time for himself. To be honest, sometimes he suggested a game and then quit when the others were busy…just to bask in his mother's love. That didn't make him sensitive, but he could see why his mother might think so.

Now Misty was all cuddled up to him. He propped his chin on top of her head and stroked her dark, silky hair, cascading down her back. And he liked it.

"Gabe?"

"Mmm?"

"Is this okay?"

"Is what okay?"

"This. Your holding me. 'Cuz if it is, I'd like to stay here forever."

He chuckled. "Forever is a long time, Misty. I might get hungry."

She pulled away just enough to look up at his face. "I'm hungry now. But not for food."

Whoa. "You had to go and make it weird." He let out a nervous chuckle.

"It's *not* weird. We like each other. We always have."

"Parker would kill me."

"And then I'd kill him. Either way, *I* get to live." The little minx was smirking.

"Oh, so as long as *you* come out of it okay…" He couldn't help laughing.

She gave him a carefree shrug.

He dipped her until she lay flat on the couch, and then he loomed over her. Without thinking, he bent down and captured her lips. Her arms twined around his neck. Careful not to put his full weight on her fragile body, he stretched out beside her. They kissed for who knew how long.

He was well aware of the erection straining his jeans. A moment later, he realized she was aware of it too. And she reached down to stroke him.

"Jesus, Misty. Stop it."

"Why? I want you, Gabe. And unless you're always this hard, I can tell you want me too."

He bolted upright. "Oh, fer Chrissakes." He stood, placed his hands on his hips, and frowned. He was losing the war inside his head. At last, scooping under her bottom and back, he lifted her effortlessly. Then, against all better judgement, he carried her to his bed.

He lay her in the middle and straightened. Arms folded, he studied her for a few moments. She wasn't afraid. Her expression was...expectant? Probing?

"What's wrong?" she asked softly.

"Nothing. That's what's wrong."

Her forehead wrinkled into a perplexed line.

Gabe unbuttoned his shirt, still holding her gaze. She didn't move as he peeled it off. Her eyes flicked to the white puckered burn mark on his ribs but quickly returned to his face.

"You can still stop me if you want to," he said.

"I don't."

She sat up and pulled her sweater over her head.

Shit. She had the most perfect breasts he'd ever seen. Granted, they were still partially hidden by her black satin bra, but the shining skin and her cleavage were tempting enough. His mouth watered. Her breasts were no less beautiful when she popped her bra open and tossed it aside.

She unbuttoned her jeans, and he quickly lay down beside her, placing his hand over hers. "Let's leave those on for now."

"Seriously?"

"Absolutely. There's a lot of feel-good fun that can be had with your pants on."

Misty rolled her eyes. "If you say so."

Gabe leaned over her. "I say so." He laved one nipple, and it pebbled quickly. Then he took it into his mouth. As he sucked one breast, he massaged the other, giving a small squeeze to that nipple. She arched and moaned.

Gabe continued to lavish attention on each breast while Misty ran her fingers through his hair occasionally, as if holding on for dear life.

"Oh God, Gabe. I swear I could come from just this."

He leaned back with a satisfied smile. "See what I mean?"

"Yeah, but what about you? I want to make you feel good too."

"I do feel good."

"I don't think so." Misty pushed on his shoulder until he lay on his back, and then she climbed on top of him. She began the age-old beat of dry humping.

Gabe moaned. "How did you learn that?"

"You'd be surprised what living with your grandparents will make you resort to."

He grinned. He didn't know if Misty was a virgin or not. He hoped *not*.

It didn't seem like the right time to ask, so he just closed his eyes and enjoyed the sensations she was creating over his clothed cock. Before long, he had to stop her, or he'd embarrass himself.

"Babe, it's time to stop."

Instead of stopping, she sped up and added more pressure.

"Whoa, I'm too close."

"Go with it. Please," she begged.

Gabe didn't really have a choice. His orgasm had already started. Then his climax hit, and he came hard in his tighty-whities.

"Jesus. Why did you…"

She placed a finger over his lips. "Shhh. Now we're even."

"Not by a long shot," he said, then he flipped her onto her back.

She shrieked and giggled. He unzipped her jeans and plunged his hand down over her black panties. He stared at her face as he massaged her covered clit.

Her eyes closed on a moan. Her breathing sped up, and she gripped his bedspread. Her moans became more frequent and soon gave way to a different sound. A strangled cry. He didn't let up until she screamed, then grabbed his hand, and yanked it out of her jeans.

Finally, her arms fell to her sides, and she panted, relaxing completely. After a few more deep breaths, her eyes fluttered open. "Wow. That was… I mean… Wow."

Grinning, Gabe propped himself on his elbow. "And you still have your pants on."

She laughed out loud. "I guess you were right. Lots of feel-good fun was had."

"Now, I'm going to leave you for a few minutes—to change my pants."

Chapter 7

MISTY HEADED HOME TO CHANGE HER CLOTHES. SHE couldn't help smiling at strangers on the subway. She'd needed that release more than she'd realized. Her first real orgasm with a guy. And she was glad it was Gabe who gave it to her.

As she walked up to her house, she received a text message. She smiled when she saw it was from Gabe. She waited until she was in her apartment before she read it. All he said was, We never made firm plans for your birthday. I can't do the spa. I'm working until 6. When should I pick you up?

She felt like saying "now," but she didn't want to seem overly eager. Or more eager than she already had been. Anyway, it was time to cool it...just a bit. Until she seemed more cool than desperate.

She consulted her calendar. There was very little to consult. Other than tests and doctor's appointments, she was wide open. Sadness swamped her. If not for Gabe, her life would suck. Living paycheck to paycheck. Working at a job she had no passion for. Even her love of dance might be in jeopardy.

She wanted to be in a better mood when she talked to him again, so she just texted back, How about seven thirty?

A few moments later, he answered, You got it.

She shuffled to her bathroom, turned on the shower, and waited for it to get warm. What was she going to do with the rest of her life? With nothing to look forward to, she was adrift.

"Turn it around, Misty," she said out loud. Her grandmother had taught her to reframe negative thoughts and feelings. But as much as she tried to look at it differently, all she could see was day after day of the same boring job and not much to show for it. She sighed deeply.

Stepping into the warm steam and hot water interrupted her train of thought. It was a good thing, because that train was on the track to doom. As she ran her hands over her head to get it wet and ready for shampoo, she thought of Gabe running his hands over her hair and down her back. Sometimes it almost felt as if he were petting her. And then his hand would move farther down…a little lower than was strictly necessary. It seemed as if Gabe was the only good thing happening to her now.

She missed him already.

Growing up down the street from the Fierros showed her how different families could be from each other. Her own small WASP family was quiet, and as children, she and Parker were expected to be well-behaved. Their home was always neat and clean, because that's the way her father liked it. Her mother had a cleaning lady come in twice a year. She helped her with the huge spring cleaning to freshen everything after a long hard winter, and a thorough fall cleaning just because.

The Fierros, on the other hand, were a rough-and-tumble bunch, always running, jumping, and tossing things around. Their home was alive. There didn't seem to be anything to refresh at any particular time of year. It would just wind up on the floor or out of place a minute later anyway.

Mr. Fierro may have been head of the household, but

Mrs. Fierro was in charge. Misty's parents commented on how they managed to keep all those kids in line. They would shake their heads and say, "How do they do it, with all those boys?" It was as if her family would have cracked under the pressure that the Fierros thrived on. Maybe they would have. But Misty secretly wished her family could be more like them.

After her shower, she toweled off and wound another towel around her hair. She barely heard her phone ringing. By the time she got there, she had a voicemail message. It was from her friend Julie in Saugus.

"*Hey, girl. We miss you. All of us are planning on getting together for a toy party.*" She giggled. "*And we're not talking about Barbie dolls. Let me know when you're available. We won't have it without you!*"

Misty called her right back. "Julie! It's so good to hear from you. I've missed you too."

"So, have you met anyone? Anyone that could replace the toy, if you know what I mean?"

Misty smiled to herself. "Sort of." She wasn't sure how much to say. She didn't want to identify Gabe as her boyfriend...yet.

"Sounds intriguing. So where did you meet this 'sort of' someone?"

"I don't want to go into details just yet. You know how it is."

"Ah. It's just at that flirting stage, right?"

Misty thought about how far past flirting they were. "Not to repeat myself, but sort of."

"Oh, come on, girl. Spill. Is it someone I know?"

"No. None of you know him. Let's just say that I'm not ready to DTR."

Julie sighed loudly. "Fine. When you 'define the relationship,' be sure to let me know first."

Misty figured she'd better change the subject. "So where are we having this toy party?"

"Well, we were thinking of doing it at your place. None of us have seen it yet, and we'd like to go into the city to kick around a bit beforehand."

Misty laughed. "Oh, so you just thought you'd invite yourselves to my place? Lucky for you, I'd love that. Maybe when you all know how to get here, you'll come and see me more often." *Or at all*, she thought.

She missed her friends and was afraid that their lives were going separate ways. The kind of separate ways that resulted in Facebook-only communication. Everyone was either going to college or engaged already. Julie was the only one whose life was as uncertain as hers was.

"Excellent!" Julie said. "So when would it be convenient to throw a party for all of us?"

Misty laughed again. "Wow. You're not nervy at all. Hang on. Let me look at my calendar." She pulled up her planner, looking further out, even though she knew there was nothing on it to speak of. More tests and doctor's appointments. Ugh. "How much notice do you need?"

"Not much. I have a party next weekend. How about the weekend after that? I can text everyone as soon as you and I pick a time."

"Don't you need to consult the hostess, or put-er on-er, or whatever she's called?"

"You're the hostess. And you're in luck, because the put-er on-er is me."

"Oh. I see how it is. You're using me to forward your career as a toy party put-er on-er."

"No! I don't want you to feel that way. I just thought it would be fun if we all got together, and doing it this way would be even more fun."

"Yeah. I was kidding. It does sound like a lot of fun. How's a week from next Saturday? The twenty-ninth."

"Perfect. What time?"

"I don't know. Do you want to have dinner here?"

"Oh, hell no. I'd never make you cook for all of us. Besides, you only eat rabbit food as I remember. We could all go out to dinner first. Nothing fancy or expensive. Maybe just someplace in Quincy Market."

"That sounds good. Want to meet at the fake Cheers at five?"

"Sure. We might need to make reservations since there are so many of us."

"I don't know if they take reservations."

"Well, I'll call and ask. If they don't, maybe I can order pizza to be delivered to your place? And salad, of course."

"Either is fine with me. You decide…since you're orchestrating the whole thing."

"Speaking of orchestras and stuff, how's your dancing going?"

Misty's good mood took a nosedive. How could she tell her friend she might never dance again? She would have to wait until she knew for sure. Hopefully they'd find out it was nothing…just some inner ear infection or something.

"I haven't really had time to do much. New job. New apartment. I'm still adjusting to the move."

"Really? I thought you'd have a dance studio lined up before any of that. I've never known you to miss a lesson…until your grandparents got sick."

"Nope. A roof over my head and a job to pay for it take priority. I'm getting practical in my old age."

"If you say so. Well, I gotta go. I'll let you know what I find out as far as who's coming."

"Sounds good. I'm looking forward to it."

And she was. She might need friends more than ever, depending on the results of the tests she was having Thursday.

⁓⁓⁓

Misty and Gabe had firmed up their plans for her birthday. Gabe had had to work overnight the night before, but he would be getting off at six that evening. She hoped he didn't get too many calls during the night and wind up exhausted. That was a common problem for firefighters, but she understood this and would go with the flow. They made arrangements to meet at his station in the South End, right around the corner from where they grew up.

When she arrived, she was told Engine 22 was battling a three-alarm fire in another part of town. Gabe was on Engine 22. *Oh well…*

Misty decided since she was in the neighborhood, she'd drop in on Mrs. Fierro. It wasn't as if she was inviting herself for dinner. She already had plans—whenever Gabe got back. She left a message with the dispatcher, so he'd know where to find her.

She was pretty sure she was always welcome at the Fierro home. How many times had Gabriella told her so? If she got hungry before Gabe was able to join her and Gabriella offered to feed her, she could have a cup of coffee and a cookie or something to hold her over.

Strolling down Massachusetts Avenue a couple of blocks, she found herself actually looking forward to visiting with Gabriella Fierro. The woman had been like a second mother to her.

When she arrived on the doorstep and rang the bell, the diminutive matriarch opened the door and almost threw herself at Misty, giving her a huge hug.

"Come in, come in! It's cold out tonight, isn't it?"

"Yeah. It's always freezing on my birthday."

Gabriella Fierro gasped. "It's your birthday? Today? I thought it was… Never mind. Happy birthday, my sweet girl!" After another tight hug, she released her. "Let me take your coat."

"I hope I'm not imposing. I was supposed to meet Gabe at his station, but they're out on a job."

"Oh, yes. We heard about a big fire in South Boston. Antonio thought he'd go watch for a while." She chuckled. "You'd think he might have had enough of fires after thirty-two years." She hung up Misty's coat and led her to the kitchen. "I was just wishing I had some company. Have you had dinner yet?"

"Not yet. I have plans with Gabe, but I guess they'll have to wait."

Gabriella sighed. "Ah, yes. Plans need to be somewhat flexible when you're involved with a firefighter. It's a shame they don't work regular hours, but fires can be very inconsiderate."

Misty smiled. The woman had such an easy way about her. She wondered if she'd ever be able to take things so calmly. Misty tended to be "wound a little tight," or so she'd been told.

"Can I get you some coffee and a small piece of cake? I imagine Gabe was taking you out to dinner, and I don't want to spoil your appetite."

"Coffee, yes. But no thank you to the cake. It might be easier if I just get takeout and save him the trouble of going out to dinner at this point."

"Tsk tsk." Gabriella shook her head as she gathered the cream, sugar, and spoons. "You can't always make everything easy on them, especially when the relationship is new. They might grow to expect it."

"Oh. I don't think we have what you'd call a relationship."

Gabriella was quiet until she sat down with two mugs of coffee and set one in front of Misty. Then she took a deep breath and held Misty's gaze. "Be patient with him. He needs you. He just doesn't know it yet."

Misty didn't quite know what to say to that. Gabe needing anybody or anything seemed implausible. He was always so self-sufficient.

Leaning back, coffee mug just below her lips, Gabriella smiled. "He's a good boy. They all are. But Gabe is the one who… Well, I worry."

"Worry? Why would you worry about Gabe? Is something wrong?"

"Oh, honey, it's not that. He's just a little stubborn. He thinks he doesn't need anybody, but he couldn't be more wrong."

"I see." She didn't see. She didn't have a clue.

"So, how are things with you? Have you found any leads on a new job?"

"Um, no. I don't think I'm going to look for a new job right now. I kind of need the insurance."

Gabriella's eyebrows raised. "Health insurance? Are you all right?"

"Yeah. Well, no. Um, maybe."

Gabriella gave her an indulgent look. "You know you can tell me anything, right? I won't divulge any secrets."

"I know. It's just that I need to have some tests first. I won't know if there's anything wrong or not until next week at the earliest."

"What makes you think there might be a problem?"

"Between you and me, I've been having trouble with my balance. I was afraid it might interfere with my dancing, so before quitting my job to find something in the dance community, I thought I'd better get it checked out."

"That's wise."

The phone rang, and Gabriella rose to answer it. They had one of those old-fashioned phones on the wall. It even had a dial instead of buttons. The Fierros were complete Yankees. What was that saying? *Use it up, wear it out, make it do, or do without.*

"Hi, honey. Yes, she's here. We're having a lovely chat." Gabriella smiled slyly. "There's no need to rush. We're fine."

As she replaced the receiver, she chuckled. "My son will be here in about five seconds."

"Oh no. Is he worried about being late? It's no big deal. Really."

Gabriella grinned. "No, darling. He's afraid of my talking to you." As Gabriella sat down, she chuckled and shook her head. Apparently she wasn't going to explain anything further. She just took a sip of her coffee and looked pleased with herself.

Misty couldn't imagine why Gabe would be afraid of his mother having a conversation with her. Was there something he didn't want her to know?

It took more than five seconds, but not much. Gabe strode through the front door and entered the kitchen. He was covered in soot.

"Hello, darling." Gabriella rose and strolled to her son. He towered over her, but she grasped his broad shoulders and pulled him toward her for a kiss on his cheek.

"Mom, I'm filthy."

"No kidding. I thought you'd take a shower at the station, but I guess you didn't want to let Misty wait any longer than necessary. That was sweet. Why don't you run upstairs and shower? I can find an old pair of your jeans and a sweater or something to change into…unless you need a suit. I don't know what your plans were."

Gabe focused on Misty for a moment. "I, uh… We were just going to get Chinese food and go back to your place to watch a movie, right?"

"Yeah. We never did decide what movie we wanted to see."

Gabriella set her hands on her hips. "Is that the best you can do, Gabriel? Takeout food and a movie at her house?"

"Butt out, Mom."

Misty had never heard him speak to his mother that way. It would have bothered her except that Gabriella was smirking. It was as if the older woman was in on some kind of private joke neither Misty nor Gabe understood.

"I really didn't want anything fancy. Takeout food and a movie sounds perfect."

Gabriella shrugged. "Well, if that's what you really want..."

"It is. I never do anything much for my birthday."

"I see. If you'll excuse me for a minute, I'll go get some fresh towels and set those out for you, Gabe."

"I'd rather shower at my place. I have something for her birthday there, and I'd feel more comfortable in jeans that fit. Not something I wore in high school."

"Okay, honey. I'll just get Misty's coat then."

When Gabriella had left the room, Gabe looked over and gave Misty a smile. "I'm sorry I'm late. It couldn't be helped."

"Oh, I know. The dispatcher told me about the fire. Saving lives is a little more important than one person's birthday."

"Well, I'm glad you feel that way. Because about a dozen people are going to be able to celebrate another birthday because of us."

Misty rose and strode over to him. She placed her hands on his dirty coat, looked up at him, and said, "My hero."

Gabe leaned down and gave Misty a quick peck on the lips.

Gabriella cleared her throat, then breezed into the kitchen, carrying Misty's coat, grinning from ear to ear.

———

Gabe had set Misty up in his living room with a movie to preview and then went to take his shower. He was just soaped up when Misty walked into his bathroom, stark naked. Her womanly body was on full display—and she was breathtaking. He stood there in the glass enclosure, not quite sure what to do, but he didn't object. How could he? He could barely speak.

"What are you doing?" he asked when he got ahold of himself.

"Modeling my birthday suit." She smiled. "Oh, I think you missed a spot. Let me get that for you." She opened the shower door.

Suddenly, her foot caught on the lip, and she toppled off-balance. He lunged forward and caught her, his hands grasping her under her arms. Instantly, every nerve in his body was alive with sexual energy. The satiny texture of her skin, smooth and flawless, resulted in the overwhelming urge to caress the rest of her.

"Are you okay?" he rasped.

"Dammit." She let out a frustrated breath. "Way to make a sexy entrance, Misty."

When he had her steadied, she reached up and put her arms around his neck. "You're tall."

Gabe gently pushed her away, despite his body protesting the loss of her warmth against him. "And you're my best friend's sister."

She answered him by taking the soap and running it over his chest, and then down, and down, all the way to his pubic hair, before he grabbed her hand and wrenched the soap out of it, replacing it in the soap dish.

"Not fair," he said.

"All's fair in love and war."

Gabe gazed at the ceiling while he decided what to do. "I'm going to hate myself for asking, but which is this?"

"You don't know?" She picked up the soap again and massaged his six-pack. After an agonizing few seconds, she said, "I love you, Gabe. I have for years."

Shit. I was afraid of that. As much as he didn't want her to feel that way, telling her not to wouldn't accomplish a thing—except to hurt or infuriate her.

This time, he didn't stop her as she caressed his pelvis and eventually reached his semierect cock. He leaned back and moaned. His shaft swelled instantly. Sensations she created within him were ridiculous. He had never felt such a strong physical reaction to a female's attention before.

Gabe gazed at Misty's full lips. Any man would kill to kiss a mouth like that. He yanked her hands from his cock and pulled her into a full embrace. His lips descended, and she tipped up her chin to meet him halfway.

He captured that sensuous mouth, and their tongues found each other easily. Heat built as they sucked and twirled, and the steam had nothing to do with the hot water. Gabe wondered what kind of strange power this woman had over him. Had she hypnotized him? He knew better, but he was unable to help himself.

He still hadn't responded to her confession of love. He should say something, but he had no idea what. He simply feasted on her lips until they were swollen. Pulling away, he took a deep breath.

"Misty—"

She reached up and stroked his cheek. "It's okay. You don't have to say anything back. I just couldn't stand not saying that any longer."

Gabe framed her face with his hands and stared into her eyes. All he saw was pure sincerity. No guile. No manipulation. *Dear God. Now what?*

"Let's get out of here," Gabe said huskily. He shut off the water and stepped over the lip of the glass enclosure.

Remembering how she had stumbled into the shower, he extended his hand to help her over the three-inch sill.

The droplets on her skin shone as the light caught them and they dripped down. He had to cover her, or he'd go crazy. He grabbed the towel he had set on the sink for himself and wrapped it around her.

"You don't like what you see?"

"On the contrary, I like it too much."

She threw off the towel and stood straight, as if offering herself to him.

"Misty. We can't."

"Yes, Gabe. We can. My brother doesn't own me."

"But he's trusting me to take care of you."

"And that's exactly what you'd be doing." She smiled. "Gabe, I never had a real orgasm until the other day. You gave that to me. I can't help wanting to give you the same gift."

He groaned.

In seconds, they were in his bed, wrapped around each other. To his surprise, he was trembling inside. The thrill of anticipation doubled his pulse. He wasn't sure who started the deep passionate kisses that fed the fire burning inside him. He only knew that she aroused him like no other woman ever had.

He hesitated to break the kiss. She tasted and affected him like wine. Gabe leaned away a little bit and nibbled her lower lip. She answered by pulling his upper lip between hers. *Okay...Either she's had more experience than she's let on or she's a fast learner.*

Chapter 8

NEVER HAD A GUY KISSED HER THE WAY GABE DID. HE WAS gentle, yet sure of what he was doing. He didn't mash his teeth against hers while fumbling around her breasts. He took his time and caressed her whole body.

The feel of his warm skin against her own aroused her even more. If this was foreplay, she'd take all she could get.

She ran her hand over his sparse, dark chest hair and circled her index finger around his nipple. Then she gave them each a little squeeze. His husky moan encouraged her to keep exploring. Her fingertips followed the muscles of his arms and shoulders while he expertly kneaded her breasts. Then he gave her nipples a little squeeze too. Her breath caught from the electrifying sensations. She tangled her fingers in his damp hair. She played with the silky strands, winding them around her fingers, being careful not to tug too hard.

Gradually, she caressed a path down his back, gliding over the dip at the base of his spine. When she cupped his buttocks and squeezed, he growled. She ached to go further but waited for a sign.

He rolled so she was lying on top of him, then placed both of his hands on her exposed buttocks and kneaded her glutes. She sighed at the intimacy of this new discovery.

"Beautiful," he murmured. "You feel like silk. So

soft… Warm perfection." He rolled her onto her back, then feasted on her breasts until the rosy tips became hard and puckered. He captured each nub between his teeth, scraped gently as he withdrew, and then flicked his tongue over the very end, creating a torturous frenzy.

Still, there was no urgency in his lovemaking. He seemed to enjoy awakening every raw nerve in her body. The length of his hard cock prodded her naked thigh. She reached down, grasped it, and he sucked in a deep breath.

"Misty…"

She didn't answer, and he didn't finish his thought—if he had one.

He rolled on top of her. Nothing stood between her and the point of no return. She couldn't stop now even if she wanted to.

Gabe said, "I'm going to tell you in searing detail what's going to happen if we continue."

"Tell me," she said breathlessly.

"I'm going to fill you up. Take you, inch by hot inch. I want to feel your legs wrapped around me while I penetrate you. I'm going to rock hard against your clit until you climax. Is that what you want?"

"Yes! More than anything."

Her next breath mingled with his as they shared a deep lingering kiss. He crawled off of her just long enough to grab something from his nightstand.

A condom, she realized. Thank goodness one of them was thinking logically. He placed the condom on the pillow, scooted between her legs, and parted her nether lips.

"Why are you—" She sucked in a deep breath as his tongue flicked her most sensitive spot. "Oh!"

Her urgent moans filled the air. A rush of sensations erupted into a powerful climax. She thought she heard screaming. *Oh yeah, that would be me.*

As soon as she had returned to earth, she let go of the sheets she had gripped in her hands as she held on for dear life. Nothing mattered now but having this man inside her.

"Gabe, I want you."

"How? Tell me exactly how you want me."

She didn't dare use the words *making love*. The L-word would probably scare him off—and she wanted him *in*. "I want you fucking me, five minutes ago. Is that exact enough?"

He laughed. "Just making sure."

He opened the condom package and handed her the rubber. "Would you like to do the honors?"

She took the condom from him and placed it over the tip of his penis but only after planting a kiss there. Then she rolled it all the way down to the root. She cupped his balls and gave them a gentle squeeze. He growled.

She wanted to come again, but this time with her lover inside her.

He positioned himself between her knees and paused at her entrance. He smiled down at her, then leaned down and kissed a path to her ear, whispering, "I want you to enjoy this fully."

She planned to.

He leaned on one elbow, propping himself up. As he entered her, slowly, he looked down at her, and his eyes seemed to glow. His free hand parted her folds so he could make contact with her clit completely.

He began a slow rhythm and did as he promised,

grinding into her clit with his pelvis. God, the sensations! Soon, she was alternately gasping for breath and moaning. She arched to meet his every thrust, and it wasn't long before she exploded in ecstasy.

She thrashed. She screamed. She left her body and saw stars. Gabe came too, with a roar.

He collapsed on top of her, and when he tried to roll off, she blocked him. "No. Stay"—*pant*—"where you"—*pant, pant*—"are."

He chuckled. "I'm kind of heavy."

"I like your weight on me."

He laid his head on her pillow and kissed her temple. They lay like that for several minutes, just breathing and recuperating. When he had apparently had enough recovery time, he propped himself on his elbows and began his rhythm again.

If she'd had any doubts about being deeply in love with this man, they had vanished.

They made love several times that night. At last, they drifted off into a very sound sleep, Gabe buried deep inside her.

———

Upon awakening, Gabe began to stretch and bumped into something. Misty. *Oh my God. What have I done? Did I really make love to Parker's sister all night?*

He glanced down, looking for the last condom he used. He searched the bed, trying frantically to find it without waking Misty.

She woke up anyway. Sitting up, she stretched lazily. The blanket slipped down, revealing the beautiful breasts he had enjoyed over and over.

"Oh God, Misty. I'm so sorry."

Her perfect eyebrows shot up. "Sorry? For what?"

"For getting so carried away. I should never have…
I mean…"

"Spit it out." Her mouth hardened into a thin line.

Shit. She knew what was coming.

He sighed.

"Yeah. I get it." She threw off the covers, snatched up
her clothes, and headed to the bathroom.

That's when Gabe spotted the condom. It had been
right under her. It might have emptied inside of her!
Fuck. Berating himself for his stupidity, he lay back
and threw his arm over his eyes. It was too late to do
anything about it now.

A loud bang came from the bathroom. *What the…*
Was she so angry that she threw something? She shouted
his name. *Time to face the music—or yelling.* He grabbed
his bathrobe off a hook and shrugged into it as he strode
to the bathroom door and knocked. "Are you okay?"

"No. A little help here, please?"

He slid open the pocket door and was shocked to see
her on the floor.

"Misty!" He rushed to her side and helped her up.
"You fell?"

"Yeah. I dropped the toothpaste and lost my balance
when I went to pick it up. Something's wrong. I'd get
up myself, but I just can't seem to make my legs work.
Especially my left one. It feels…well, like it fell asleep."

"It wasn't like that a minute ago?"

"Yeah, but no. It tingled, but not as bad as now."

"Let me help you," he said, even though he felt pretty
helpless himself.

"No. Wait a second, maybe it's not too bad." She waved him off. "I think I can do it." She tried to drag herself up by grasping the edge of the pedestal sink.

He let her try for a moment, but the first responder in him couldn't let her struggle. He picked her up off the floor and carried her back to the bed.

"We have to get you to a doctor."

She hung her head. "I know. I have that MRI in a couple of days, but I'm not sure I should wait."

"You sit here and rest."

"Okay." She had started rubbing her left leg.

"Does it hurt?"

"No. It's more like pins and needles."

He was still alarmed, but at least she wasn't cringing in pain.

"Do you have a laptop?" she asked.

"Of course."

"Would you be willing to bring it to me?"

Uh-oh. "Why?" *I hope she's not looking for an internet diagnosis.*

"So I can Google these symptoms. That doctor wasn't telling me anything helpful."

"I don't know how smart Googling this will be. You can get a lot of misinformation off the internet."

"Please."

He sighed, but relented and brought his laptop to her. "Where do you want to start?"

"Uh…" She scanned the screen for an inordinate amount of time. At last, she said, "You decide."

This wasn't the Misty he knew. She wasn't indecisive. If anything, she knew exactly what she wanted and wasn't shy about expressing it.

"I'm not just going to Google symptoms. WebMD has a pretty good reputation, and it has the most introductory information."

"Okay. I'll start there." Misty typed for a few minutes while Gabe ruminated over his misgivings. Maybe he should have refused to let her use his computer for this.

At last, she clicked on a video. He didn't know why she picked that one. The doctor droned on about myelin. Lesions. Antibodies. It was dry, but he understood the important stuff. He glanced over at Misty. Her eyes were closed.

"What's wrong?"

"Um, just a little trouble focusing."

"As in mentally, or with your eyes?"

"Both?"

Shit. He took the computer and paused the video.

"Oh, no, Gabe. I wanted to finish listening to that. I think it's what I have."

"Let's not jump to conclusions."

She restarted the lecture. As the video went on to explain how a lesion in a specific part of the brain affected a person's nerves, which affected the muscles—including muscles of the eyes—well, it didn't look good.

He turned her head so he could study her eyes. All he could see was water gradually filling her inner corners and spilling over. He wiped a tear away with his thumb and whispered, "Don't panic." He wasn't sure if he was talking to her or himself.

"How can I not? What if they see those lesions on my MRI?"

"We'll deal with it then."

"Oh, will *we*?"

Her sarcasm was hard to miss. "Yes. *We* will," he stated firmly.

"Don't tell Parker anything. Please."

"Why not?"

"Because there isn't a damn thing he can do from where he is except worry," she said. "They use live ammo in training, you know. I'd rather he concentrate on his surroundings, not on what's happening here." She placed her hands on her forehead and closed her eyes.

"Headache?" he asked.

"No. Despair."

"Misty…" He gathered her into his arms and let her weep.

Misty had to take some time off from the bank for her MRI. When she explained the reason to her boss, Adam was understanding—a little *too* understanding.

He dragged his chair around his desk and leaned forward to place his hand on her knee. "I'm here for you if you need anything, Misty. Anything at all."

"I, uh, appreciate that, Adam."

"Would you like me to go with you? I have a meeting with a client, but I can reschedule."

"No. Gabe is taking me. Thank you, though."

Adam leaned back, and his expression grew chilly. "The firefighter who's responsible for destroying our vault?"

She knew he wasn't fond of Gabe, but seriously? "The damage is covered by insurance, right?"

"Uh-huh. So was the cash. How do you know him, anyway?"

"We grew up together. He was my brother's best friend, and his family lived down the street from us."

"Was? I take it they aren't friends anymore."

"No, that's not what I meant. We moved when I was twelve, but he and Gabe stayed in touch all those years. Parker would take the T into the city once in a while."

"Didn't you go too?"

"I was too busy. Dance classes, field hockey, and school stuff… I would have been welcome, though."

"Hmph. Well, since your brother isn't around, the other guy is probably acting as his surrogate. Another big brother, in other words."

Thinking about the incredible night they'd spent together, Misty almost laughed. "I know what a surrogate is, and no. Gabe isn't a big brother to me. He's a friend."

"Just a friend?"

"Why all these questions about Gabe? I like to keep my personal life kind of private."

"Of course." He rose and dragged his chair back behind his desk.

She rose too, a little more slowly. "Can I go? He'll be here—" She glanced out his glass office wall just as Gabe strode in. "Oh! There he is." She couldn't help the grin that spread across her face.

Gabe spotted her, smiled back, and waited outside the office.

Adam just waved her off. "Let me know how it goes." He opened a folder and looked bored as he went back to work.

She strode over to Gabe. "Hi!" she said brightly.

"Hi, yourself. I didn't expect you to be in such a good mood."

She leaned in and whispered, "Getting out of work early always puts me in a good mood. I'll just get my things and be right out."

She knew not to admit just seeing his handsome face was enough to thrill her. She walked briskly to the back room to get her jacket and purse and was relieved when she didn't even list to one side. Standing behind the counter wasn't too bad. Any time she felt unsteady, she could just grab the edge.

When she returned he said, "I'm double-parked outside."

"Oh, I didn't know you had a car."

"I don't. It's Dante's."

She followed him to the steps, and as he jogged down, she walked over to the handrail. He noticed she wasn't beside him when he got to the bottom and turned.

Slapping his forehead, he said, "Sorry. I should have helped you."

"No. I've got it."

Just then, she stumbled.

He rushed over and caught her, even though she had a death grip on the railing and wouldn't have hit the pavement.

"Damn," she muttered.

"Don't be mad at yourself. It's not your fault. You can't help it."

She realized that Gabe had already given her a diagnosis in his head. "You can't help it" or "it's not your fault" meant there was some medical reason for her clumsiness.

She was relieved that he'd brought a car and she didn't have to ride the subway to Brigham and Women's

Hospital. If it was crowded and she had to stand while compensating for shifting floors, she'd be in trouble.

The car ride seemed long and quiet. She tried to initiate conversation once and he told her he really had to concentrate. He hadn't driven a car in several months… or maybe a year.

She didn't know what to make of that. Maybe that's all it was. Driving in Boston could be a nightmare even for commuters who did it every day. Or maybe he was avoiding conversation. The way they'd left things on the day after her birthday made her wonder. He was fine when talking about superficial things, like making plans to take her to this appointment, but he clammed up when she casually tried to bring up the topic of their relationship.

Please don't be an asshole, Gabe. Don't lose interest as soon as I put out and the chase is over. That's what my stupid high school boyfriend did.

What chase? She suddenly realized because she was the one who had been chasing him, he'd never had the thrill of the chase at all. Well, that had to change. She wouldn't chase him anymore. Let him come to her… but would he?

Gabe had regrets. Huge regrets. He was supposed to be looking after Parker's little sister, protecting her from guys like him. Instead, he wound up being the guy who took advantage of her.

Well, that had to stop. She needed him as a friend, not a lover. Especially now.

"We're almost there. Why don't I drop you off at the

front door and find a place to park? I'll meet you in the waiting room."

"No need," she said. "I can handle it. Why don't you go do something you feel like doing? I'll text you when I'm done."

Surprised, Gabe glanced over at her. She was staring straight ahead. Something had changed. "What's wrong?"

She looked over at him. "Nothing."

"I am not very good at woman-speak, but I've heard that nothing means something."

She smiled and said, "Sometimes nothing means nothing. Seriously, there's nothing to worry about. I want you to know that I can handle these things on my own. I'm sure there will be times when you can't be there."

"Okay, if you're sure."

"Yes, I'm sure."

Gabe pulled up to the front entrance and let her open her own door. She wanted to be independent, and now he was in flux again. Should he insist on walking in with her, making sure she got to the office all right? Or would that just be making her dependent on him? *Shit*.

"Misty, I should go with you."

"No, you shouldn't." She slammed the car door shut and ambled down the sidewalk. He watched as she entered the revolving door. She held onto the bar in front of her, but she seemed to be walking okay.

He sat there for a few moments, debating with himself. At last, he decided to park the car and meet her at the MRI unit. And it wasn't because he had to. It was because he wanted to.

When he found her, she was in the waiting room, scanning a magazine. She didn't seem to be reading, just glancing at the pictures. Maybe she was more nervous than she had let on. He was glad he didn't just take off and leave her.

"Hey, beautiful," he said as he sat next to her. "Is this seat taken?"

She glanced over at him and shrugged. "I was saving it for some good-looking dude, but you'll do."

Gabe laughed. She still had her sense of humor. At least he hoped that was a joke.

"Misty, if you think you're being a burden, don't. I'm not here because Parker asked me to look out for you. Well, not completely."

She closed the magazine and faced him. "Then why are you here? I told you I could do this on my own."

"I know you can." What could he say? *I'm here because I care about you?* He didn't want her to take that the wrong way, although it was true. He simply didn't elaborate.

She went back to gazing at her magazine. He wondered how much concentration she had, since she flipped the pages frequently.

When she got to the end of the magazine, she tossed it back on the table next to her, and instead of picking up another one, she slid down in her chair. Leaning her head against the top of the backrest, she stared at the ceiling.

"Bored?" he asked.

"Yeah."

This wasn't the Misty he knew. Her answers were short and not so sweet. Something was up. Maybe it was simply the stress of her impending appointment.

Fortunately, at that moment, a nurse opened the door

and called her name. She got up slowly and seemed to be a little unsteady. Gabe shot to his feet and grasped her arm. She shook him off. "I'm fine," she snapped.

He backed away with his hands in the air. "Okay, okay. I'll be here when you get out." He watched as she followed the nurse through the door toward the first step in finding out the truth.

That's got to be it. She's got to be scared out of her mind. That's why she's not herself.

A big part of him sensed there was more to it.

Chapter 9

MISTY PLANNED TO OUTSMART ANY CLAUSTROPHOBIA THEY warned her about by closing her eyes before she entered the MRI tunnel and not opening them until she was out. As far as her body was concerned, she could've been lounging on a sandy beach. Despite the circumstances, she'd try to meditate and calm herself down.

Then the noise started. They'd given her headphones, but she didn't feel like listening to music. *Ping, ping, ping. Pong, pong, pong. Boom, boom, boom, boom, boom...*

Random thoughts drifted through her mind. Gabe, sitting in the waiting room. She pushed the thought away and went back to her happy place. She wondered how Parker was doing. She pictured him safe, maybe playing cards with his buddies. Gabe in bed with her, rolling her over. Kissing her.

Ping, ping, ping. Pong, pong, pong, Boom, boom, boom, boom, boom...

Damn. As often as she tried to push thoughts of Gabe away, her mind returned to him. She set that thought aside again and pictured herself in a dance class. In her mind, she could execute every turn and even the acrobatic moves perfectly.

Ping, ping, ping. Pong, pong, pong. Boom, boom, boom, boom, boom.

Dear God, I hope I don't wind up in a wheelchair.

And on it went until at last the techno-torture was over. When the white-jacketed guy reentered the room, she sat up and asked, "What did you see?"

"I don't interpret the results. That's up to the doctor."

She studied him for any sign of discomfort. Apparently, he was used to the question, because he didn't seem to have much of a reaction. She wanted to press him for some kind of hint, but chances were he'd just practice avoidance again. Men were good at avoidance. She rolled her eyes.

As she changed out of the hospital gown and back into her jeans and sweater, she wondered if Gabe was really waiting all this time. *Of course he is. He promised Parker he'd look after me.*

But would he be there if he hadn't?

She sighed and pushed open the door to the waiting room. Yup. There he was, reading a magazine.

She wandered over to him. "Anything good in there?"

He flipped the magazine over and said, "Yeah. Some new cars coming out this year."

He had been reading *Consumer Reports*. Fascinating. "Are you thinking of getting a car?"

He shrugged. "Depends."

She knew she was supposed to ask "On what?" but instead, she just waited to see if he'd elaborate on his own.

He didn't. Instead, he rose and dropped the magazine on the table. "Ready to go?"

"More than ready."

He dug the car keys out of his pocket. "Where to?"

"Home, I guess."

"How about Starbucks?"

"Really? You're going to take me out for ice cream because I was such a good girl at the doctor's?"

He looked puzzled. "Starbucks doesn't have ice cream."

"I know. I meant..." She sighed. "Never mind. Coffee sounds good."

On the way there, he turned toward her and asked, "How did it go?"

He seemed more comfortable driving—and talking— than he had before. That helped her relax a bit, but she was still aware that something had changed. "It was okay. About what I expected."

"Did they give you any results?"

"No. Apparently the only one who can be trusted to interpret the results is the doctor, and I guess I'll hear from him sometime soon."

"When's your next appointment?"

"Next week. Wednesday."

"I'm working Wednesday through Friday."

She shrugged. "No problem. I think I can go to a simple doctor's appointment by myself."

"Are you sure?"

What choice did she have? Her friends at the bank were working. Her friends in the suburbs were working. "Yeah. I'm sure."

"Okay then. Let me know how it goes."

"Sure thing."

He glanced over at her again. She kept her eyes straight ahead. She thought he might ask if something was wrong—again—but he didn't. Maybe he really didn't care.

Gabe met his older brother for a drink that night. They found a quiet table, and before they even sat down with their beers, he asked, "Can we keep this between the two of us?"

Jayce adjusted uncomfortably in his seat. "I don't keep secrets from Kristine, but you can trust that whatever you say won't go any further."

Gabe chewed his lip and thought it over. He didn't know his new sister-in-law very well, but if Jayce trusted her completely, it was probably safe. One thing their parents had impressed on all the Fierro boys was finding women they could trust with a *big* secret.

Come to think of it, a public bar might not be the place for this conversation. "Jayce, can we go out on your boat?"

"In the middle of winter? Why? Do you want to do some ice fishing?"

Jayce. Always the joker. Maybe I should have called Ryan—in Ireland. Yeah, that would help, he thought sardonically.

"No. To clear my head." He lowered his voice. "I need to fly. You know we can't do that where our ridiculously colorful tail feathers will be spotted."

"Why don't you just do what I do? Find a chimney to fly down and coat your feathers with creosote?"

"Yeah, and getting that crap off is so easy. Even in the shower, scrubbing with castile soap, it doesn't like to come off."

"What's going on, Gabe?"

He sighed and raked his fingers through his hair. He wouldn't have been surprised to see some falling out from stress. "It's Misty. I don't know what to do about her."

"Ah. I should have known." Jayce smirked. "You've still got no game, do you?"

Frustrated, Gabe set his beer on the table a little too hard. "It's not that."

After a long hesitation, Jayce tipped his head. "Well, are you going to tell me what it is or not?"

Gabe took a deep breath, then spit it out. "I know I told Parker I'd look after her, but I've been doing a piss-poor job of it."

"What do you mean by doing a piss-poor job of looking after her?"

Gabe glanced around the bar. No one was paying any attention to them. He just hoped his brother wouldn't give him a stern lecture and embarrass the shit out of him. "This is just between us, right?"

Jayce nodded.

"Okay. No. I don't want to get overinvolved, but I think I made a mistake."

"Go on," Jayce said as he swirled his beer.

Gabe covered his eyes and mumbled through his hands, "I slept with her." He removed his hands to take in Jayce's reaction. Or maybe he should say his nonreaction. His facial expression hadn't changed. He was just staring at his beer.

"Well?"

Jayce placed his beer on the table and smiled. "And I thought you had no game."

He let out a heavy sigh. "It's not a game, Jayce. She's vulnerable, and I was supposed to be looking out for her. Instead, I slept with her. By the way, does that make me her boyfriend?"

Jayce laughed. "Man, you are clueless."

"Give me a break. I know you slept with women before Kristine, and they didn't all become steady girlfriends."

Jayce stared at him for a few seconds. "We're different people, Gabe. I let them know up front I wasn't looking for anything serious, then left them laughing and remembering our time together fondly. I don't think you can do that."

"Yeah, I don't think so either. And what did you tell women who wanted to see you again?"

Jayce shrugged. "I would say I wasn't ready to settle down with just one woman. Then I'd compare them to one beautiful flower in a bouquet and say I couldn't pick my favorite."

Gabe mimed sticking his finger down his throat. "Yeah, that's not my style. How about making up some excuse to disappear, like joining the French Foreign Legion?"

Jayce burst out laughing. "Is that what you came up with? I don't think that would work for you...unless you do plan to join up."

"I'd rather not."

Jayce reached over and placed his hand on his brother's shoulder. "I'm glad to hear that. I'd miss you." When he sat back, he added, "Frankly, you could do a lot worse than Misty Carlisle."

"You're right, but she could do a lot better than me."

Jayce straightened his spine and frowned at Gabe. "What the hell makes you say that?"

"Have you forgotten what we are? I wouldn't know how to tell her. You, Ryan, and Miguel all lucked out. You and Ryan wound up with women who had their own paranormal identities, and Miguel...he was really lucky to have found Sandra in high school. By the time they were ready to get married, she knew him well enough to know he would never hurt her or anyone else, no matter what shape he took."

"And Misty has known you all her life. I understand your stumbling block, but it's clear to anyone who has eyes that she adores you."

Gabe hung his head. "Yeah. I'm screwed."

Jayce laughed, then quickly schooled his features when Gabe glared at him. "All right, Bro. We'll go for a very cold boat ride, and you can fly until you put some of the pieces together. I could do it for you, but it wouldn't mean much. You have to figure this out for yourself."

"Like Dorothy having to go all the way to Oz to figure out she'd rather be home in Kansas?"

Jayce smirked. "Something like that."

"If only it were that easy. Unfortunately, there's more."

"I figured as much. What is it?"

"She might have MS."

"Jesus. That's horrible—for her. Is that what's making you want to run?"

"Hell no. I'm not that much of an asshole. If anything, it would prevent me from running when I really want to."

"So, what makes you think she has MS?"

"She noticed some weird symptoms. She even fell in my bathroom when she went to pick up something she dropped. After that, we looked at some YouTube videos. It sure sounds like MS."

"Whoa. Diagnosis by internet?"

"No, of course not. She saw a doctor. I guess they're still ruling out other things, but it sounds like the doc suspects MS. The last thing I want to do is add to her burden right now."

"Is there anything else?"

"Does there need to be?"

"Nope. I'd say that's plenty to deal with."

Two hours later, Gabe was gliding on the wind. Yes, it was cold, but his feathers covered every bit of skin, so he barely felt it. His mind was so preoccupied, he wouldn't have thought about the weather anyway.

What must Misty feel like? He hadn't even tried to put himself in her shoes. Her slippery, klutzy shoes. He knew she wasn't a klutz, though. He remembered her twirling down the sidewalk. He and Parker were asked to watch her while her mother was entertaining friends. She was light on her feet and nearly acrobatic. She could cartwheel down an entire city block without appearing dizzy at the end.

In feathered form, Gabe couldn't sigh, but he was doing a lot of that in his mind. *So, what does Misty feel like, knowing she might never dance again? Shit.* She would be devastated if the doctors told her that.

And what about physical pain? She never complained about it—never showed it—except for the time she fell in his bathroom. She'd winced. Could she have been keeping that to herself?

He pictured her on the floor, naked, massaging her left leg. Then he pictured her in his bed, the sheet slipping down to reveal...

Focus, Gabe!

It didn't matter how many times he tried to forget what they'd shared on the night of her birthday. The feel of her soft skin under his fingers, her rounded breasts and bottom, her responsiveness to his every touch...it was all burned into his brain.

Yup. If he couldn't find a way to put that behind them, he was well and truly screwed. At least he had his job to keep him occupied for the next few days.

Gabe landed on the deck of Jayce's boat and shifted back to his human form. He shivered the minute the freezing wind hit his skin and couldn't get his clothes on fast enough. Jayce came up from below with a blanket and wrapped it around him.

"So, little brother. Did you get any answers?"

Gabe shook his head.

"I guess you'll just have to keep following the yellow brick road. Watch out for those flying monkeys."

"Thanks for that."

Gabe hadn't called in nearly a week. Misty would be damned if she was going to call him. There were more tests and appointments, but her friend Julie said she'd take an afternoon off and go with her to the next one.

Misty really didn't want to tell her friend anything was wrong, but fortunately, a plausible excuse was built into her eye exam. They asked her to have someone with her, because the medicine that would dilate her pupils for the exam could interfere with her vision for a little while.

She'd rather be able to see Gabe when she was with him, anyway. Picturing his tall, solid body and his naturally brooding expression didn't help. She missed him like crazy. But letting him come to her would answer the only question she had about him. Unfortunately, she was getting the answer she didn't want.

She wanted him to care. To call her and ask how she

was feeling—at the very least. The truth was she was feeling better, and she wanted to tell him so.

The last thing she wanted was to become a burden on anyone. That scared her more than any disease or problem. And she knew that would scare away almost any guy. Except, apparently, her boss, Adam. He'd been asking if there was anything he could do to help make her life easier. The only thing she wanted him to do was to stop asking.

Julie arrived, and Misty greeted her with a huge hug. Then she leaned back and stared at her friend. "Your hair! It's purple!"

"Yeah. I wanted something different. It's been too long, girl. What have you been doing with yourself?"

"You know. Work, work, work."

"Ewww. No, I don't know. I work as little as possible."

Julie jogged down the stairs to the narrow sidewalk. Misty managed to get into her friend's car without incident. She fastened her seat belt. "So, why are you doing the toy parties, if you don't like to work?"

"For that reason exactly." Julie started the still-warm car. "The parties are more fun than cleaning houses any day."

"I'll bet. You're so fun and friendly. Isn't there something else you could be doing instead of maid work?"

As Julie pulled away from the curb, she confessed, "Yeah. I thought about becoming a flight attendant… Hey! We could become flight attendants together!"

Shoot. That would be nice, but with numbness in her hands and feet, that might be a problem. "I don't know about jet-setting all over the world. I mean, I can see you doing it, but I like Boston and want to stay right here."

"Too bad."

"So, what are you doing to make the flight attendant dream come true?"

Julie rolled her eyes. "Promise not to tell anyone?"

"Of course."

"I went for an interview at Delta, and they offered me a ground position. Just what I want to be doing. Driving into Logan every day and checking in bags," she said sarcastically.

"I'm sorry. Do you think the purple hair had something to do with it?"

"Nah. There was only a purple streak in it then. Something I could have easily dyed back. To be honest, I was so mad, I just did the whole thing bright purple to spite them."

"Really? Don't get me wrong—I like it. But I doubt they're losing any sleep over your hair color."

Julie chuckled. "I know. I never said I was logical." After a brief silence, she changed the subject. "So, are you ready for the Tantalizing Toys party?"

"Is that what it's called?"

"Yeah. I was going to send you a hostess kit, but since I was seeing you today, I just brought it with me. Dig around in my tote bag until you find it."

Misty rummaged around in the huge bag. She pulled out a brochure with vibrators, roses, and nipple clamps on the cover. "I found it." And she promptly dropped it in her lap. Her fingers were numb again. Dammit.

Julie grinned. "Are you shocked?"

"Not at all."

"To be honest, I wasn't sure if you'd want to do this. I mean, you were kind of a good girl in high school."

"I was just involved in a lot of activities. That doesn't mean I wasn't interested in, um, other activities." She turned the pages with the feeling of pins and needles in her hands.

"Okay. Well, good. It's good to know you're normal."

Misty rolled her eyes. "Thanks."

"So, how's the kinda sorta boyfriend?"

Misty snorted before she realized how it might be interpreted.

"Oh crap. That's too bad. Well, we're in the same boat, then. Are you sure you don't want to run away and see the world? I hear that European men love American women."

Misty wanted to run away, all right, except that wherever she went, the body she was trying to figure out would be going with her.

―――

The eye exam resulted in a new pair of glasses and a suggested MRI. When she said she'd already had one, the eye doctor said she'd send for the results.

At last it was the weekend, and Misty's old high school friends were coming over. She hadn't cared what the reason was. Julie's adult toy party was as good an excuse as any. Now it seemed like the perfect suggestion. She needed to cut loose and have some fun.

As she was opening the red wine to breathe, she poured herself a glass. "Breathe this," she said aloud and toasted the empty air in front of her. She took a generous swallow.

"Oh! I have to order the pizza." She grabbed her purse out of the closet in her bedroom and called the pizza place down the street.

"Hi, can I order three large pizzas now but not have them delivered until seven? Yeah? Great." She placed the order for one cheese, one pepperoni, and one vegetarian—and a salad. *That should cover the bases*.

She glanced down at what she was wearing. Her work clothes were much too fancy for this crowd, so she quickly changed out of her white silk blouse and gray suit and put on a pair of tight-fitting jeans and a purple sweater. Perfect. If she splashed some wine on it, no one would be the wiser.

At six sharp, the doorbell rang. Julie led the pack into her living room. They came in two cars but arrived together. Hugs were happily given all around.

Robin also sported a new hair color, but she went with pink. Misty wasn't sure how she felt about the color. Robin's had been such a pretty shade of golden blond.

Nanette had a new tattoo—this one on her wrist. Misty saw it as she took her coat.

"Can I get you guys some wine?"

"Hell yeah!" Nanette said.

Soon, the party was in full swing. She had put out appetizers and more wine. A lot more wine. They were joking and laughing, and Misty was fully relaxed for the first time in what felt like months. It had been a couple of weeks since Gabe had relaxed her into a sexual stupor.

She had briefly wondered if the party would affect her in a sad way. Gabe still hadn't called. She'd called him a few choice names in her mind, however.

"C'mon, Misty. Let's get this show on the road. Where can I set up?" Julie asked.

"Oh, I didn't know what kind of space you needed. Is the ottoman enough room? I can get a tray if you need a flat surface." Julie's expression said it wasn't ideal. "Or I have the dining table. We'll have to make room when the pizza comes." She checked her watch. "That will be in about half an hour."

Julie shrugged. "I guess the ottoman will have to do. I need to leave the stuff out so everyone can touch it afterward."

"You mean, we get to try it out?" Jordan asked.

Everyone laughed.

"Yeah, right," Julie said. "I'll just pull down the shades so the neighbors don't get a free show."

Julie began her demonstration, using a lot of double entendres, making her friends giggle and outright laugh. The wine didn't hurt, either. Everyone was in a frisky mood when the doorbell rang.

"Oh, that must be the pizza!" Misty yelled out, "Be right there!" She walked briskly to her bedroom to get her wallet.

"I'll get the door," Nanette said.

Misty heard her friends squeal and murmur their approval. *The pizza must smell delicious*, she thought as she rounded the corner. Or the delivery guy might be a hunk.

Gabe stood there, like a deer in headlights.

"Take it off! Take it all off!" Robin shouted. Nanette was running her hands over his chest, and Jordan was pulling his coat off…or trying to.

Julie gave her a big grin. "You didn't tell me you hired a stripper!"

"I didn't! That's my…" She felt helpless. She couldn't say boyfriend. She didn't have time to explain he was her brother's friend.

Gabe yanked his coat out of Jordan's hand, turned, and fled.

"Crap."

"Uh-oh. Was that your kinda sorta boyfriend?" Julie asked.

"Not anymore."

Chapter 10

GABE WAS HORRIFIED AT FIRST, THEN AMUSED, THEN PHILO-
sophical. Apparently, Misty wasn't pining over him at
all. It was nice to be mistaken for a stripper, he thought,
until... *Wait a minute*. Misty hired a stripper? For what?

He almost turned around and marched back to her
house, but he got ahold of himself. Shit. He had no
right. He was trying to squash a boyfriend/girlfriend
relationship, and acting like a caveman wouldn't
exactly accomplish that. He needed to talk to someone.
Not one of his firefighter buddies. He'd never hear the
end of it.

His real brothers might understand—or not. Luca was
too young. It was Saturday night, so Noah and Dante
were out playing wingman for each other. Jayce... Well,
as much as he respected his older brother, he'd find it
funny as hell.

Maybe Miguel. Crap. Miguel was so serious and had
been married so long, he probably had less experience
with this than Luca had. That left Ryan, who was in
Ireland. Was it worth an international phone call?

Gabe kicked at the ice patches on the sidewalk and
decided he'd figure out what to do by himself. He
usually did.

Stopping at a busy coffee shop, he made his way
inside and got in line. When his turn finally came, he
ordered something a little more decadent than usual. A

giant chocolate chip cookie and coffee with a double shot of espresso, instead of just the usual cup of joe.

When he'd paid for it and joined those loitering at the other end of the counter, waiting to pick up their orders, he was surprised to find a familiar face.

"Sandra?"

"Gabe! How are you doing?"

His sister-in-law was the last person he'd expect to see out in the world. Wasn't she attached to his brother's hip? He glanced around the store, then out the windows. "Where's Miguel?"

She laughed. "We aren't together every minute, you know. I'm taking a class."

"A class?" he repeated.

She chuckled. "Yes. An art class."

"I didn't know you were into art."

At that moment, Sandra's name was called, and she picked up her frothy drink. He watched her put a packet of sugar substitute in and grab the top. When she came back, his name was called.

"Would you mind waiting a minute?" he asked.

"Sure. My class is over. I was just getting this for the ride home."

Gabe nodded and went to grab his coffee and the bag that held his cookie. He added a generous amount of milk and sugar then returned.

"Do you want to get a table? Or take a walk?" he asked.

She looked around and saw all the tables were full. "We could take a walk or sit in my car. Whatever you feel like doing."

"I'll walk you to your car. How's that?"

"It's only down the street. And to be honest"—she

tipped her head so she could glance up at him as he held the door open for her—"you look like you need to talk."

He created a column of fog with his long exhale. "Is it that obvious?"

"You looked pretty preoccupied when you walked in." She turned toward the city lights and wandered in that direction. He caught up and walked beside her.

"You always were the perceptive one."

"So, what's going on?" she asked.

"It's Misty."

"Oh dear. Girl trouble?"

"Huh? Oh, ah… We're just friends. She's not doing so well. Having trouble with balance, vision, walking, and forget dancing."

"Oh no! Poor thing. I remember her as a little girl dancing up and down the street in front of your house. Miguel and I would have to dodge her sometimes to get inside."

Gabe smiled. "Yup, that was her. Always dancing. Now, I guess she might not be able to."

"Dear Lord. What a disaster. Is she okay? She must be devastated."

Gabe frowned. "Yeah, I would've thought so. But I just went to her house, and she was having a party. Some of her friends thought I was a stripper and practically tried to tear my clothes off."

Sandra giggled and slapped her hand over her mouth. She glanced up at him and giggled some more. Eventually, tears leaked out the sides of her eyes.

"Yeah, yeah. Hilarious."

"I'm sorry, Gabe. It's just that, knowing you…"

She wasn't going to finish that thought, apparently, but he couldn't help being curious. "What?"

"Well, you know…"

"No, I don't. What aren't you telling me?"

She let out a long sigh. "Gabe, you're almost as serious as Miguel. And that's not a bad thing. Not at all. It means you care. You'll take a minute to think things through and keep your comments to yourself, if you don't think they're helpful. That's a good thing."

He stared at her. He'd never thought he had much in common with Miguel. Miguel was so quiet, nobody really knew what he was thinking. Everyone was too busy joking and laughing and trying to one-up each other.

She took his hand and gave it a squeeze. "But still waters run deep. If I were facing something difficult, I'd much rather have you or Miguel by my side than anyone else in your family."

Gabe realized his mother had said something similar to him. But she had used the word *sensitive*. That's probably why he'd dismissed it. He didn't mind taking a minute to think things through, and yes, he cared. Sometimes he cared too much.

"Maybe you can help me figure this out. I want to be there for Misty, but I don't want her to get the wrong idea."

Sandra looked at the stars and let out a snort. "You guys." She shook her head. "What do you think will happen if you give a girl a hug when she needs one? Do you think she'll plan the wedding? Honestly, I don't know what you're so afraid of."

"You mean, she won't?" He was only half joking. "I know. I know. It doesn't make sense. But neither does her having a party right now."

Sandra sighed. "She probably needs to blow off steam and have some fun. Are you hurt that you weren't invited?"

"Ha. Not at all. I don't think I would have fit in. It was all girls, and they were pretty giddy. I was just glad to get out of there in one piece."

"So, why were you there in the first place?"

"I was just going to check on her. She had a couple of appointments during the week, and I wanted to know how they went."

"You didn't call her?"

Gabe shrugged. "I'm not very good on the phone."

Sandra stopped and folded her arms. She gazed at him for a few moments before speaking. "Gabriel Fierro, I think you're lying to yourself. Not that you aren't good on the phone—I believe that. Miguel isn't either. But you could have just asked 'how did it go?' That's what most people would do."

He shrugged.

"You know, I work at Brigham and Women's Hospital. I'm in OB-GYN, but if she ever needs support and you're…being you, tell her to call me there."

"Hey! I'm not that heartless."

She let her hands drop to her sides and smiled softly. "I know. I've known you since you were thirteen. Misty was about ten. She'd say, 'Hey, Gabe. Look!' and cart-wheel down the sidewalk. She didn't call to Parker, or Miguel, or even me. And you didn't ignore her. You watched and gave her a thumbs-up.

"I think you want to give her that hug. Maybe you need a hug yourself. Gabe, you love the girl. You may not want to admit it, but that's what I see when you look at her or talk about her. And I don't blame you. She's a kind, sweet, beautiful girl. And she needs you. If you let her down, you'll hate yourself."

How could his sister-in-law know all that? He didn't even know it himself. But it rang true. Everything she said.

"I…uh…"

She held up her hand. "You don't need to say anything. Just think it over. My car is right here." She pointed to the dark-blue Toyota they stood beside.

"Oh. Well, I guess it's time to go home. Thanks for talking to me."

Sandra pulled him into a hug and didn't let go. Eventually, he relaxed and hugged her back.

"See? I hugged you for a long time, and I don't want anything from you. It's okay. You can hug her, and she won't plan a wedding." Sandra hit the unlock button on her key fob and opened her car door. "Unless you want her to." She closed the door, winked, and waved as she drove away.

Misty's party didn't break up until after midnight, so she wasn't surprised when she woke to the sting of the fully risen sun. She sat up and rubbed the sleep from her eyes. The evening came flooding back, especially the part where Gabe made a quick appearance and disappeared like a magician in a cloud of panic.

Her friends apologized and giggled and wanted to run after him, but thank goodness, she talked them out of that. He would have been mortified. Correction, *more* mortified. "Should I call him? I was waiting for him to come to me," she muttered to herself. Well, he'd done that.

She wandered out to the kitchen and made her morning coffee. Her one splurge was good coffee. She'd bought one of those special French presses that made two cups of strong, dark Kona roast. She needed it this morning.

As she waited for the water to boil, she tried to phrase what she would say. *Hey, Gabe… Was that you who barely escaped with your underwear last night?* She couldn't help giggling. Maybe she could tease him, saying he could have a part-time job delivering strippergrams.

She shook her head, picturing the big somber guy he'd become handling any of that well. He would probably stammer and change the subject. How had he become so serious? She didn't remember him that way. He was always on the quiet side, but with Parker, he was able to talk and laugh. She guessed that in a family of nine, *somebody* had to be quiet. *But it's not like he needs to be with me.*

Well, whatever she said, it had to happen soon. If she let it go, it would look like she hadn't cared what her friends did. If the shoe were on the other foot, he'd be right there apologizing for his friends—probably after he knocked down anyone who touched her. That made her smile…then wonder at herself. She certainly wouldn't want to inspire anyone to violence. But it would be nice to know he cared. A little.

She sighed deeply and finished making her coffee. After a few fortifying sips, she located her phone. On her way to her closet, she realized she had forgotten to charge it. "I guess that dumb landline will come in handy after all, Parker."

She felt a little foolish talking to her brother as if he were in the room instead of far away. What to tell him had also been weighing on her mind. The tests weren't looking good. She'd been told there were lesions and she should see a specialist. They needed to know if the disease was active or not.

The disease. Yeah. They'd ruled out everything except MS. They hadn't made it official yet, but it seemed only a matter of time before they ran out of other tests and explanations.

Suddenly, she felt ill. Nausea was an early symptom, but she hadn't had that one yet. Chills invaded her, and a sweat broke out on her forehead. She dashed for the bathroom and made it to the toilet bowl just in time.

Last night's pizza made a reappearance along with a lot of pink fluid. *Ugh. Too much wine.* It must have been the wine.

When she was able to get up, she brushed her teeth viciously, trying to get every crevice and taste bud clean. Then she dressed in jeans and a sweater, her usual Sunday morning attire. Even if she did feel like going to church, which she didn't, she could go like this. No one got all dressed up at the church she belonged to. *Boy, am I feeling lazy.*

"Well, I have to call him," she said and strolled to the living room where she kept the landline on an end table.

After a couple of rings, Gabe answered. "Misty?"

"Yeah, hi. Sorry about last night. Are you okay?"

He laughed. "I'm fine. It was flattering in a bizarre way."

"Well, I'm glad you're looking at it like that. I'm really sorry for my friends. When we all get together, we can act a little…wild."

"You probably needed to go a little wild."

She relaxed. "I did. But I wasn't feeling too great this morning. I didn't think I had that much to drink, but I must have. Oh well. Live and learn."

"Are you feeling okay now?"

"Yeah. Perfectly fine."

"Good. Would you like some company?"

Her brows shot up. "Seriously?" That popped out before she had a chance to think it through. *Of course* she wanted his company!

"Unless you're busy," he added.

"No. I was just planning on having a lazy, do-nothing day. I'd welcome your company."

"Okay. Maybe I'll bring a board game. Do you still like Risk?"

"You're kidding. You still have that?"

"Yup. We're Yankees, Misty. Perfectly good games aren't thrown away, even if nobody plays with them much. You know the Yankee motto…"

"Yeah, I've heard it. Use it up, wear it out, make it do, or do without. Okay then. Bring it. I guess you got over your aversion to taking a risk?" She almost slapped her hand over her mouth. *Did I just say that? Way to sabotage yourself again, Misty.*

After a brief pause, he said in a quiet voice, "I might be getting there."

After he hung up, she ran around like a demon, cleaning up after the party, vacuuming, dusting, and paying special attention to the bedroom. By the time he got there, she was pooped.

Gabe had spent quite a while thinking about what Sandra had said. She was not wrong. He just didn't know what *love* meant—especially when it came to Misty. He hadn't felt this way about any other woman and didn't even want to.

Yes, he loved Misty…but how? As an old family friend?
As a newfound friend? As a lover? He was terrified to find
out, but he'd promised he'd try to be honest with himself.

He'd decided that spending some quality time with her
would help them get to know each other better as adults,
meaning not at doctor's appointments and not in bed.
Like hanging out or—dare he say it—*even actual dating*.

That's why he'd brought a game with him. It was
funny he'd suggested Risk. He hadn't even thought
about what the name implied. But if what he felt for
Misty was real, he could decide what to do from there.
Risk it or stay in his safe isolation. In the meantime, he
didn't want to behave like an ass. That made him feel
worse than anything.

Then he thought of something that made him laugh and
allowed him to be an ass because it was part of the game.
So instead of Risk, he brought Cards Against Humanity.

Misty let him in and reached for his coat. "Army
green looks good on you," she said.

Anything looks good on you, he thought. But instead
of voicing the compliment, he just smiled.

"Where's the game?" she asked.

"In my pocket."

"Risk? They make a pocket version now?"

He chuckled. "No. I didn't feel like playing Risk. I
brought something we've never played together before." He
dug the sleeve of small square cards out of his deep pocket.

When he produced the game, she grinned. "I've
always wanted to try that, but I thought it was for more
than two players."

"We can make up our own rules. That's what I like
about it."

"Awesome!"

"That's right. We play for awesome points. When it's only two people though, there's no card czar. We have to agree on which person's answer to the question is the funniest. Think we can do that without arguing?"

She looked up at him and smirked. "Is this a test?"

Maybe. He hadn't thought of it that way. Until now. "I don't like tests. I just think we both need a good laugh. But if we can't decide on which is the funniest answer without debating, it won't be fun anymore. Would you rather not try it?"

"No. I'd like to see what happens."

"Okay. Got paper and a pen? One of us needs to keep score."

"I'll be right back. Make yourself comfortable."

Gabe looked at the sofa and chair. Hmmm... It didn't really matter where they sat as long as they behaved themselves. He picked the chair.

"So, how was the rest of your party?"

She laughed from the other room. "It was fine. The girls were just a little worked up, because it was an adult toy party."

Did she just say what I think she said?

When she came back, she gave him a sticky note pad and a pen with the bank's name and logo on it. "Do you want anything to drink?"

"Just water."

"Water sounds good." Misty left to go to the kitchen.

While she was gone, he glanced around her apartment. He didn't see any "toys" and wondered if she'd bought anything. He wasn't about to ask, though.

He hadn't really looked closely at her apartment

before. A bookshelf held not only books, but a vase and some home decor stuff. There was a large photo book facing out. He opened it and saw some pretty pictures of waterfalls, rivers, streams, and lakes.

Misty returned with two glasses. She put one on a cork coaster on the end table and found a second coaster for Gabe's glass. Then she sat on the end of the couch closest to his chair.

"This is great photography," he said.

"Yeah. Parker gave me that."

"Really? It doesn't strike me as something he'd like."

"He didn't. I did. We were kicking around Rockport one Saturday, and I wanted a souvenir. While I was looking around, I thumbed through this book and remarked on how much I liked the photographs, but it was kind of pricey. I don't know when he bought it without my noticing, but he gave it to me for Christmas last year."

"Very thoughtful guy, your brother."

"Yeah. He has his moments." She smiled wistfully.

"Have you talked to him recently?"

"Not for a few days."

"Have you told him about the tests you're having?"

She worried her lip. "I will. Probably as soon as I get the official diagnosis and prognosis." She waved away the air in front of her. "I don't want to think about that now. There's nothing I can do until Thursday."

"What's Thursday?"

"Another appointment. No biggie. You don't have to come with me."

"Are you sure?"

"Positive. Hey, let's play this game." She leaned forward, like she couldn't wait to get started.

"Okay." He opened the box and dealt ten white answer cards to each of them. Then he placed the smaller pile of black question cards between them. "We can take turns reading a question."

"Okay. Ladies first?"

"Always." He smiled.

She peeked at her white cards and chuckled. He surveyed his too. Oh boy. He forgot how politically incorrect this game could be. Hopefully she wouldn't be shocked. Or if she was, maybe that meant she wasn't the right girl for him.

She pulled the first black card from the top of the pile and read, "What gets better with age?"

Misty picked an answer card and held it out, ready to plop it down at the same time he picked his. He found one that fit, and they both showed their choices. Hers read, "A bucket of fish heads," and his read, "Not wearing pants."

They both laughed. Misty decided his answer was funnier since hers was just gross. He marked his column with one awesome point.

He pulled the next black card and read, "And the Academy Award for blank goes to blank. Oh, it's a pick two."

"Okay." She perused her cards for a moment, then chuckled and separated two from the others. He did the same.

"You first," he said.

"And the Academy Award for poor life choices goes to chunks of dead hitchhiker."

He laughed.

"Okay, so what do you have?" she asked.

"And the Academy Award for science goes to an erection that lasts longer than four hours."

She giggled. "Mine, again, is just gross. I must be a disgusting person."

"Nah. That's the point of the game. You can be as immature, disgusting, or politically incorrect as you want. How about if we don't keep score?" Gabe suggested. "We can just enjoy trying to make each other laugh."

"That sounds good. Okay. Next one… 'The CIA interrogates enemy agents by repeatedly subjecting them to…'"

He laid down his answer right away. "A Super Soaker full of cat pee."

She pulled a face while she was laughing. "Ewww… Now who's disgusting? Sorry. We said no judgment, didn't we?"

"Yup. This is a judgment-free zone. What does yours say?"

"The CIA interrogates enemy agents by repeatedly subjecting them to"—she read the card in her hand— "German dungeon porn."

He almost swallowed his tongue and wondered if she even knew what that was. At least she was laughing.

She drew another question card. "What will I bring back in time to convince people I'm a powerful wizard?"

They shuffled through their remaining cards, and Misty snorted.

"Got a good one?" he asked.

She shrugged. "Bio-engineered assault turtles with acid breath."

He chuckled. "Okay. That I'd like to see."

"Now show me yours," she said suggestively.

"'What will I bring back in time to convince people

I'm a powerful wizard?' My collection of high-tech sex toys," he said and winked.

Her eyes rounded. "You have some?"

Gabe laughed. "Not unless you bought something for me last night."

"Hell no."

He sighed dramatically. "Oh well. A guy can dream."

"Next question," she said, smirking.

Was it his imagination, or did she seem shocked by the idea that she'd buy him a sex toy? Or that he'd even want one? Maybe…especially if she wanted to *be* his sex toy.

Oh well. Moving on. He drew a new question card. "I got ninety-nine problems, but blank ain't one."

She scanned her last few cards and picked one. He did the same. Before he had to ask what her card said, she laid it down.

"Three dicks at the same time."

"Wow. You *are* a wild woman." Then he laid down his card. "I got ninety-nine problems, but getting married, having a few kids, buying some stuff, retiring to Florida, and dying, ain't one."

"Wow. That's a lot on that itty-bitty card," she said.

"And some people act like that's all there is."

She tipped her head and looked at him thoughtfully. He sensed an uncomfortable question coming his way, so he shoved the pile of black cards toward her. "Your turn."

She drew another question card and asked, "What's that smell?"

Gabe started going through his cards.

"No, really! What's that smell?"

Gabe sniffed the air. "Gas. Grab your coat, and let's go!"

Misty popped up and ran to the closet by the front door. She tossed his jacket to him first, then grabbed her own. "I need my computer," she said and started toward her room.

"Leave it. Is your landlady home?"

"Oh! Mrs. Patterson. Yes. We have to get her out too."

Misty grabbed her purse, and they rushed down the stairs. When they reached the door leading to the first-floor apartment, Misty banged on it.

"Mrs. Patterson! Mrs. Patterson!" She rushed to the small window that looked out on the driveway. "Her car is here."

Gabe knocked again. When there was no answer, he tried the knob. "The smell of gas is stronger here. Get outside and talk to EMS." He handed her his phone. "I already dialed 911."

He checked to see which way the door opened by checking the hinges. If the door opened toward him, kicking it down was going to be next to impossible. Fortunately, this door would swing away from him.

He hadn't had to kick a door in for a long time, but he remembered to kick the side where the lock was mounted near the keyhole. This would typically be the weakest part of the door.

He quickly checked where Misty was and saw her standing on the sidewalk with the phone up to her ear. Apparently, she was doing what he'd asked, and she was clear.

Today, most doors are made of soft wood and are hollow. They give way fairly easily, especially since the lock's dead-lock bolt extends only an inch or less into the doorframe. He hoped the landlady had replaced this door at some point and he wasn't trying to break through original solid hardwood.

He backed up, and using a front kick, he rammed the heel of his boot into the door. He gave the kick forward momentum and kept his balance by driving the heel of his standing foot into the ground.

The wood began to splinter. Regardless, he had to kick it again. And again. *Damn it. The thing is solid pine.* At last, his foot went through. The smell of gas flowed through the hole he'd created.

He was able to reach in and turn the dead bolt. Opening the door, he called out "Boston Fire Department," as he entered.

No answer. He still had to be on guard in case it was a trap. He didn't think Misty's landlady was one of those sick individuals known to lie in wait for firefighters. Those were genuinely horrible people against humanity. But Misty had said the landlady didn't own a gun. Just a baseball bat.

He edged around a narrow doorway to a kitchen. A thin woman was seated at a tiny table, slumped over a cup of tea.

"Shit," he muttered. He didn't see any pilot light on the stove under the teapot and feared it had gone out. There was no way of knowing how long gas had been leaking. Now he just prayed he could get the woman out without creating a spark.

He draped her arm around his neck and scooped his hand under her denim-clad thighs. So far, so good. As he lifted her, static made her short hair fan out toward him. He held onto her and ran as fast as he could over the dirty shag carpet toward the front door.

BOOM!

Chapter 11

MISTY SAT BY GABE'S BEDSIDE AND PRAYED. *Hi, Lord...whoever you are. It's me, Misty. I've spoken to you recently about the possible MS symptoms I've been having. It's funny, but I'm more worried about Gabe than I am about myself. Please help him recover from his recent accident. You know the one I'm talking about, right? Well, of course you do. While he was rescuing my landlady, he was almost blown up and landed headfirst in the snow. How could you miss that? Oh! Please help her recover too. Amen.*

Call it coincidence, but at that moment, Gabe opened his eyes. Misty rose quickly and leaned over his hospital bed's safety railing.

"You're awake."

"Where am I?" he asked.

"In Boston General. Do you remember the accident?"

Gabe rubbed his forehead with his free hand; the other one was hooked up to an IV. "Do you mean the gas explosion?"

"Yeah. Thank goodness you got out of there just in time. I was terrified for you." *And terrified for myself. I'd die if I lost you.*

"How's your landlady?"

"Still unconscious last time I checked, but alive, thanks to you."

He closed his eyes and nodded slowly. "I imagine she's going to have one hell of a headache when she wakes up. I have one now, and I wasn't even exposed to the gas that long."

"Your head hurts because you landed on it."

"Oh."

A knock at the door was followed by Jayce entering the room. "Don't worry about him, Misty. It's not the first time he's been dropped on his head."

"Ha ha," Gabe said. He reached for Misty's hand. "How long have you been here?"

She clasped his hand gratefully. "Ever since they brought you in yesterday."

"Jesus. You're probably more than ready to go home. Wait a minute. Do you have a home to go to?"

She shook her head. She'd promised herself she wouldn't worry him. If she had to, she could move in with her friend Julie, out in the 'burbs. Commuting to work would be a bitch, but she could do it.

Jayce looked over at Misty. "I'd offer you a guest room, but Kristine and I don't have one. We have a couch you can crash on."

"No, no. I don't want to put you out."

A female voice said, "Nonsense. You're staying with us. We have lots of room." Gabriella Fierro brought flowers into the room and set them on Gabe's side table. "Hi, honey. How are you feeling?"

"Hi, Mom. I'm doing okay, I guess. I imagine the doctor will tell us something soon." He looked at Misty. "Did he say anything to you?"

"Not much. They took some X-rays when you came in and said there weren't any skull fractures or internal bleeding. No broken bones. And that you probably just have a concussion. You're lucky."

"Did you hear that Misty's been here all night?" Jayce asked his mother.

Gabriella crossed to Misty and gave her a kiss on the cheek. "You must be exhausted."

Misty nodded. "It's okay. I had to know he was going to be all right. Now that he's awake and I can see he's okay, I can go back to work and make the money I need to rent a new place." She checked the clock on the wall. "I should either get going or call in sick."

"I told you," Gabriella said. "You can stay with us—for as long as you like. Call in sick. Your home blew up! You must be traumatized."

"Thank you. Really. But I don't want to impose longer that I have to. I really appreciate the offer of a temporary spot to land, though. If I could take you up on that..."

"Absolutely." Gabriella looked at Gabe and smiled. "Don't worry. We'll take good care of her."

Gabe smiled. "I have no doubt of that. Misty, why don't you go with my mom and get some sleep? When I get out of here, I'll take you shopping or something. I imagine you'll have to replace everything."

That was just like Gabe. He was thoughtful of others. It was true he didn't want to get married and have kids, but he would have made a terrific husband and father.

While she had sat by his bedside during the night, Misty had come to the conclusion that he really didn't want those things in his life. And she wouldn't push it. At the same time, she couldn't see herself with anyone else. She had even let the nurse believe she was his fiancée so they'd let her stay at the end of visiting hours.

She'd just stick with him as long as he let her and hope she never had to move on.

"Hey, Mom," Jayce said. "Why don't I stay with my lazy brother while he's just lying around in bed doing nothing? And you can take Misty home."

"Why is everyone trying to get rid of me?" Misty asked.

Gabriella tapped her on the end of her nose. "No one is trying to get rid of you, darling. Everyone is just concerned about you. You were here all night. The rest of us went home, had a good night's sleep, and said we'd check back in the morning. Now that I know Gabe is getting well and under good care, I insist on taking care of you."

Misty smiled. "Thank you."

"Be careful. She'll feed you to within an inch of your life," Gabe said, smiling.

"Thanks for the warning. I'll have to buy new clothes one size larger."

There was an awkward moment right before she left. They gazed at each other, not knowing how to say good-bye. A quick peck on the lips? Did his family know? His father had caught them in the kitchen, kissing. Did he tell anyone? She thought Gabriella would be happy about it if he had.

Instead, Misty extended her hand, and Gabe grasped it. For a moment, she worried that he might shake hands, and that wouldn't look awkward at all, she thought sardonically. But he just squeezed her hand and held on for a bit longer. She left with his mother, who looked delighted.

Gabe watched them leave. *Well, she always wanted a daughter. Now she has one.* Hopefully that wouldn't make their relationship weird…or weirder.

Another knock on the door was followed by Kristine poking her head in. "Anybody home?"

Jayce's face lit up when he saw her. "Hi, honey. I didn't think you were going to be here. You said you had a million things to do."

Kristine crossed to her husband and gave him a sweet kiss. "One of those million things was visiting your brother."

"I'm glad you came." They were grinning at each other and gave each other another kiss before wrapping their arms around each other's waists and facing Gabe. A united front.

Gabe rolled his eyes. "Newlyweds," he mumbled.

Jayce laughed. "You should try it sometime, little brother. With the right woman, there's a lot to recommend it."

"Yeah, like getting Mom off my back."

Kristine stuck her free hand on her hip. "Come on, Gabe. Maybe people just want the best for you… especially your mom. She and your father have had a wonderful marriage for thirty-five or forty years. Right? Why wouldn't she want the same for you?"

"Thirty-four next month," Jayce supplied.

"Just because marriage is right for them and you guys doesn't mean it's right for everyone. So get off my back, and take Mom with you."

"Fine. Just so you know what you're missing," Jayce said and swiftly dipped Kristine, giving her a long, passionate kiss. When he righted her, she giggled.

Gabe groaned. "Come on, guys. You're making me nauseous."

"That's just the concussion," Jayce said.

Gabe closed his eyes and feigned exhaustion. "Guys? I think I need to rest."

"Sure. Of course," Kristine said. "I'm sorry if we stressed you out."

"Do you want me to call off the rest of your visitors using the group text or telephone tree?" Jayce asked. "Otherwise, you'll see Dad and three or four more brothers soon."

"Yeah, tell them to give me a couple of hours."

"Sure thing."

He took Kristine's hand, and as they walked toward the door, she called over her shoulder, "Get better, Gabe."

"I will. I'll probably be out of here this afternoon."

Finally alone, Gabe mulled over what everyone was saying. And demonstrating. Misty had stayed with him all night. Was that just because she had nowhere to go? She had friends. She had his family. She had plenty of places she could have gone.

But she stayed with me. Knowing that made him think. He didn't know if he liked her actions or not. On one hand, it was nice that someone cared that much. On the other hand, maybe she cared too much. She deserved someone who would love her unreservedly and be there for her—always.

He just wondered if he was up to the job. At some point, he was bound to disappoint her.

—w—

Several days later, Misty was seeing doctors again. Her friend Julie took the day off and drove her. Misty could have taken public transportation, but she had a foreboding feeling and wanted her friend there. Besides, Julie made her laugh. She had an appointment right after this one with a gynecologist named Dr. Ingalls. Julie decided to rename the gynecologist they hadn't met yet Dr. Tingles.

In her internist's waiting room, Misty's name was called.

"Do you want me to come with you?" Julie asked.

"Nah. I'm all right. Thanks, though."

She followed the hefty nurse through the busy office area. This time, she didn't complain when she had to step on the scale. The number shocked her, and she gulped. *120 pounds? Oh my God! I've gained ten pounds? How? When? It must be the lack of exercise. Or water weight. Yeah, one of those.*

"No need to get undressed," Dr. Warren's nurse said. "In fact, you don't even need to go into an exam room. He wants to meet with you in his office."

Misty wasn't about to complain, even though the formality concerned her a bit. She followed the nurse to a door with Dr. Warren's nameplate on it and ushered her in. The walls were lined with books, and her doctor sat behind a dark wood desk. Two comfortable chairs sat in front of it.

"Have a seat, Misty." His expression looked grave.

She lowered herself slowly into one of the blue upholstered chairs. "Hi."

"I have some news, and I'm afraid it isn't good."

"Oh?" Her mouth went dry, and she steeled herself for whatever he was about to say.

"I'm afraid you have multiple sclerosis."

She knew this was a possibility, but hearing it confirmed seemed surreal. "That's…that's what's responsible for all my symptoms?"

"Almost all." He smiled. "When you called to say you were experiencing nausea, I had the lab run another test on your blood."

"Really? I didn't know you could do that."

"Sometimes we hold onto the samples for a while. I see you have an appointment with Dr. Ingalls right after this."

"Yeah. I haven't seen a gynecologist in a few — Wait! What are you saying?"

"I'm not saying anything. I'm letting Dr. Ingalls explore the new findings with you. It's her area of expertise."

"New findings… What did the blood test show?"

He paused until she thought she might throttle it out of him. At last, he said, "You may be pregnant. We'll need that confirmed. I expect your gynecologist will want to do a more definitive test and an exam before confirming anything."

Internal shock waves knocked Misty back in her seat. "Are you sure?"

"Again, I'll let Dr. Ingalls be the one who determines that. Don't you want to know more about the MS?"

She pinched the bridge of her nose. "Yes. Of course. I'm just…overwhelmed at the moment."

He didn't get up or even extend a hand across the desk for comfort. He simply nodded. "Well, the good news — if there is any — is that pregnancy can alleviate the symptoms of MS for a while. But I don't want you thinking the diagnosis must have been wrong. It isn't."

"Is there any medication I should be taking?"

"Not yet. I'll let your neurologist and Dr. Ingalls decide what to prescribe and when."

"Will I ever be able to dance again?"

"You'll probably be able to waltz, depending on how you feel. But anything more strenuous than that may become progressively more difficult. What you have is relapsing-remitting MS or RRMS."

She made herself concentrate on his words, despite her mind's desire to wander off on its own.

"RRMS is characterized by clearly defined attacks of new or increasing neurologic symptoms. These attacks—also called relapses or exacerbations—are followed by periods of partial or complete recovery called remissions. During remissions, all or most of your symptoms may disappear. However, there is no apparent progression of the disease during the periods of remission. Approximately 85 percent of people with MS are initially diagnosed with RRMS. So you have the most common type."

"Yay, me," she muttered sarcastically.

He sighed. "I'm sorry. If you have any questions at all, you can call me, but I think working with your neurologist will be more important going forward."

"I'm okay. I think it's just the shock of it all."

"I'll get a nurse to help you out."

Misty felt as if she were walking through a fog as she was escorted to her next appointment. She latched onto Julie as they walked through the waiting room. After she'd made it through the new waiting room, the nurse she was handed off to made her stop at the restroom and give a urine sample.

She hadn't gone to her gynecologist in the suburbs for a few years, so when she was making appointments for everything else under the sun, she took the nurse's advice and scheduled that too. By the time the appointment rolled around, she'd been experiencing nausea, and her always reliable period was absent.

Misty didn't smile or answer some question she barely heard, and Julie frowned. "What's the matter?"

"Oh, you know…MS, new mysterious symptoms, the whole nine," she said as she changed into the hospital gown.

"You definitely have MS?"

Misty nodded.

Julie stood there with her mouth hanging open for a moment. "What new mysterious symptoms?"

"Nausea. And I should have gotten my period by now. My internist didn't want to commit to anything, so he's letting Dr. Tingles give me the news."

Her friend remained quiet for once.

A pretty redhead in a white lab coat entered the room and introduced herself as Dr. Ingalls. Misty had to remind herself not to add the T to her name—ever! She had Julie stick her nose in a magazine during the internal exam, but it was over quickly.

Her gynecologist confirmed the bombshell Dr. Warren had dropped earlier by saying, "You're pregnant. Congratulations! That means I'm your new best friend."

Julie's eye rounded, but she quickly hid behind the magazine again.

"I'll let you get dressed, and I'll be back in a few minutes. I'll prescribe some prenatal vitamins, but you shouldn't take anything else unless you check with me first," the doctor said as she whipped off her exam gloves and tossed them into the trash bin.

Now Misty lay on a cold exam table in nothing but a hospital gown. "How the hell did this happen?" she asked in a trembling voice.

Julie's eyes widened. "Um, you don't know? Well, when a man and a woman like each other very much—"

"Shut up." Misty draped an arm over her face as she lay on the exam table. Tears were leaking out of the corners of her eyes.

I have multiple sclerosis and *I'm pregnant. How the hell do I deal with this?*

Since her feet were still in the stirrups, Julie patted Misty's bent knee. "Cheer up, Mist. It could be worse."

"How?"

"I don't know. Maybe if this were happening during the zombie apocalypse? The doctors and nurses would be way busier, and you'd have to wait forever to get an appointment."

"Oh God!" The mention of nurses reminded her that Gabe's sister-in-law worked in this hospital. "Sandra must know. She's a nurse here. Or maybe she doesn't. Is there any way you can find Dr. Ingalls? I need to ask the doctor if she can keep it to herself."

"I'll try. Will you be okay by yourself?"

Misty moved her arm and stared at her friend. "What do you think I'm going to do? Give myself a coat-hanger abortion while you're gone?"

"I...oh, hell. I don't know. I was just trying to... Never mind. I'll go find the doctor."

"I'm sorry, Jules. I'm angry, but not at you."

Julie left, thank God. Misty had to think. What could she do? This was a disaster. If only she didn't have MS too. It would still be a disaster, but less of one.

Why did things have to happen all at once? She was just preparing herself for the diagnosis of MS. Now this. She'd almost rather deal with a zombie apocalypse.

A few moments later, Dr. Ingalls returned, with Julie right behind her.

Misty waited until her friend had closed the door. "Sandra Fierro is the father's sister-in-law. I'm not ready to tell him yet. Does she know? Is there any way you can keep her in the dark for a while?"

Dr. Ingalls gave her a sympathetic look. "I don't know if she's aware of it or not. I can't keep her from peeking at your chart if she decides to."

"Isn't there something about doctor–patient confidentiality?"

"That pertains to people outside the hospital. Hospital personnel have to communicate with each other regarding patient care. They sign a form saying they'll keep any information they learn about patients confidential. I can remind her of that."

Misty nodded sadly. "Thank you."

"May I ask why you're not ready to tell the father?"

Misty was tempted to say "No, you may not." But there was no reason she couldn't tell her doctor that Gabe had just been released from another hospital with bad news of his own. He couldn't work until the fire department's doctor cleared him. And he wasn't happy about waiting around and twiddling his thumbs.

"It's just bad timing. I'll tell him as soon as the time is right."

Dr. Ingalls patted her arm. "If you need anything, give me a call."

I need a miracle, Misty thought. She couldn't get an abortion—this was Gabe's child, and on a deep, secret level, she wanted it. Desperately.

It might be the only part of Gabe she could have and love long-term. She wouldn't expect Gabe to marry her. Others might, but that's not how she wanted her relationship with him to play out.

The doctor left as soon as she was confident Misty was in a stable frame of mind. Julie agreed to stay with her all afternoon. Misty got up off the table and made Julie turn around while she put on her underwear.

"Seriously? We're both girls here. I'm probably going to be your birth coach, and I'll see a whole lot more of you, if you know what I mean."

Misty halted with her arm half in her sweater. "What makes you think you're going to be my birth coach?"

"I thought Mr. Handsome disappeared after the night of your party, never to return. Did he come back?"

"Yeah. He came over the next day. He was there when my house blew up."

Julie smiled. "I'd say something about the sparks between you two setting off that explosion, but it's probably too soon."

Misty pulled her sweater over her head. "Ya think?"

"So, how are you going to tell him? And when?"

She sat down to put on her jeans. Her balance was still questionable. "As I told the doctor, I don't know when. And I don't know *how* either."

Misty started tearing up again. She tried some deep breathing and fanned her face.

Julie looked over her shoulder. When she saw Misty falling apart, she rushed to her and put her arms around her. "It's gonna be all right. It's okay to cry. I'll be here for you no matter what happens. Okay?"

Misty swallowed the rest of her tears. "I know. Thank you."

Julie was sweet but not who she really wanted. Then she remembered someone else she had to tell.

"Oh, crap."

Julie leaned back and gazed at her. "What is it?"

"Parker. I'll have to tell Parker too."

She took a few more deep breaths and pulled her jeans up as far as she could before standing. When she rose and tried to pull them up the rest of the way, she wobbled and grabbed Julie's arm.

Misty burst into tears. "Oh, I can't do this. I just can't."

"Relax. I've got you," Julie said. She held her shoulders steady while Misty zipped up her jeans. "You see? We can do this together. We can do anything together. We're women, dammit! Hear us roar!"

Misty appreciated the feminist leanings of her friend but doubted her own at that moment.

There was a knock at the door, and it opened partway without her saying *Come in*.

Sandra peeked around it. "Are you decent?"

Misty gave her a halfhearted smile. "Depends on what you mean by decent."

Sandra entered and shut the door behind her. She strode over and enveloped Misty in a warm, tight hug. "I want you to know I won't tell anybody anything. Not even Miguel. I won't even say you came in today."

Misty exhaled a deep breath. "Thank you. I appreciate your telling me that."

Sandra stepped back and rubbed Misty's arms. "How are you holding up?"

Misty dropped her gaze to the floor. Tears threatened to spill again.

"Oh, honey. I know how you're feeling, but it'll be all right."

Misty glared at Gabe's sister-in-law. "What do you know about how I feel?"

Sandra smiled, albeit sadly. "I imagine you're overwhelmed, scared, and feeling alone. I've seen this before, Misty."

She sagged. That's exactly how she felt. Misty nodded. "You forgot feeling sorry for myself, but other than that, you nailed it."

"I know one person who won't be sorry."

"Ha. If you say Gabe, you're dead wrong."

Sandra tilted her head. "I was going to say Gabriella. She wants a grandchild so badly, she's bugging all her younger sons to get married and have kids. The older married ones have already said they won't be providing her with grandchildren."

"Well, she'll be disappointed on that front with Gabe. He has no intention of getting married. Ever."

Sandra lifted her chin as if sure of something. "He'll do the right thing."

"I want him to do the right thing *for him*. For *all* of us. That doesn't mean marrying me out of pity. He'll resent me for it. He might even resent the baby too."

Sandra's lips thinned. "Okay. I can't predict the future, but there's one thing I know about the Fierro men. When the chips are down, they'll come through. Only an asshole would walk away from your situation. These guys are *not* assholes."

Misty nodded sadly. "I know that. I'm afraid of that, actually."

Sandra tipped her head and gazed at Misty for a moment. "Don't be. I can't divulge the details of the conversation I had with Gabe recently. But I think you may be surprised by his reaction."

Misty's brows shot up. Had Gabe had a change of heart? *Oh Lord, I hope so.*

Chapter 12

GABE PACED THE LENGTH OF HIS STUDIO APARTMENT, GOING stir-crazy. It had been a week since his discharge from the hospital. Couldn't the captain at least assign him to light duty? Nope. He was off the roster until cleared by the fire department's doctor.

He needed a distraction. Some pleasant company would do the trick. Misty popped into his mind right away. It would fit in with his plan of getting to know each other better.

He took his phone off the charger and called her as he paced around his apartment.

She answered on the second ring. "Hi, Gabe. I was hoping you'd call."

"Oh yeah? I guess we're on the same wavelength. How are you?"

Misty hesitated. "The question is, how are you? You're the one who took a big bang to the head."

"I feel a lot better physically, but I'm bored. If you're free, we could go somewhere…or hang out and do something at my place."

"Umm, I don't know what you're thinking of doing, exactly. I have to go to work tomorrow. I shouldn't be out too late. And I can't stay the night."

Stay the night? "Whoa. That is *not* what I meant at all. I…I shouldn't have called."

"Huh? Why not?"

"I just meant doing something this afternoon. I… uh…have plans with Jayce this evening."

"Gabe? There's something I have to tell you."

"Oh? Okay. So tell me."

"It's not a conversation for over the phone."

"Uh-oh. Are you dumping me?" He laughed. "Not that we're really a couple, even."

She must not have found his joke funny. Her voice became stern. "How about if we meet for coffee and discuss it this afternoon?"

"That sounds good. Starbucks? The one on Cambridge Str—Oh, sorry. I was thinking of the one close to you in the North End. You must be at my parents' house in the South End, right? I can pick up a copy of the local entertainment paper on the way."

"Actually, I'm at my friend's house in Saugus."

"Hi, Gabe," a faint voice yelled in the background.

He chuckled. "Hi, whoever you are."

The voice got louder, as if she'd grabbed the phone. "My name is Julie. Actually, I'm one of the girls who thought you were a stripper. Sorry about that."

"Ah. No worries. It was kind of flattering—I guess. Can you put Misty back on the phone?"

"Sure."

He heard Misty frantically whispering to her friend to give her privacy. A moment later, Misty said, "Hi."

"Maybe I can meet you out there—wherever you are."

"Saugus. There are all kinds of places we can go, but why don't you meet me here at my friend's house and then we can decide where to go to talk."

"Okay. Give me the address."

Misty gave him the address and some simple directions.

"I just have to borrow a car. I'll be there in forty-five minutes—maybe longer, if I have to rent one."

"Good. I'll see you in an hour or so. I would actually like some time to shower and change my clothes. I slept in them last night."

"Should I be worried?"

There was a hesitation. Finally, Misty said, "No. Not for the reason you're thinking. No walk of shame or anything."

And before she could say any more, he said, "I'll meet you there around eleven."

She disconnected, leaving him to wonder what she was being so mysterious about. Whatever it was, he'd find out later. Right now, he had to call Dante and hope his little brother wasn't using his beloved sports car.

———

Misty had just enough time to wash her underwear and blow-dry it. Then she showered, brushed her teeth and hair, put on mascara, and borrowed some clothes from Julie. She was glad they found something cute that fit. A pair of skinny jeans and a pretty magenta sweater. She was also glad she wasn't back at the Fierro house waiting for Gabe.

She didn't want to chat with her future child's grandmother. Gabe needed to know first, and his mother seemed to have some kind of psychic power or something. She always knew what other people were feeling. And she had a way of getting them to spill their guts.

When the doorbell rang, she jogged downstairs to answer it, but Julie had gotten there first.

"Surprise, Misty. It's Parker!"

She froze halfway down the stairs. "Parker?"

"Hey, Sis!"

"How are you here? And how did you know where I was?"

"I have a short leave between training and shipping out."

"He called me to arrange a little surprise for you. I didn't know if I'd have to kidnap you to get you here, but fortunately, you were easy to convince." She winked.

Crap. Now she'd have to tell Parker and Gabe at the same time. There was no way she could keep this to herself until she saw each one alone. In a way, it was a good thing Parker was here and not half a world away. He might need to see for himself that she was really all right.

"Don't I get a hug?" he asked.

"Of course!" She ran into the foyer and hugged her brother hard. "I missed you!"

"I missed you too. More than you'd think."

"Oh yeah? You must have been really homesick."

"That's putting it mildly."

"Holy shit!" Gabe exclaimed. "Is that Parker?"

Parker whirled around and met his best friend coming up the walk. They gave each other a man hug with many slaps on the back.

"Good to see you! Hey, Julie, I didn't realize you knew Gabe."

"I don't. Well, not really. I thought he was a stripper, and then he ran off before proper introductions could be made."

Parker's brows rose.

"Jeez, Julie," Misty interjected. "It's not what it

sounds like. I was having a party at my apartment for Julie and my friends from high school, and Gabe just showed up to check on me. I thought he was the pizza delivery guy and went into the other room to get my wallet and, well…the girls thought I had arranged something else—which I didn't, by the way."

Parker laughed hard. "So, I guess you're still looking after my little sister, Gabe. Thanks."

"What are you doing here?" Gabe asked. "Did you get emergency leave when you heard that Misty's house blew up?"

Parker took a step back. He grabbed Misty's arm. "Your house blew up? How? When? Why didn't you tell me?"

"I was going to. It just happened, and there was a lot of other stuff going on." She realized she'd inadvertently introduced subjects she didn't want to get into just yet. "Hey, let's go inside. Why are we all standing in the foyer with the door open? It's February, for God's sake." She grabbed Parker's hand and tugged him inside.

As soon as Gabe had closed the door, she quickly addressed Parker's concerns. "It was a gas leak. Gabe saved both me and my landlady. He was in the hospital, knocked unconscious for a while." There. Put the focus on Gabe. That should buy her a little time.

Parker let go of Misty and clamped his hand on Gabe's shoulder. "I knew I could count on you, man. Thank God you were there."

Gabe offered a weak smile. Maybe he was just being humble, or maybe he didn't want Parker to know how close they had become. Either way, it was time for another distraction.

"Let's get out of the chilly hallway." Misty made a point of shivering.

Julie laughed. "No shit. If my father were here, he would have yelled, 'Do you want to heat the whole damn neighborhood?' ten minutes ago. Let's go into the kitchen where it's warm. I'll make some coffee."

They all tromped into the kitchen and found seats at the round glass table in the corner.

"Nice house, Julie," Gabe said.

"I'm a squatter. Sort of. My folks are in Germany. My dad got transferred, and they're looking at houses. Until they buy one, they won't put this one on the market. I get to live here until the new owners evict me."

Misty brightened. "Maybe you and I can get a place in the city when they sell this out from under you."

Parker groaned. "That's a recipe for disaster."

"What do you mean?" Gabe asked.

Parker laughed. "When these two get together, you never know who's going to call you. The towing company, the cops, or—"

Gabe held up his palm. "I don't need to know the details." He gave Misty the hairy eyeball.

"Hey, we're not that bad." Julie giggled as she filled the coffeepot with water. "At least we're no longer underage."

Parker smiled. "I guess it's just harmless girl fun. Nothing to be concerned about. But what does concern me is where are you living now, Misty? Can you get to your job from here—or wherever?"

"The Fierros took me in. I just have to commute from the South End to the North End. It's nothing the subway and a CharlieCard can't handle."

Parker glanced at Gabe. "You're still at your place near the theater district and Chinatown, right?"

"Yeah. Why wouldn't I be?"

"Just making sure."

Misty sensed her brother's discomfort. Or maybe it was her own worry she was projecting. Parker obviously didn't want them together. She and Gabe shared a quick glance and looked away.

Julie joined them at the table while the coffee was brewing. "Hmmm… Something is going on here." She pointed to the other three in turn.

"Oh? Is there something I should know?" Parker asked.

Oh, crap. Julie was always too observant and never could shut the hell up. Misty had to get her brother and Gabe alone and tell them her news soon—before Julie blurted it out at the worst possible moment.

"Julie, can you please give us some time alone?"

Julie straightened and looked offended. "You don't want me here? I would think you might need my support."

"No! What I need is for you to disappear for a few minutes." Misty felt bad as soon as she raised her voice to her friend, but it had to be done. Her well-meaning friend would probably add her two cents and just complicate things.

"Fine." She sounded hurt as she rose and stomped out of the room. "When the coffee is ready, you can help yourselves."

"I'm sorry," Misty called after her.

"No, you're not, but you might be when I'm not there to help you figure out what you're going to say." Julie's voice trailed off, but it looked as if the guys caught the gist of it.

Misty muttered, "Jesus."

"What's she talking about?" Parker asked.

Misty leaned back and crossed her arms. "There's something I have to tell you. Both of you. I didn't want to do it here, like this, but it seems like I have no choice now."

Parker narrowed his eyes. "Spit it out, Misty. What did you do?"

She straightened and glared at her brother. "What makes you think I did something?"

"Whoa. Relax, Parker," Gabe said. "Misty hasn't done anything. She's had some bad news, and if you'll just shut up, she'll tell you what it is."

Gabe was trying to help, probably thinking she had to tell him about the MS. Boy, was he in for a rude shock.

Misty took a deep breath. "Actually, there are two things I have to tell you, Parker. And one of those things you don't know yet, Gabe. But you need to."

Gabe sat up straighter. "What is it?"

Misty's lower lip began to quiver. *Oh no, Misty. Do not cry. Do. Not. Cry.* She had to get out the words before she couldn't talk past the lump in her throat.

"Parker, I have MS. Multiple sclerosis."

"Damn. You said you were going to the doctor for some weird symptoms. Is that what they found? I don't know much about it, but it's pretty serious, right? Are they sure that's what it is?"

Misty nodded. "Yeah. They did a bunch of tests. They ruled out everything else. The MRI showed a few lesions in certain places in my brain."

"Why am I just finding out about this now? Did you know, Gabe?"

"Yeah. She didn't want me to tell you, and it wasn't my place to do that, anyway."

Parker reached over and took Misty's hand. "I'm so sorry, Sis. I should have been here for you. But at least Gabe was. Thanks, buddy."

Oh boy. Wait until part two of the news... "There's more."

"Yeah, what was that other thing that I don't know about yet?" Gabe asked.

Misty took a deep breath, closed her eyes, and said, "I'm pregnant."

Parker jumped up so fast, his chair fell over. "What? How the hell? No. Never mind that. Who the hell is the father?"

Misty looked at Gabe. His mouth was hanging open, and he was staring at her, dumbstruck. Parker would probably figure it out at some point, but maybe she could buy Gabe some time.

"It's none of your damn business, Parker, who the father is. This is my problem, and I'll handle it."

Gabe looked like he just swallowed a bug. "Shit."

Parker glanced from Gabe to Misty and back. "Jesus. Fucking. Christ. Are you telling me my best friend knocked up my little sister?"

Gabe said nothing. He just folded his hands and stared at her.

Parker's face reddened. He grabbed Gabe by the collar and yanked him out of his chair. "Did you?"

"Yeah. I guess so."

Parker took a swing at him, and Gabe ducked, narrowly missing his fist. He wasn't so lucky the next time. Parker aimed for his stomach and hit him hard enough that Gabe doubled over.

Misty jumped up. "Stop!"

"Hell no," Parker yelled. "I'm just getting started."

"He has a concussion. You could kill him!"

He kicked Gabe in the shoulder and sent him sprawling into the cabinets.

Gabe just sat there, staring at the floor.

Parker loomed over him. "Get up."

"I'm not going to fight you." Gabe rubbed his shoulder and stayed where he was.

"I said, get up!"

"Parker, stop it!" Misty demanded. "Leave him alone."

Julie rounded the corner. "What happened? I heard a crash."

Misty burst into tears. Julie took her by the shoulders and led her out of the room. "I knew you'd need me."

"Get up. Let's finish this," Parker was saying.

"No!" Misty broke away from Julie. She stopped in the kitchen doorway and held on to the trim. She swayed and felt like she was going to faint.

Gabe jumped to his feet and got to her in time to lower her slowly to the floor. "Are you okay?"

Misty shook her head. "No." Then she started crying openly.

"Jesus," Parker muttered. "It's not bad enough she has some kind of disease, but you had to go and get her pregnant too? You're a monster."

"Maybe you can wait until we get her lying down before you finish kicking the shit out of me." Gabe lifted her and walked into the living room, where Julie stood watching. "Where can I put her?"

"Upstairs. In my bedroom."

"We're not done here," Parker yelled.

———

"I'll be down in a minute," Gabe snapped. He carried Misty up the stairs, with Julie leading the way. As soon as she opened the bedroom door, he strode in and laid Misty on the bed. "Stay with her," he said to Julie.

He didn't wait for any acknowledgment. He stormed back down the stairs and into the kitchen. Parker was sitting at the table with his head in his hands. Gabe sat across from him. "I'm sorry. I don't know what else to say."

"Don't. Don't say anything." He took a deep breath and let it out in a whoosh. "I can't believe it. I asked you to look out for her. I figured she'd probably attract guys who were just trying to get into her pants. I never thought that guy would be you."

"I didn't seduce her. She… It just happened."

Parker jumped up and rushed toward him. "What were you about to say? She started it? She seduced you? Liar!" His fist connected with Gabe's jaw and knocked him over. "You piece of shit. You're not good enough for her."

Gabe stayed down and rubbed his jaw. "You're right."

Parker paced back and forth, raking his fingers through his short hair. At last, facing away from him, he said, "Get out."

Gabe didn't hesitate to comply.

He stopped halfway down the walk and turned around. He had to know if Misty was okay. Jogging around to the backyard, he inspected the area. It was fenced in, high enough so neighbors couldn't look right in. It seemed about as private as he was going to get, so he stripped off his clothes and shifted. His six-foot frame shrunk down to about the size of a hawk with long, colorful tail feathers.

Fortunately, there was a mud puddle nearby, and he was able to roll in it until his feathers were dull looking and disguised. He picked out the window that belonged to the room where Misty lay and flew to the nearest branch.

Misty was still lying down, and now Parker was sitting by her side. Julie was just stepping out and closing the door. They must've asked for privacy. Gabe doubted Julie would leave voluntarily. Misty's friend seemed pretty protective.

"Misty, I lost my head. I didn't mean to upset you."

With Gabe's paranormal hearing, he was able to hear the conversation, even through the closed window.

"Well, you did. I can't believe you would hurt him like that. I love him, you jerk."

Parker hung his head. "I don't think I really hurt him. He got right up and managed to carry you upstairs with no problem."

"And then you hit him again. I heard the crash. Where is he now?"

"Gone," Parker said. "I threw him out."

"You can apologize later. That was the first he'd heard it, and he probably needs some time to process the news. I know I did."

"Didn't you use protection?"

Misty glared at her brother. "Not that it's any of your business, but yes. Of course we did."

Parker's posture sagged. "I don't really want the

details, but was he… Is he… Never mind." He shook his head. "It doesn't matter. What's done is done."

Misty rolled toward the window. She seemed to be staring right at Gabe's bird form and blinked a couple of times.

He flew onto the roof, where he could still listen but not be seen.

"I hate to ask you this, but have you thought about what you're going to do now?" Parker asked.

"I've thought about it, but I haven't decided anything. I really need to talk to Gabe before I make any plans."

"I don't want you marrying him."

"I don't think he wants to marry me, so you're in luck."

"What's that supposed to mean?"

"It means he doesn't want to marry anybody."

"He told you that?"

"Yeah. I wasn't pregnant at the time, or I didn't know I was, anyway. He's always been honest with me about that. No wife. No kids. That's how he wants it."

"All right. Try not to get mad, but if you want help paying for a procedure, I can—"

"Don't! I don't want to discuss this with you. This is not your fault or your problem. I need to talk to Gabe. And *only* Gabe," she said, strengthening her voice.

Gabe imagined Julie was probably listening with her ear against the door.

There was some rustling, and she spoke again, this time in an assertive tone, but without anger. "I know I'm in trouble. I know you're worried about me. But don't. Whatever happens, I'll be fine. After I got over the shock, I realized I'd love to have Gabe's baby. Even if I raise the child on my own… And don't think I can't.

Mothers figure out how to take care of their kids in all kinds of difficult circumstances. I imagine I can too."

Gabe was full of emotion. He wanted to fly through the window, shift, and take her in his arms. But that would only make things worse, since neither Misty nor Parker had any idea what he really was.

He could fly down to where his clothes were, change, and go knock on the door again. But he knew that was not a good idea, either. Not yet. He needed to give brother and sister some alone time to process. He could use some time to figure out the whole mess too. Especially why his best friend was so against her marrying him. Did Parker really think he'd be bad for her?

He flitted to the ground, shifted into his human form again, brushed the dirt off his backside, and dressed quickly.

He strode past the house to where he'd left the Zipcar he'd rented. Jumping in, he decided to visit his brother Jayce a little sooner than expected.

Chapter 13

GABE LEFT THE ZIPCAR NEAR THE BUS STATION WHERE HE'D rented it. He was in the mood for a long walk anyway. Travelling from there to Charlestown on foot should wear him out. Hopefully more mentally than physically.

Unfortunately, the exercise never did kick him into that natural high that runners experienced, and he still arrived on his brother's doorstep a little early. The condo was in an older building right near the Charles River. Even though it was only a one bedroom, Jayce loved it, probably because he could dock his boat so close by.

It was only him and Kristine anyway, and there would never be any children, since his dragon bride could only produce children with another dragon. And she'd never be unfaithful. He was sure of that. They'd made it pretty clear that they adored each other.

"Gabe! We didn't expect you for another hour," Kristine said. "Did we get the time wrong?"

"No. I'm early. I need to talk to Jayce. Is he here?"

"Right here, buddy," Jayce said as he exited the only bathroom, zipping up his jeans.

Gabe winced at the nickname, even if it was said as an endearment. That didn't matter right now. He had to talk to someone sane, because he certainly wasn't.

"Can we go out on your boat before dinner?"

"Sure. I thought you'd want to wait until dark so we

could do a little flying without freaking out the fishermen. We don't exactly resemble seagulls."

"I need to talk."

"Go ahead," Kristine said. "Dinner can wait."

Jayce kissed his wife, then gave a sharp nod to Gabe. "Okay. Let's go."

Following his brother across the street, Gabe tried to pick out any of the mentally rehearsed speeches he could use. Telling his older brother, who would be head of the family someday, was a little unnerving but only practice for the big revelation to the rest of the family—probably at the next Sunday dinner.

As soon as they'd cast off, Gabe let out a sigh of relief. In no time, they would be far off the coast and into open water. As the land disappeared behind him, so did some of his stress.

Finally breaking the silence, Jayce asked, "So, what's eating you?"

"I need to talk and just want you to listen. No advice that I 'do the right thing,' please."

"Uh-oh. You'd better tell me where this is going before I jump to conclusions."

Gabe sighed. "You'd probably jump to the right one but only conclude part of it."

Jayce was quiet but focused on him intently.

He had to spit it out. "Misty's pregnant."

"Shit. Does she know?"

"Huh?"

Jayce chuckled. "Sorry. Just trying to lighten the moment with a little humor."

Gabe looked skyward, then remembered why he'd gone to Jayce. He wouldn't give him a lecture, like he

would get if he went to Miguel or his father. He wouldn't
get an inappropriate pat on the back from Dante or Noah
for "bagging a babe" like Misty.

"Jayce, I appreciate your trying, but there's no way to
lighten this load. In fact, it gets heavier."

"Crap. What else is there?"

"She has MS." Gabe scrubbed a hand over his face.
"I'm freaking out, and you're the first person I've talked
to about this."

"Okay. So, now that you've gotten that much out, is
there any more?"

"No. That's it. As far as I know."

Jayce looked thoughtful. "I hate to ask this, and
please don't bite my head off…"

Gabe nodded. "Go ahead. I'll try to control myself."

Jayce let out a deep breath. "Is it yours?"

Gabe laughed. "Yeah. It is."

"I didn't think you'd find that funny."

"I guess I know Misty well enough to know she
wouldn't be involved with anyone else. We only slept
together once, but that's all it takes, right?"

Jayce's brows shot up. "Only once?"

"Well, not exactly. Just one night, but it was all night
long." He waited for Jayce to make some kind of joke,
but he didn't. Thank God. He didn't want to attack his
older brother.

"Look, Gabe, I know how you feel about responsibility. I'm not taking this lightly, believe me. But the thing
is, ready or not, here it comes."

Gabe let out a deep sigh. "It's not just the responsibility.
I really didn't want to bring a child into a world like this.
You know as well as anyone how fucked up people are."

"Yeah. Some people suck. But not everyone. Whatever asshole let your dog off its leash on a busy street like Mass Avenue is a sick fuck. I'm pretty sure that's when you lost all faith in mankind—and yourself."

Gabe hung his head and nodded.

Jayce put his arm around his brother. "I'm not going to tell you what to do. You already know what you can and can't control. But one thing I can tell you is that whatever you decide, I hope you'll be true to yourself. Not the fearful part of you, though. The best part of you."

Gabe looked over at his older brother and saw sincerity in his eyes. Jayce believed in him. He probably believed in him more than Gabe believed in himself.

"Thanks." Gabe rose and whipped his sweater over his head. Then he dropped his pants, shifted, and flew.

———

Misty had had it. She was actually glad to get back to work where she could think about something besides disappointing Parker, messing up Gabe's life, and probably messing up her own. There were no words to express how she felt. She had cried herself to sleep and probably looked like hell. Putting on the first clothes she could find, she had bolted out the door before the Fierros saw her.

Adam did a double take and asked her to see him in his office. It was a few minutes before the bank opened, so there would be limited time to talk. Good. She had no idea what to say to him. If she told him she had MS and might not be able to do her job, she could lose it. Not that he could fire her for a medical condition. He couldn't. But he could find another way...like layoffs. Even if it were solely based on seniority, she'd be the first to go. *Last one hired, first one fired*.

She wasn't a good liar. If he asked point-blank what was going on, she'd have to tell him some part of the truth. There were plenty of parts to choose from.

He pulled the chair across from his desk around to his side so they could sit closer. She hated it when he did that, but as long as he didn't touch her or proposition her, he skirted the sexual harassment line.

"Something's up with you, Misty. What is it?"

He held her gaze until she couldn't stand it anymore and looked at her lap. She wasn't showing yet and wouldn't for a few months. It was still early, so she could probably skip the pregnancy part.

"Uh...did you hear about the house in the North End that blew up a couple of nights ago?"

He looked at her askance. "No. Why?"

"Well, there was a gas leak in the house I lived in. I rented an apartment upstairs. All my stuff burned in the fire. I've been borrowing clothes and going without my usual makeup. All I have is what was in my purse."

He leaned back, openmouthed. To Misty, he looked like Billy Bass, the talking fish, mounted on some redneck's wall.

"Holy moly!" When he finally got ahold of himself, he said, "You know, if you need a place to stay, I have a lovely home in Medford."

Ack! Misty needed to shut down that shit right away. "No! Thank you. I'm staying with Gabe's parents."

His face looked as if he'd bitten into a lemon. "Oh.

Well, that doesn't sound ideal. What if the two of you break up? You know which one they're going to side with. You'll be out on your—Well, you'll be homeless."

She *had* thought of that, but as awkward as it would be at family get-togethers, she couldn't imagine the Fierros tossing her out on the street. Besides, she was going to find her own place. Just a little one-bedroom apartment so the baby could have undisturbed naps. When the little tyke got older, she'd give up her bed and get a pullout couch to sleep on.

She couldn't help picturing a mini Gabe running around, and she loved that baby already. Of course, if Sandra was right, the Fierros wouldn't let her go. They'd want her to move in permanently so they could enjoy their only grandchild. She couldn't let that happen, either.

Misty wanted—no, *needed*—to be her own woman. She had friends and family who could help, but she'd never let anyone step in and take over. She wanted this child, desperately, and wanted to be the kind of mom Gabriella Fierro was. Someone who taught values but wasn't so strict that a child couldn't make mistakes. She wanted to be warm, supportive, and welcoming to the child's friends. Hell, she even wanted to bake cookies.

"Misty?" Adam snapped a finger under her nose.

"What?" Oops. She had taken a little mental vacation. Did he ask her something? Other than to move in with him, that is. *Ugh*. She threw up in her mouth a little bit. "Adam, excuse me, but I have to hit the ladies' room before work."

He straightened his spine, looking affronted. "Go ahead. Just think about my offer. I know it might sound like a bad idea since I'm your boss, but I assure you, it would be fine."

She jumped up and almost lost her balance. *Oh, great. That would have been enough for another interrogation.* And off she hurried, as fast as her unreliable legs could carry her.

In the ladies' room, her coworker Terri was applying some lipstick. "Hi, Misty. How are—"

When Terri got a better look at her, she stopped talking and just stared. Just as well, because Misty's stomach was roiling. She ran into the stall and tossed her breakfast.

"Oh dear," Terri said. "You don't look so good. Are you sure you should be here?"

When she was through retching, Misty wiped her mouth with some toilet paper. "Yeah. I'll be fine. Sorry you had to hear that."

"Oh, don't worry about me. I was barfing in here every morning during my whole first trimester."

Misty's eyes widened, and she tried to school her expression right away. She moved slowly to the sink and splashed some water into her mouth, swishing and spitting it out.

"Wait a minute. Are you—"

Shit. Terri's putting two and two together.

"Misty! How exciting. Is it with that gorgeous fireman we've seen you with?"

She held onto the sink and swayed. Her balance seemed to desert her too.

"Oh no. It's more than that, isn't it? What's wrong, hon? Here. Sit down. I'll go get your purse, and you can call somebody."

Misty grabbed her arm. "No. Don't go anywhere. I'm fine. I just need a minute."

"Okaaay." Terri continued to stare at her with concern. "Maybe Adam can call a cab or limo or something."

"Limo?"

"He can afford it, and you look like you need some pampering."

Misty couldn't put up with that response all day long. She glanced into the mirror to see what everyone else had been reacting to.

Ugh. Her hair was sticking out in several places from when she'd pulled off Julie's knit hat. She had raccoon eyes from yesterday's mascara meltdown, and the middle button of Julie's borrowed blouse had popped off. She would have loved to call a limo to come and return her to her town house so she could call her stylist and start the day over.

Alas, reality bit the big one. No stylist. No clothes but the bare essentials at the Fierros' town house. Not even certain essentials! All the Fierros had were men's tighty-whities, a few BFD sweat suits, and Gabriella's petite clothes. She had to go shopping soon, but she didn't feel like it. *What size should I buy? I'm so screwed.*

Terri was rubbing circles on her back, maternally. "How can I help?"

Misty smiled at her friend and coworker. "I don't know. I guess I need to clean up before going out there. You don't happen to have an extra blouse or cardigan lying around, do you?"

Terri smiled. "As a matter of fact, I do. It may not be your style or size or go with what you're wearing, but..." She shrugged.

But beggars can't be choosers, Misty finished for her in her mind.

Terri hurried off, leaving Misty feeling truly about as low as she could go. "Hold that thought," she muttered to herself. If she'd learned anything in her twenty-three years, it was that things could always get worse—especially if all a person focused on was negative.

She had to talk to Gabe. This time without an audience. She was pretty sure she knew how he felt, but where to go from here was the question. Even though he didn't like the circumstances, he was part of it.

As soon as Terri handed her the bright-orange sweater and Misty's purse, she said, "Don't worry. It's not busy out there. I can cover for you for a few minutes."

"I'll be right out. Thanks, Terri."

She dialed Gabe with one click, but he didn't answer—at first. When she was about to hang up, he said, "Hi, Misty. I'm waiting at the fire department's doctor's office. I should be getting cleared to go back to work. What do you need?"

He was busy. He'd have to make time for her, since no one could help her but him. Oh well. It sounded like he was getting a clean bill of health. At least one of their problems was solved.

━━━∿━━━

Gabe was waiting for her at Starbucks in the South End. He was perusing the free newspaper and didn't notice her come in. She wanted to turn and run…if her feet cooperated. But this conversation absolutely had to happen.

She'd half expected him to drop in and visit her at

his parents' house last night. Talking to him there would have been awkward. She was nervous, but bringing up the pregnancy in a public place where he couldn't make a scene helped her relax. A little. Until he saw her.

He rose, unsmiling. Realizing she had changed his whole life, she hesitated. He strolled over to her and kissed her cheek. Stepping back, he indicated a table with two coffees on it. "Have a seat."

"You already ordered something for me?"

"Yeah. I hope you don't mind."

"No. Not at all." It was a good thing Starbucks didn't serve wine. She'd be tempted.

"Yeah. I think I know what you like. You take your coffee with cream and no sugar. Right? I also ordered decaf. I thought you might be avoiding caffeine now."

She smiled at him. "Yeah. Thanks." He remembered how she liked her coffee. Most guys weren't that observant. And he'd taken her pregnancy into consideration. Maybe he *did* care.

They sat opposite each other, and he stared at her for a moment. Briefly shaking his head like something was unbelievable, he leaned back and took a sip of his coffee.

"What?" she asked.

"Nothing. You're just sort of…glowing?"

Well, that may have been because as soon as she'd made it back to his parents' place across the street, she'd scrubbed her face clean, changed into the outfit she'd bought on her lunch hour, and had hurried across four lanes of traffic to get here on time.

Misty fidgeted in her seat. He still hadn't smiled. She couldn't figure out how she felt now that he'd had a chance to digest the news. And as scared as she was to hear the answer, she had to ask. "Gabe, are you okay?"

He sat up straight and focused an intense stare at her. "You mean because you're pregnant?"

She bit her lip and nodded.

He set his coffee down and covered his face with one big hand. "I hate to ask, but are you sure? Could you be mistaken?"

"I went to my gynecologist the same day I got diagnosed with MS. So, yes. I'm sure. I guess I could've started off by saying 'I have good news and bad news,' but I wasn't sure if there was any good news."

Gabe just stared at her, biting his lower full lip. He sat there saying nothing for the longest time. At last he rose so suddenly, the table tipped a bit.

"I can't do this, Misty."

She held up one hand. "You don't have to. I'm the one who has to deal with this. I just wanted you to have a say. But if you don't want one, don't worry about it. I'll take care of myself."

Gabe let out a long exhale. "No. I don't mean that. I need to think." He strode out the door, leaving her sitting with two coffees in front of her and no Gabe.

A few patrons turned her way and gazed at her curiously.

A tear formed in the corner of her eye. She took several deep breaths, willing it away. She'd known he wasn't going to like talking about it. She'd expected that. There was no way he would jump up and down and pull her into his arms, declaring his undying love. But a little part of her had hoped...

She took a few more sips of her decaf coffee and tried

to compose herself. At last, she rose, poised to leave, but her knees gave out, and she sat down hard.

"Oh, hell," she muttered. *How am I going to deal with MS and single motherhood? How can I do this alone?* After a long deep breath, she just knew she'd find a way.

She decided to wait a few minutes to see if her unsteadiness was just the shock of Gabe walking out on her before she tried to stand again. She didn't know how her MS responded to stress. She imagined it wasn't good for anybody and maybe especially for people with her diagnosis.

She sat there with her hands clasped, elbows on the table. It must have looked like she was praying. She probably should. In a few minutes, she'd be all right. She'd go back across the street and take a moment to lie down and rest before she told anybody else.

She imagined Gabe had tried to wrestle with this alone. He didn't strike her as the type to confide in anyone. Or would he? Just about anyone in his family would listen. But she imagined that after talking to them, he'd probably offer to "do the right thing," because it would be expected. That's *not* what she wanted.

She took a couple more deep breaths and then pushed herself to her feet. Other than feeling a little numb, everything seemed fine until she tried zipping up her bomber jacket. She lost her balance and fell into another table. A couple of patrons jumped up and grabbed her.

"Are you all right?"

"Yeah. I'm fine," Misty said. "I just need to make it across the street."

"Do you need help?" one of the patrons asked. "You know...Narcan or something?"

She was shocked speechless. "No! I'm not drunk or on drugs. I'll be fine."

She took a few steps toward the door and paused. At that moment, the door flew open, and Gabriella rushed in.

"Misty! Honey, are you all right?"

"Did Gabe tell you?"

"Yes. He wanted to make sure you were okay, and I told him to stay right where he was. I can't guarantee he'll be there when we get back, but he'll come to his senses. Don't worry, honey."

"There's nothing wrong with his senses. I know what his problem is. It's not a big deal. I can do this without him."

Gabriella made some sound of disgust. "Let's get you across the street. There's no use talking about it here."

The woman was a powerhouse. Despite being three inches shorter, she led Misty out of the restaurant with an arm firmly under her elbow, the other grasping her waist. They walked across the street that way. Misty was being lead as if she were blind. Maybe that was in her future too. Another lovely perk of MS.

The lights cooperated, and they got to the other side without incident. "If Gabe doesn't want to talk yet, don't make him," Misty said.

"He's a big boy. He can face all kinds of challenges. This included. And I don't want you to let him off the hook. This is half of his doing."

"I'm really not sure about that."

Gabriella laughed. "You do know how sex works, don't you?"

Why is everybody asking me that?

Antonio opened the door, and Misty walked up the steps, holding on to the railing just in case.

"Gabe?" Gabriella asked.

Antonio shook his head. "Not here."

"Damn. I thought he'd man up and stick around."

Misty straightened to her full height. "Just because he needs to think doesn't make him any less of a man. In fact, maybe it's a good thing he's not here. I don't want to talk to him while he's upset."

"I suppose you're right." Gabriella sighed. "He's not particularly good with change at first, but he'll adjust. He always does."

Antonio closed the door behind them, then smiled at Misty. "I'm not sure what's going on, but I take it my fourth son has something to do with it."

"I don't want his whole life to change. If he doesn't want to be a dad, he doesn't have to. There are plenty of men who are biological fathers and nothing more."

"Oh no." Gabriella shook her head hard. "No son of mine is going to be just a 'biological father.'"

Antonio's brows shot up. He looked shocked for a moment. His expression returned to a gentle smile quickly enough.

Gabriella escorted Misty to a comfortable side chair, and as soon as she was seated, she crossed to her husband, putting her arm around his waist and stepping into the space under his arm. "It looks like our family will be expanding again. Misty and Gabe are having a baby."

"That's wonderful! I'd offer to toast to the occasion, but…" He pointed at Misty's middle.

"There's just one little problem," Gabriella said. "Gabe is being quite an ass about it."

"What? Where did he go?"

Gabriella patted his arm. "Now don't go getting all upset with him. He's just out for a walk. He came and got me and asked me to stay with Misty until he got back."

"I'll go find him." Antonio strode to the closet, grabbed his coat, and was out the door before anyone could stop him.

"Oh no. Is he going to yell at Gabe?" Misty asked, concerned. "I don't want anyone getting angry with him about this. It was not intentional."

"Of course not. They'll just talk. We know how it feels to be in that position ourselves, but don't let anyone else in on that." She winked.

"Oh. Don't worry. I'll keep it to myself."

"I'm sure Antonio remembers how it feels. I think it'll be good for Gabe to talk to his father right now. Meanwhile, it will be good for you and me to talk a bit. Can I get you something to drink or eat? Milk? Some homemade cookies?"

"No, thanks. I just had a cup of coffee."

She smiled. "It's the Italian mama in me. I want to feed you as a sign of love."

Misty chuckled. "That's sweet, but I really don't need anything." *Other than a miracle*. "Sandra didn't tell you anything, did she?"

"No. Does she know?"

"Yes. She was there when the diagnosis was confirmed."

"Diagnosis. That sounds so clinical."

Misty stared at her lap. "Well, I've been to a lot of doctors recently. I guess I've picked up some of the clinical lingo."

Gabriella reached over for Misty's hand. Misty took it, and they just held hands in companionable silence for a moment.

"They made a positive diagnosis of MS the day before yesterday, too," Misty added quietly.

The Fierro matriarch leaned forward and clasped Misty's cheeks. "Oh my goodness. You've really had a bad week, haven't you?"

Misty's lower lip trembled. She did not want to cry, especially not in front of Gabe's mother. She took a few deep breaths and got herself together.

Gabriella gave her a knowing look. "You're not alone. You understand that, right?"

Misty smiled weakly. "I know. I can always count on you."

"And you can count on Gabe too. We'll be hearing wedding bells soon. Long before the baby is born. When are you due?"

"Sometime around the end of November."

"Ah, Thanksgiving. A perfect time to be grateful for one's blessings, especially for a baby who's bringing a young couple together. It's meant to be."

Misty sighed. "I'm not sure about that. Gabe never wanted to get married, have kids, and all that."

"I'm well aware," Gabriella said. "That's why it's meant to be. It would take something like this to make him realize he can do it."

Misty was confused. "Of course he can do it. But whether he wants to is a whole different question. I don't want him to feel forced into something he doesn't want. He'll just resent me and the baby."

Gabriella laughed.

Misty didn't expect that reaction. She didn't think her situation was funny at all.

"Oh, honey. Men don't know what they want. Sometimes they have to hold their child to know how much they love and want one—or seven," she said and rolled her eyes.

"And sometimes they have to lose things to really value them," Misty said glumly.

Gabriella stared at her, looking concerned. "You can't be saying you're going to walk away from him. There's no way you're going anywhere with my grandchild."

"I...I don't know what to do."

Gabriella stroked Misty's hair and tucked it behind her ear. "Oh, darling. My mother taught me, and now I'll teach you, that when you don't know what to do, the best thing to do is nothing. Soon enough, the answer will present itself."

Misty nodded. "Well then, I guess I'll go to my room and lie down. If you don't mind my calling it my room. I still don't have my own place yet, but I will."

Gabriella sighed. "Please don't rush off. We enjoy having you here."

"Really?"

"Honest and truly."

Gabe heard his father calling his name. "Oh, shit."

"Gabe, hold up."

There was no way he could pretend he didn't hear him. A supernatural being has no excuse to ignore anyone for that reason. So he stopped, turned, and waited for his father.

The elder Fierro slowed his steps and walked up to his son calmly.

Maybe he wasn't in for as bad a chewing out as he'd thought he was.

"I hear congratulations are in order," his father said and slapped him on the back.

"Or condolences."

His father narrowed his eyes and stared at him shrewdly. "You can't change the situation, Son. You can only change your attitude. If you look at it one way, you'll be miserable. If you look at it as a blessing in disguise, you might be surprised by how true that is and how happy you'll be."

Gabe let out a deep breath and hung his head. "I'm scared, Dad. What do I know about parenting? What do I know about marriage? I've spent years trying to keep relationships casual and breaking them off as soon as the woman got 'that look.'"

Antonio smiled. "What do any of us know about anything before we're knee-deep in it?"

Gabe crossed his arms. "I know they don't let us fight fires until we've had quite a bit of education and training. Maybe that's what's wrong with so many parents. No training."

"Well then, take a parenting course. Read a book. Do whatever makes you feel more comfortable, because *you're doing this*."

"Just like that, huh? I have no say in it. Is that right?"

"You bet your ass that's right. You did the deed. Who else should clean up your mess?"

He sighed. "It was just one night. And it was her birthday. She wanted it more than I did."

Antonio set his hands on his hips. "It doesn't matter if it was her idea or not. I'm guessing she didn't rape you."

Gabe dropped his gaze to the sidewalk. "Of course she didn't. It was my fault for going along with it, but at the time, it seemed innocent enough. I used condoms. It's just that I fell asleep and... Never mind. I guess it doesn't matter how it happened."

"Now you're getting it. The point is, you need to come to peace with this, and soon. That beautiful girl is going to need your help. Of course, your mother and I want you to do the right thing and marry her."

"I can't, Dad. I just can't."

"And why is that? Do you think you have to be in love first?"

"It has nothing to do with love."

"Good. Do you have any doubt that your mother and I love each other?"

Gabe's jaw dropped. "Of course not. How could I? You show it in a million little ways all the time. Are you saying you *don't* love her?"

"Don't be an idiot. Of course I love her. Desperately. More than anything on earth, including myself. The point is, it wasn't always that way."

Gabe had to think about that for a minute. "When did you know you loved her?"

"There wasn't any kind of lightbulb moment. It was just a gradual knowing. And it got stronger over time."

"And you think that's how it will happen for me?"

His father laughed. "Hell no. I think it's already happened. You just need to stick with it, nurture it, and let it grow. You could easily destroy it at this point and break that poor girl's heart. I forbid you to do that."

Gabe sighed and shook his head. "I don't want to be an ass, but I don't want to be a martyr either."

"Good. Because you don't have to be either one of those things. You can man up, get your head in the game, and allow yourself to enjoy the happy accident."

"You make it sound easy, but there's one little detail you've forgotten."

"What's that?"

"Misty doesn't know what we are. And none of us knows what's growing inside her. She could be pregnant with a phoenix."

"You think I didn't have that same situation with your mother? Where would we be if we hadn't taken a chance? More importantly, where the hell would *you* be?"

"I...I guess I wouldn't be anywhere."

"Exactly. Now answer one question for me. Do you like Misty?"

"Hell yeah. Of course I like her. She's awesome."

"Good. That's more important than being head-over-heels crazy in love. That stuff fades. If you're left with affection and friendship, you're in good shape."

"I feel more than affection for her."

"Oh?"

Gabe struggled with what to say next. "I—I guess I love her, but..."

"But what?"

Gabe shrugged.

"Damn, you're stubborn."

Chapter 14

MISTY WAS CURLED UP IN A FETAL POSITION, IRONIC AS THAT seemed. She was occupying Gabe's old room on the third floor. There were still trophies from his football days. A few pennants. They must've been from college teams he supported. As far as she knew, he never went to college himself. There was so much she didn't know about him.

A knock at her door made her stop ruminating and sit up. "Come in."

Gabe opened the door. "Am I allowed in here?"

Misty smiled sadly. "It's your room, Gabe."

He entered and sat beside her on the bed. He took her hand and seemed to be studying it. He kissed her palm and then laced his fingers with hers. Looking at her intently, he said, "I'm sorry. I shouldn't have left you at the coffee shop."

Misty squeezed his hand. "I understand. You needed a few minutes. I needed that too, but I had time to think at the hospital and later at Julie's, and I still didn't know what to say to you."

Gabe looked at her, concerned. "About the hospital… I'm not sure that's the best place for the birth of our child."

Misty skipped over the part where he wanted to avoid the hospital and was just thrilled that he said "our child." When she'd caught up to the whole sentence, she asked,

"Why? I would have thought you'd be more comfortable with the doctors and all the emergency equipment right there if anything were to go wrong."

"I guess we can talk about that later. But there's something we really need to talk about now."

She waited.

"I'm glad you're sitting down. What I have to tell you may come as a shock. There's a family secret that you have to know. Now, not later. It's part of why I didn't know what to say or do."

He had her attention, so she just said, "Go on."

He scratched his head. "I don't quite know how to say this, so I guess I'll just spit it out and then answer the hundred questions you'll have after that."

Her brow furrowed. *What could they possibly have as a family secret?*

He cleared his throat. "We're shape-shifters, Misty. All of us, except my mother. We can take the shape of a bird called the phoenix. We have very long lives, unless we spend a lot of time in bird years. Then we age faster."

She leaned back and stared at him. He seemed to be sincere. Had he lost it? Had he gone around the bend due to the shock of her situation? She patted his arm. "It's okay, Gabe."

His eyes rounded. "It's okay?"

Misty shrugged. "Yeah, well… I'm sure there are doctors who can help you. I wish I knew what to do, but I don't. All I can say is"—she glanced at her lap then up at him again—"I love you, anyway."

Gabe fell back on his elbows. "I'll be damned. I never thought it would be that easy. But what did you mean about doctors? This isn't something we're infected with."

"Oh, I know that. I'm sure there's a perfectly good explanation for why you believe this whole phoenix story. Maybe it's just the stress."

Gabe dropped down the rest of the way till he was lying flat and covered his face with his hands, mumbling through them, "Shit." Then he started laughing.

He sat up and shook his head at her. "It's not that you accept me or don't. You just think I'm crazy. Is that right?"

Misty worried her lip. "I don't think the word *crazy* is exactly right. I think there might be some psychological thing…a kind of delusional escape from the stress of reality or something."

"If my parents back up my story, would you believe it then? We can't all be delusional, right?"

Misty just stared at him. Either the whole family believed this nonsense, or they were just humoring him. It was probably best to find out which it was. "Okay. Let's go talk to your parents."

"Wait. Before that." Gabe slid down onto one knee. "There's something else I have to say."

Misty jumped up. "Oh, no. No, don't do that yet. I need to know more about what you just told me first."

Gabe rose. "Of course. I understand. Let's go downstairs and find my parents."

"No need," Antonio said, and the door opened wider. "We're right here."

Gabe frowned. "You were eavesdropping?"

"We just thought you might need some help, dear," Gabriella said. "I remember when Antonio first shared the family secret with me. I doubted his sanity too. I think it's probably best if we all talk about it together."

"Is it okay with you if they come in?" Gabe asked Misty.

What could she say? It was their house. She had nowhere else to go. Unless she moved back to the suburbs to hide from the baby's crazy family. "Of course. Come in." She rose.

Gabriella crossed over to her and took her hands in both of hers. "I know what you're thinking. You probably think the whole shifter story is crazy. And that I'm crazy for believing it. But they can prove it, if you want them to."

Misty was scared now. Either all of these people were nuts, or she was about to witness something so bizarre, she never would have believed it otherwise. But she had to know—one way or the other. She gulped and straightened her shoulders. "I think I need a demonstration."

"As you wish," Gabriella said. She turned to her husband and son as she put her arm around Misty, grasping her tightly. Part of Misty was uncomfortable, and yet part of her thought it was a good idea to keep from falling if she fainted.

"Are you ready?" Gabe asked.

"As ready as I'll ever be," Misty said.

In the blink of an eye, the man she loved shrank, shifted into a colorful bird, and flapped its wings to get free of his clothes.

She gasped and recoiled. Gabriella tightened her grip on Misty's waist and arm. Then Antonio followed suit but let his sleeves drape over extended wings. The bird that was Gabe shifted again and became the man she thought she knew.

He asked her to turn around so his father could shift and yank up his sweat pants. Meanwhile, he put on his jeans again.

When they were dressed, Gabe asked, "Are you okay?"

She turned back and faced them. "I…I think I am."

Antonio nodded sagely. "You're a strong, brave woman, Misty. I give you a lot of credit for not fainting away. We need women like you in this family."

Gabriella placed her hands on each side of Misty's face, then kissed her on both cheeks. "I knew you'd be all right. That you'd understand."

"Oh, I understand nothing. How do you do this? Why did this happen? Where do you come from?"

"It's time for a brief history lesson," Antonio said.

Misty's mouth was suddenly dry. "Can I have a drink of water or something?"

Gabriella nodded. "I'll go get you something, dear. You'd probably like something stronger than a glass of milk or a cup of coffee, but…"

Misty snorted. "You got that right. No, it wouldn't be good for the baby. You don't have to get it for me. I can go downstairs."

Gabe took her hand and smiled. "I'll lead the way."

She wasn't afraid of him. She had just witnessed something she'd believed he couldn't make happen. But he did. And according to him, everyone in his family except his mother could shift like that. All six brothers. She had grown up knowing every one of the Fierros and was never afraid of any of them. She liked them all.

Come to think of it, Sandra had married Miguel years ago. She must have known. Ryan and Jayce were married too, although she didn't know their wives. So it wasn't just Gabriella and Antonio who'd had to navigate the revelation of a major secret. This was startling.

When they were all settled around the dining room table, Antonio began his story.

"The first reference to a firebird was in ancient Rome. However, the legend has roots in different cultures around the world. That should tell you there's something more than legend to it. The Native Americans never met the ancient Romans, but both cultures believed strongly in a bird that can rise from the ashes after it's engulfed in flames."

"And as you can see," Gabriella added, "it isn't a legend at all. This is the family I married into. They were kind enough to tell me before Antonio proposed. I had some time to think it over and come to my own conclusions and decisions. Gabe can give you that time too."

Gabe watched Misty sipping her water when she abruptly set her glass on the dining table. "Wait! The baby... Will he or she be a phoenix and able to do that shifting thing too?"

"We don't know for sure," Gabe said. "If it's a boy, probably. But we haven't had a girl born in the family for generations. No one can remember if the last girl shifted into a phoenix or not."

Misty paused for a few moments, then shrugged. "Well, if he or she can fly, that might come in handy with my MS. Maybe I can teach the baby to fly where I want him to go instead of worrying about my unsteadiness."

Gabe leaned back and laughed. "Always looking on the bright side. I love that about you, Misty." Quietly, he added, "I love a lot of things about you."

They gazed at each other. He could tell he'd surprised her. Hell, he'd surprised himself. His parents smiled at each other. He hadn't said, "I love you." And he wouldn't just tell her what she wanted to hear. He hoped everybody would understand that and not force the issue.

After a respectful pause, Antonio cleared his throat. "That brings up an important point. We're not supposed to shift in front of humans. Ever. It's a general rule of paranormal beings that they never display their powers to unsuspecting mortals, and that rule is hard and fast."

"Well, except for spouses," Gabriella was quick to add.

"Paranormal beings?" Misty repeated with a shaky voice. "Are there more than just phoenixes?"

Gabe, Antonio, and Gabriella all took turns glancing at each other. At last, Antonio spoke. "We're not at liberty to say, Misty. At least not at this point. I could see if you married into our family, there might be a little more information we could give you—"

"In other words, yes," she said.

Antonio chuckled. "You've always been a smart kid. The only reason that's not a problem is your ability to respect people's boundaries. Just accept that you're perfectly safe. Paranormal beings have some very good reasons for staying under the radar."

Misty bit her lip. "Are you afraid of scientists trying to experiment on you? Maybe the government finding secrets they can use in war?"

"Yes. That's a major threat," Antonio said. "Believe me, nobody wants that."

"Well, that's a lot to take in," Gabriella said. "I'm

glad you're staying with us. If you ever have any questions, anything at all, you can come to me."

"I have one question right now."

"Go ahead."

"Well, since everyone in the family has these powers or whatever, except for you, why do they obey you?"

Antonio laughed. "Apparently, it hasn't escaped Misty's notice that my little spitfire of a wife rules the roost. Pun intended."

Gabriella smiled. "I have to be honest, dear. They don't always listen to me—but if they want a big piece of tiramisu instead of the first little one that crumbles on its way out of the dish, they behave."

Misty gaped at her. "Really? You control them with food?"

The men laughed.

"I was just being silly. No, darling, our boys are taught to respect their elders from the cradle. And there's no mistaking who rules this family. It's Antonio."

Gabe smiled. "Dad lays down the law, and then we complain to Mom."

"Does it help?" Misty asked.

"Sometimes she gets him to lighten up. Be reasonable."

"Hey, I'm always reasonable," Antonio protested.

"And if I can't get him to listen, he gets the crappy piece of cake," Gabriella joked.

Antonio wrapped an arm around her waist and kissed her cheek. "Her cooking is worth behaving myself for."

"Do you like to cook, dear?" Gabriella asked.

"I—I never really learned how. I mean, I can put together something simple without poisoning anyone, but that's about it."

Gabe groaned.

"Maybe while you're here, you can learn to cook," Antonio offered. "You couldn't find a better school than the Fierro kitchen. Not even in Paris or Rome. Even Gabe has learned a thing or two."

Misty gave Gabriella a grateful smile. "I think I'd like that. My own mother didn't have a chance to teach me anything more than how to use the microwave. This is one of those times when your generosity—" Her voice cracked, and she couldn't finish her thought.

Gabriella reached over and squeezed Misty's hand. "We're here for everything and anything you need. Remember that, sweetheart. Just let us know when you're ready to plan the wedding, and we'll arrange to pay for whatever you'd like. A big church wedding or a small family gathering. It's up to you two."

"One problem," Misty said.

Gabriella tipped her head. "What's that?"

"Gabe hasn't proposed."

"I was about to."

Misty straightened her spine. "Well, don't. I'm not sure I can accept right now."

Gabe's brows shot up. "Is it because I left you at the coffee shop? I'm sorry. I really shouldn't have done that, I know."

Misty shook her head. "That didn't help, but no. That's not all of it." She faced Gabe's parents. "I don't want Gabe to ask just because 'it's the right thing,' according to everyone else." She used air quotes to indicate it might not be the right thing at all. "I don't think he'd be proposing if I weren't pregnant. Even if I am a catch." She winked at him.

He grinned. "You are that, and more."

"Yeah, but my *more* comes with major drawbacks."

"Do you mean your MS?"

"Well, yeah. I don't know what's in store for me. You watched those videos. This disease can be devastating."

"I feel bad for you, but I'm looking at it philosophically. Sometimes life slaps you in the face. It's how you react that matters. I hope I can always behave like a good person, even though I'm far from perfect. I promise to make sure you get the care you need."

"Yeah, medical care."

"If you're talking about moral support, I seem to remember holding you while you cried. I imagine it won't be the last time."

She worried her lip and was quiet for so long, he felt the need to fill the silence.

"Why don't we see how it goes? I understand your reluctance. I can do better. I *will* do better." He stood and moved behind her chair. "I can give you killer massages." He kneaded her neck and shoulders while she sighed, and everyone watched the tension melt away.

After a few moments, Misty said, "I'm exhausted. Would you mind if I go upstairs and take a nap?"

"Of course not," Gabriella said right away. "I remember how tired I got during my pregnancies. It's been a stressful day."

Misty snorted, excused herself, put her water glass in the dishwasher, then left.

"Antonio, would you excuse us for a couple of minutes? I'd like to talk to Gabe alone."

Gabe's father rose and pushed in his chair. "Have at it. I'll be in the man cave downstairs."

In a few moments, Gabe was alone with his mother, who looked over at him and smiled sweetly. *Oh no*. That smile could mean a number of things. Not all of them good.

"Gabriel, dear, do you remember my telling you that someday I would sit down and introduce you to yourself?"

Gabe chuckled. "Yeah. Something about my being your most sensitive son or that kind of bull—I mean, baloney."

She reached over and patted his hand. "That's right. You may not believe it, but I do know my sons."

Gabe leaned back in his chair. "Why wouldn't I believe it? Dad's the one who gets us mixed up."

She chuckled. "That's not what I meant. All of my sons are special—and not just paranormally. Ryan is rebuilding a castle in Ireland with his wife, Miguel and Sandra are preparing to take over as heads of the family along with Jayce and Kristine. In some ways, you're the one I worry about the most and the least."

"Now I'm even more confused."

Gabriella sighed. "Listen to me carefully. I don't need to worry about you, because you're content to be who you are. And I'm worried about you, because you're content as you are. Think about this. Right now, you're happy living in a studio in downtown Boston and working as a firefighter. But is that what you want to do for the next five years?"

He shrugged.

"How about five hundred?"

Gabe sat upright. "Five hundred? I think the fire service might catch on after a couple hundred years or so. I know I'll have to do something different eventually."

"Okay. Let's just advance five years, then. You and I both know you have a lot of long-term goals to think about."

Gabe shrugged. "Well, in five years, I might be a lieutenant or at least studying for and going after a promotion."

Gabriella nodded. "And that's a fine goal. So, what else will you be doing?"

Gabe squirmed in his chair. "I don't know, Mom. Do I have to decide right now?"

"No, you don't. But if you just drift along and wait for something to happen, you're letting fate decide where you'll go, what you'll do, and who you will be. I want you to be happy."

"I *am* happy."

"You could've fooled me."

Gabe leaned forward and rested his elbows on the table. He stared at his hands, turning them over and then clasping them in front of him. "I think I know what you're saying, but look at what's happening right now. Life is throwing something at me that I didn't ask for."

"Consider yourself lucky. You could have had a lot worse things come your way."

He sighed. "I know, I know. I'm lucky I have shoes on my feet. I'm lucky I have feet to walk on. And right now, I feel like walking right out the door. Maybe you could just say what you're trying to say without all the subtle messages."

"If I tell you what to do, it won't mean anything. You need to examine your own life, look at the possible outcomes, and choose a path. The sensitive boy I know is probably scared, going around and around in his own mind, trying to figure out what he should do and what other people think he should do. And you're thinking of things in terms of avoiding the worst."

He just stared at his hands.

"And there's nothing wrong with that. A couple of my sons take too many risks. They just dive in, barely looking to see if there's water in the pool. You, on the other hand, stand beside the pool, watching everyone else. I don't know what you're thinking half the time, but I do know what you're doing. Nothing. Zero. Zilch. Nada."

Gabe held up his hands. "Okay, okay. I get it. I need to make a decision about my future."

"And it should be a decision you feel good about. If you can follow that plan, I think you'll find your way into at least the shallow end of the pool. Who knows? You might even have some fun. But I guess you'll have to learn to splash before you can swim."

"Or sink." He smirked.

She leaned back and swatted his arm. "Now you're just mocking me."

"Yeah. I am." He looked over at his mother shyly. She was a beautiful example of someone who made good decisions and traveled a happy path. But she couldn't have guessed at the circumstances that would touch her life.

"How did you do it, Mom?"

"Do what?"

"Deal with all this? Us? Did you really want seven sons? Seven *paranormal* sons?"

She laughed. "Sometimes you don't get what you want, you get what you need. Isn't there some song about that?"

"Who the hell needs seven kids?"

They both laughed.

His forehead wrinkled. "So, are you satisfied?"

She smiled broadly. "If I were any more satisfied, it would probably kill me."

The two of them smiled.

Gabe rose. "Good talk, Mom." He leaned down and kissed her on the cheek.

She reached up and stroked his face. "I love you, you know."

"Well, duh. I'm going to go home now to make some decisions and plans."

Chapter 15

Misty went on her break at work. She had no sooner put her feet up than she heard some kind of commotion from the lobby. *What now?* Of course, another robbery popped into her head, but she couldn't imagine it. Not so soon after the other one—especially with all the news coverage and the fact that they hadn't gotten the big prize they were going after.

Misty carefully peeked around the corner to see what was going on. To her surprise, one of her coworkers was arguing with Adam...loudly.

"She's on break. She can go outside if she wants to."

"People can't just walk into the bank and expect my tellers to drop what they're doing...or not doing...and walk outside."

"Adam? Do you hear yourself?"

Misty figured it had to be about her since she was the only one on break. She didn't usually stick her nose in, but it seemed to be where she belonged. So she entered the teller area and asked, "What's going on?"

When she looked over at Adam, she saw Gabe standing behind him, holding a bouquet of flowers.

Her jaw dropped. "Gabe?"

"Hey, Misty. I was hoping to talk to you for just a minute and show you something outside."

"Well, how fortunate. I just happen to be on my

coffee break." She glared at Adam and smiled at her coworker, Betsy, who was trying to defend her.

As she entered the lobby area, Adam stomped off to his office. Gabe handed her the flowers. Some red roses, some white lilies, and some other floral that she couldn't identify, but they made pretty purple splashes among the rest. She took a deep whiff.

"They're beautiful. Thank you. What's the occasion?"

He extended his hand. "You'll see."

Taking a couple of moments to step outside was not unheard of. One of her coworkers smoked and regularly took his breaks outside, so she didn't know why Adam was having such a fit.

She took Gabe's hand and walked confidently to the front doors. Outside, she caught sight of Engine 22 with a huge banner all across its side.

It read, *Marry me, Misty!*

"Oh my God!"

Gabe's captain was hanging out the shotgun window, smiling. "Hurry up and give him an answer, Misty. We have work to do."

She stuck her hand over her heart and took a step back, repeating, "Oh my God."

"You don't have to answer right now," Gabe said. "I just want you to know that I'm not doing the right thing." He gave her a rare silly grin.

She laughed, more from relief than amusement.

Gabe stepped closer, leaned down, and gave her a deep, toe-curling kiss. One that caused passersby to stop and applaud. It must've looked like she'd said yes. She wouldn't embarrass Gabe by contradicting them, but he must know there was a lot to consider.

When he finally pulled away, she placed her hand over his heart. "Thank you," she whispered. "I still have a lot to think about, but I appreciate the gesture."

He swept her hair behind her ear and whispered back, "Take your time. I can do this as often as I need to until you believe me. Well, not with the truck. I was lucky to finagle that once."

"What are you going to tell the guys?"

He shrugged and gave her a cocky smile. "I won't say anything, except what a lucky girl you are. They'll expect something like that."

She cupped his cheek. "It would be true."

A quick peck later and Gabe was jogging back to the truck, jumping into the driver's seat. She inhaled the fragrant flowers as she walked back inside. *Who knew Gabe could do something so romantic?* Would that change Parker's mind? That thought put an immediate damper on the elation she'd experienced only a moment before. Tough. It was her decision. Her brother didn't have to like it.

She wandered back inside. *Now, what am I going to tell my coworkers?*

The truth, of course. She wasn't a good liar. She knew that. After she had put the flowers in a generic vase, kept under the sink for just such occasions, she returned to her window. Her coworker Betsy excitedly asked, "What did you say?"

Misty decided to play it cool. "About what?"

"Don't play dumb. We saw the fire truck—and the banner."

Adam appeared to be checking the flyers on the wall advertising the other bank products. He might as well have been wearing a sign that said *I'm eavesdropping.*

Misty shrugged. "I said I'd think about it."

Adam let out a deep breath in a whoosh.

"Think about it?" Betsy exclaimed. "What's to think about? He's gorgeous, a firefighter—a real-life hero—and he loves you. A lot! Obviously."

Misty wished it was as obvious to her as it seemed to be to everyone else. Maybe Gabe had had a change of heart with all his "thinking." But was that what she really wanted? A change of heart? She would've preferred his heart be in it all along—with hers.

What was it he'd said? "*I'm not doing the right thing.*" That could be taken a couple of ways. Either he meant he was doing this because he wanted to, not because he had to, or maybe he just thought it wasn't the right thing, but he was doing it anyway. *Oh, man. This is going to drive me crazy.*

Until she was sure exactly how he felt, she really couldn't make a decision. She wouldn't be pitied. And even though there might come a time in the future when she would need to be taken care of, there were professionals for that. She didn't need to force a man into marriage for the part about "in sickness and in health."

The baby was another matter. She would welcome his financial help in order to give the child a better life. As long as they both put the child's needs first, that part would work out…somehow.

She could picture Gabriella wanting to have both her and the baby under her roof. But she didn't know how Antonio would feel about that. She had heard that he wanted to move to the Caribbean for his retirement. And he certainly deserved to do that, if they wanted to. He had been with the fire service for many years and retired long ago. Suddenly, she wondered how old he was. Was that also part of the family secret?

Misty had to get her head in the game. A customer stepped up to her window with a few different transactions, and she had to concentrate on more than just her own complicated life.

Adam gave her some kind of hand signal from behind the customer.

She glanced over at him and frowned. "Did you want to say something?"

He cleared his throat and stepped a little closer. "Stop by my office later. I have a favor to ask."

"Sure." *Oh my freakin' God. What kind of favor could my jealous boss want?*

"What? Do I need to get down on my freaking knee?" Gabe was trying to keep his voice down as he spoke to his brother on the phone.

"No, I just figured she would've said yes." Dante pitched his voice high and silly as he mimicked, "Yes, yes, a thousand times yes!"

If Gabe could've punched him through the phone, he would have. Actually, he should've punched Jayce for telling everyone about his proposal. Without knowing her answer, it was getting a bit sticky.

"Look, Gabe, I know you guys have had a bit of a weird history—"

"Weird? What do you mean by weird?" Gabe kicked at the chunk of ice beside the fire station wall. The weather was starting to get to him. Long winters didn't bother him when he was a kid, but now it must be a sign of his actually getting older. *Twenty-six. Almost twenty-seven. Since when is that getting old?*

"Well, from what I understand, your being with Misty put your relationship with Parker in the toilet. He asked you to look after her because he thought you were his best friend, most trusted man on the planet."

"Yeah, yeah… So, what are you saying?"

"I'm saying, Bro, that she still loves her brother, and now he hates you. That's gotta be tough for her. Have you even asked how *they* are doing?"

Gabe rubbed his forehead as he paced. "No. I figured it was none of my business. I'd just wait until Parker wanted to talk to me, and then we'd talk."

Dante made a sound that conveyed his disappointment. *Well, tough.* Gabe didn't know what else to do. In truth, he'd expected the same thing. Misty would jump into his arms, and they would have that blissful moment of acceptance and mutual agreement.

Now he not only didn't feel accepted by his best friend, but it didn't even seem like the person he most wanted to be accepted by was interested in him any longer. "Maybe she's just getting back at me for being such a jerk in the first place. I didn't know what I wanted, and during that time, I may have made her feel like she wasn't that special."

"Damn. If that's the case, you've got some backpedaling to do."

Gabe heard the tones go off in his brother's fire station a moment before the tones rang out in his own.

"Gotta go, Gabe."

"Yeah. Me too." He shoved the phone into his pocket and strode through the open bay, meeting his buddies at the truck. He didn't usually drive, but for some reason, he wanted to. He wanted to feel in control of *something*. "Mind if I drive, Captain?"

The captain glanced over at the probie who usually drove for experience and said, "Sure. Think you can remember where you're going?"

Everyone snickered, because Gabe had grown up in that neighborhood, and now working in the South End, he could pretty much claim his whole life had been spent in it.

"I think I can find my way around." He jumped into the driver's seat, and as soon as everyone was in, he pulled out onto Tremont Street and headed around the corner. The area they were heading to wasn't the best, but it was far from the worst the city had to offer.

"Might as well get the Narcan out now," the captain said.

"Did they say anything about a possible OD?" Gabe asked.

"No. But we're supposed to meet someone at a car, and it seems like more than half of our calls lately have been about overdoses, not fires."

"I wish they'd come to us. It would be a lot easier." Only three minutes later, Gabe was pulling in between a gas station and a fast-food place. A car parked behind the restaurant had been identified as the location they had to investigate.

An anxious woman strode up to the truck's window. All of them except Gabe exited the vehicle while the captain spoke to the woman.

"I tell you, we smelled gas. There's some kind of gas leak."

Gabe almost groaned aloud.

"Where?" the captain asked.

"My husband and I are parked right over there." She pointed at a parked car with a man in the driver's seat.

"Why is he just sitting in the car?"

The woman made a sound of disgust. "He thinks I'm being ridiculous."

"It's not ridiculous to investigate something that might be dangerous," the captain said.

The woman stuck her hands on her hips. "Thank you. That's what I was thinking too. Would you mind coming over and telling that to my husband?"

The captain smiled. "I should talk to him anyway, but not necessarily about how right you were." He waved over the probie, and the two of them went to the car in the distance. Gabe couldn't hear what they were talking about, but he saw some nodding and pointing. Eventually, they returned to the truck.

Gabe rolled down his window. "What is it?"

The rookie, a guy they called Fritz because his last name was German, said, "We have to poke around a while and make it look like we're investigating a gas leak."

Gabe's brows shot up. "Why wouldn't you?"

The guy shrugged. "The husband thinks it's just the gas station smell and that his wife's not used to it. She doesn't even drive, never mind pump her own gas."

The captain added, "He said the odor smells no worse than any other gas station. But we'll go and sniff around, just to make sure. Sit tight."

Gabe thought he'd take the opportunity to call Misty.

Maybe he could get her to give him some kind of preliminary or tentative answer. Then he glanced at his watch and realized she'd still be at work. Damn. He didn't want to get her in trouble with her douche bag boss.

He sighed as he thought about who else he could call. *Parker*. His mother's words were stuck in his head. He had thought about standing next to the pool while everyone else was in there splashing around and having a good time. That got him off his ass enough to propose.

But there was more she got him thinking about. And that was how he just sort of let life happen to him, instead of deciding what he wanted to happen and making it so. Right now, he wanted Parker's forgiveness, blessing, or whatever else would get them back into each other's favor.

"What the hell," he muttered. A moment later, he dialed Parker.

"I didn't think I'd hear from you after the other day." Parker hadn't even bothered to say hello. Maybe he was anxious to talk too.

"I'm extending an olive branch." That was all Gabe could think of to say at this point. Hopefully, his friend would know where to take it from there.

"Oh yeah? I'll take your olive branch and raise you a beer."

Gabe grinned inwardly. "That sounds good, but will I be safe if we talk about your sister? Or are you going to break that beer bottle over my head?"

Parker chuckled. "We'll see."

That wasn't exactly the answer Gabe had hoped for, but it was better than he'd expected. The two of them made plans to meet up the next day. Gabe wouldn't get off until six, and he'd need a few minutes to make it home, shower, change clothes, and steel himself for whatever would follow.

At least there would be an end to this. Just knowing that much gave him a sense of relief. Not that he would ever admit it to her, but maybe his mother was right. He needed to take the initiative a little more often.

The guys returned to the truck and hopped in.

"Nothing?" Gabe asked.

"Not that we could find," the captain answered. "Let's go."

Gabe put the truck in gear and began driving around the back of the gas station when he saw some familiar sparks and slammed on the brakes. "Fire." He pointed to a small pile of wood and newspaper…and the backside of a fleeing arsonist.

"Fuck. That must've been the gas the woman smelled." All four of them jumped out. The captain addressed Gabe before he slammed his door. "You can put that puppy out with the fire extinguisher. I'm going after that bastard."

"I'll go with ya, Captain," yelled Donahue.

Gabe grabbed the fire extinguisher and followed Fritz to the mini bonfire near the propane tanks. "It's a damn good thing we saw this here… Stand back."

He had just started to aim it when the pile exploded. Fritz swore and jumped out of the way. Gabe felt like everything was happening in slow motion.

The probie's eyes rounded, and he lunged for Gabe, pushing him to the ground. It was about that time that a thousand bees were stinging his face—at least that's what it felt like. He closed his eyes and covered them with his hands out of instinct. Soon, the smell of gas was joined by another horrible odor. Gabe smelled his own flesh frying.

He heard two sets of voices yelling. Even as he was on fire, he was concerned about the probie who had dived right on top of him and was probably also getting burned. That was no ordinary bonfire. Something had to have been planted and set to explode as soon as the arsonist had cleared the scene.

He heard the captain yelling instructions, saying he'd use the snow to smother the fire until Tom returned with the fireproof blanket. That's the last thing Gabe remembered.

"Thanks for driving me to the dealership, Misty," Adam said.

She shrugged. "You're the one driving. Why didn't you pick up the neighbor whose car you borrowed this morning? She could have dropped you off and gone right home."

"Oh, I was going to, but she called and said one of her kids came home sick. She has to stay with him. You know how to drive, don't you?"

Misty laughed. "Yeah. If I didn't, I wouldn't have gone much of anywhere when I lived in the 'burbs."

"Oh, that's right. I forget you went from living in the city to the suburbs and then back. What was that like for you?"

She shrugged. She didn't really want to chitchat with her boss. Truthfully, she didn't even want to be in a car with him. It seemed too personal. Where Adam was concerned, she'd rather keep things strictly business.

After an uncomfortable silence, he cleared his throat. "Um, Misty. I wanted to talk to you alone. Outside work. Not as your boss, but as your friend."

She glanced over at him and raised her eyebrows. *Friend? Since when?* She didn't interrupt him though. Part of her was curious about what he wanted to say.

"It…well. It's about that firefighter."

"Gabe?"

"Yeah. I hope you're not getting too involved with him. I mean, I know he proposed, but I was relieved to hear you didn't accept. I hope you'll say no altogether when you hear what I have to say."

What could he possibly have to say? Did he put a private investigator on Gabe who saw him shift into a bird and fly away? She remained quiet.

Adam squirmed in his seat. "I just don't think he can offer you much. He's a firefighter. Probably didn't go to college. Everyone knows they don't make a lot of money…and they get hurt. Then what?"

She felt her ire rise. Fortunately, she remembered who was talking and caught herself before she went off on her boss. When she could be civil, she simply said, "And?"

"And…" He glanced over with a mixture of trepidation and hope. "And I know I could offer you more. I'm not always going to be just a branch manager. I finished my MBA last summer."

Online, Misty added to herself.

"Anyway, you're a girl with a good head on her shoulders. I think you're classy as hell too. You'd be much happier as a bank president's wife than some woman who barely exists above poverty level and whose main goal is to get all the soot out of her husband's clothes."

"That's it!" Misty shouted. "Stop the car."

"What? Why?" Adam glanced over at her with genuine astonishment and kept right on driving.

"Because I said so. Now stop! If you want to fire me, go ahead. I'm not going to let you insult me, my boyfriend, and every other brave firefighter in the city. Hell, in the world! Where would people like you be without people like him? Even if your house never catches fire, other things can and do happen, every day. These are the brave first responders who run *into* danger while you're running away."

"Now, Misty—"

Just his patronizing tone of voice was enough to refuel her fire. "If you're so concerned about the families of first responders not having enough money to live on, why don't you do something about that?"

He snorted. "Like what? What could I possibly do?"

"Write to the mayor! Start a petition! Sheesh, you could even be an example to others by collecting funds for the widows and orphans of firefighters who are no longer with us."

"A drop in the bucket," he muttered.

"Yeah, with an attitude like that. Listen, my relationship with Gabe is none of your business. None!"

"I realize that. And I was afraid of a reaction like this, but what kind of friend would I be if I said nothing?"

"And that's another thing." *In for a penny, in for a pound.* "Since when are we friends? I haven't encouraged your 'friendship' in the least."

"I know you haven't. And I admire that about you. I know I can trust you around other men."

Misty couldn't stand it any longer. She burst out laughing.

He frowned at her, then focused on the road, his lips compressed into a thin line. When her laughter had bubbled down to tiny titters, he glared at her.

"Look, Adam, it's not that I'm not flattered. I am. But you don't have the full picture. It's not a matter of money or prestige."

"Oh, you mean because you're pregnant?"

He delivered the line with a tiny lift to the corner of his mouth. Like *I know something you don't know I know*.

"How did you... What makes you think..." she sputtered.

"You think I'm stupid? A guy shows up who obviously wants you all to himself, so much that he locks you in a vault with him, which I will address later—"

"Please don't."

"Fine. Anyway, a couple months later, you start taking time off for doctor's appointments, then he shows up with flowers and a proposal? Seriously? I mean, some relationships are quick, but that's a little too quick—especially for a playboy like him."

"Playboy?" Misty was too confused to laugh.

"Yeah. You know what they say about firefighters, don't you?"

She leaned away from him and studied his face. Smug. Arrogant. Whatever he had to say, it was going to be nasty. "You know what, Adam? I don't care what 'they' say. I know my boyfriend and his whole family. Every one of them is above reproach. And every one of them is a firefighter. Well, except his mom and one sister-in-law. But his father was a captain, his oldest brother is a captain, and the next one down is a lieutenant. The rest will get there soon enough. They make good salaries. They live in nice homes. They go on vacations. Yup, the whole nine yards. I resent whatever you're implying."

"Fine. Fine. It's your life," he muttered.

"Damn right it is." She was fuming. She had to shut up before she said anything about Adam's character. She was apt to take nasty to a whole new level.

Chapter 16

GABE HEARD THE SIRENS AND KNEW THE AMBULANCE WAS coming. He was in and out of consciousness. Parts of his body were numb, but his face and hands were so painful, he figured he must be passing out from the agony.

He came to for a short while as he was being loaded into the ambulance and then felt the jostling that meant they were getting his boots off. Then he heard a ripping sound followed by a stab—they were getting an IV into him. Was his femoral artery the only part of him untouched?

After that, he must have been out for quite a while.

He woke in the hospital. At least that's what he figured, because there were monitors beeping, but he couldn't see. He tried to move until a female voice said, "He's awake."

Whose voice is that?

"Gabe. You're in the ICU. You had an accident."

Gabe tried to talk, and his throat was extremely sore, but he managed to eke out, "I can't see."

"Your eyes are bandaged, honey."

Ah, his mother. A familiar voice was probably the most comforting thing he could hear at the moment.

"Mom?"

"Yes, honey?"

"Is Misty okay?"

"Yes, honey. Why wouldn't she be?"

"Someone said I was in an accident. Was she with me?"

"Oh, it wasn't a car accident, sweetheart. Do you remember a fire and getting hit with burning gasoline?"

"Sort of." Then after a short while, he said, "Yeah. Yeah, I remember now."

"Hang on. Your captain asked us to call him as soon as you were awake."

"Did they get the guy?"

"You can ask him. Your father is talking to him in the hall."

"Oh? When you said you had to call him, I thought he was back at the station."

"No. He's off duty. But he came in to see you, hoping you were awake. He'll have to put on a mask and sterile gown. It may take a minute."

"Are you wearing all that sterile stuff?"

"Yes, honey. Everyone who comes into your room has to. I'll be right back."

He heard her little feet scurry off. He was groggy. He felt like going back to sleep, so they must've put some sort of pain medication in him. Considering he wasn't feeling much of anything, that was a good bet.

"Gabe?" The captain woke him out of his drowsiness. "Hey, buddy. I'm glad you're still with us."

"How bad is it?" Gabe asked. "And did you get the guy?"

His captain cleared his throat. "We went after him and got a good look, but you were in trouble. We dropped the pursuit and came to your aid."

"Thanks. I think. Am I going to lose my eyesight?"

A female voice chimed in. "I'm your doctor, Mr.

Fierro. Dr. Ella Carpenter. I can tell you more when you're ready."

"I'm ready now."

"In front of your captain? And there are other people just outside the unit, all asking about your condition. So far, I've only spoken to your parents. Are you all right with my telling visitors the details?"

"How many people are here?"

"A lot!" the doctor said.

"Jayce, Noah, your father, and me," Gabriella said. "Sandra is here in the hospital but not just outside your door. Miguel is with her and asked us to call when you wake up."

"We can probably move you to a regular room soon, but the same protocol holds. Visitors have to wear sterile gowns and masks, and—"

"Gabe, it's me, Dante," his younger brother's voice called from a distance. "Sorry I'm late. I just had to get a nurse's phone number on the way."

Gabe chuckled. "Why am I not surprised?"

He heard a nurse chastising his younger brother and telling him to wait outside with the others.

"Where's Dad?"

"He's in the hall on his phone, talking to Ryan."

"Ryan? In Ireland? Am I dying?"

A couple of chuckles dissipated quickly. "No, darling. You're not dying." He felt his mother's amusement in her warm voice. Then her tone returned to serious. "You're severely burned. The doctor can tell you more."

"Dr. Carpenter? What's going on?"

"You have third-degree burns on your face, neck, and hands, basically everything that wasn't covered.

And second-degree burns managed to get through your clothing. About fifty percent of your body is involved in some way."

"Shit. I was barbecued." He pictured himself with a spit shoved up his ass, turning slowly, roasting over an open fire.

"I should let you know there's a bit of a disagreement as to your care," the doctor said.

Gabe imagined the family wanted to take him home. He knew what that meant. They probably wanted to finish the job and let him reincarnate. But without discussing that in front of a mere mortal being, he just had to play dumb. "What's the disagreement?"

The doctor sighed. "Well, I'd like you to stay in the hospital where we can keep you in a sterile environment, give you IV antibiotics to prevent infection, treat your pain with IV meds, do proper wound care, and get you ready for skin grafting. All of that may take several weeks."

"And we," Antonio's voice said authoritatively, "want to take you home, where we know how to deal with burns just as well as any medically trained stranger. Doctor, six of my seven firefighter sons are also trained EMTs. Plus, Gabe will be more comfortable in our home with people he knows."

"Am I going to be given a vote?" Gabe asked. "If so, I'd like to go home. No offense, Doctor."

"I'd have to advise against it. Strongly," his doctor stated. "Perhaps we can come to a compromise. If he stays just to get past the worst of it, and the family members who will be taking care of him get some instruction from the head nurse, I'd feel much better about his leaving."

Somebody was running down the hall. It sounded like high heels clicking. A moment later, that someone burst through some doors.

"Gabe! Gabe, are you all right?" It was Misty's voice.

"I'm okay, Misty."

He could almost feel shockwaves coming from her. She had stopped short. The gasp and the silence that followed spoke for her.

"Your brother may be upset with me though, Mist. We were supposed to meet for a beer. Can you tell him what happened for me?"

"Oh… Of course."

"I'm afraid you'll have to wait outside the door too," the doctor said.

After a few hesitant moments, she whispered, "Is he really okay?"

"He will be, honey," Gabriella said. "We want to take him home as soon as possible and care for him there. You can help if you want."

"Absolutely. I'll do whatever I can."

Gabe wondered what he looked like. The way people who weren't related to him reacted, it sounded like they thought he was a goner. And Misty, who was aware of the reincarnation possibility, probably didn't understand it well enough.

"I…I wish I could hold your hand," Misty said. "Apparently, I can't even stay in the room with you, but I'll be back as soon as I can."

Gabe wished she could hold his hand too. He didn't realize how much he wanted that until he was relieved to hear her voice. How much time had passed? Did she just come from work?

"How long have I been lying here?"

"You arrived in the ER in the early afternoon. It's about eight o'clock now," the doctor said. "Miss, you really need to leave the room until you're wearing a mask and sterile gown."

He wondered why it took Misty so long to get there. Maybe she went out to dinner with Julie or had errands or something. He was pretty sure she would have dropped whatever she was doing and come as soon as she was called. Maybe people were waiting until they had more information about his condition. Yeah, that was probably it.

Her heels clicked across the floor a few paces, then stopped.

"Gabe? Remember the question you asked me?"

"I do," he said, letting her know he understood that she was referring to his proposal.

"Well, my answer is *yes*."

A few hours later, Misty and Parker put on sterile gowns and masks to enter Gabe's room. She was nervous about her brother and her...her...fiancé. Using that word was still a little strange. Considering how they had left things, she didn't know what to expect.

"Are you sure he'll want to see you?" she asked.

"He said he would meet for a beer, right? Why wouldn't he?"

"Well, it's just that you tried to beat the shit out of him last time you saw him, and now he's helpless and lying in a hospital bed."

Gabe's voice called out, "I'm not that helpless. I may

be blind and wrapped up like a mummy, but I can still whoop your ass, Parker."

Parker laughed as he entered the room. "I guess you must be feeling better."

"It's the drugs," Misty mumbled.

"So, I hear you've decided to make my little sister an honest woman."

"That's the plan."

"Good. Otherwise, I'd have to tell you to get out of that bed, you lazy shit, and fight me."

"I thought we already did that," Gabe said. "And wasn't it because you *didn't* want me to marry her? I think you said I wasn't good enough for her."

"Yeah. I said I was sorry, right? If not, then I apologize. Seriously. I was just shocked, because, you know. She's my little sister."

"She ain't little anymore, bro."

Misty cleared her throat. "Hey. The sister is standing right here, guys."

"Misty," Gabe said. "I didn't know you were here. I didn't hear your high heels."

"Yeah, I'm wearing sneakers. It's my day off."

Parker carried a chair over. "Here, Misty. Sit down." As soon as Misty was comfortable, Parker continued. "I heard we almost lost you, Gabe. I would've felt terrible if that happened, especially after the way we left things."

"No. I'm way too tough to die. I'll just look like a piece of warmed-over meat when I get out of these bandages. Misty may not even want me anymore."

"Hey. Don't talk like that," Misty said.

"Yeah," Parker echoed. "One thing my sister is, is

loyal. She'll probably stick with you even when you're an ugly fuck."

"Thanks, dude."

"I'm just kidding. You know that. At first, I was pretty surprised about what happened—the pregnancy, I mean. More like shocked out of my boots. But I figure my little sister has to grow up at some point and marry somebody. I'm actually glad it's you. I don't have to get used to another brother."

"Yeah. There's that," Gabe said. "Remember how I said I was sorry I got her pregnant? Well, I'm not sorry. I'd probably never get married at all if this didn't happen. I'm kind of glad it did."

Parker was quiet for a little bit. Maybe he was trying to decide if that was an insult or not. But Misty knew it was just the truth.

Finally, Misty said, "I wish I could do this differently too, but I might not have any kids at all if this didn't happen before the MS diagnosis was made."

"Are you worried about taking care of a kid, Misty?" Gabe asked. "Because you don't have to. If we need to hire a nanny to help out, so be it."

"You can't afford that," Parker said.

"How would you know?" Gabe fired back.

"Well, can you? You might think it's none of my business, but if she needs help, I want her to get it. I can chip in."

"That won't be necessary."

After a poignant silence, she rose. "I need some air." She began walking out of the room, then remembered Gabe couldn't hear or see her leaving. "I'll be back in a few."

Her balance had been slightly better in recent days. She figured it must be due to the sneakers with better traction. She could probably get away with those at work, since most customers didn't see her feet, but she'd certainly miss her sexy shoes.

She took off her protective gown and mask and stuffed them in the trash next to the cart outside his room. Padding down the hall, as she passed the nurses' station, one of the nurses spoke up. "Hey. You're Gabe's friend, right?"

Misty looked at the pretty nurse and decided to define the relationship, quickly. "He's my fiancé."

"Congrats. I was just curious about something. There are more good-looking guys visiting him than I've seen in one place for a long time."

Misty giggled. "He has several brothers, but the one who is in there now is *my* brother."

"Oh," the nurse said. "I'm sorry. I didn't mean to—"

"No, please. Take him off my hands. Let me introduce him to you. He's been a pain in the ass for the last few days. You would do me a big favor by distracting him."

The nurse laughed. "Maybe I'll see him on his way out."

Misty waved and stepped onto the elevator. She still needed some time to think, so she pushed the button for the lower level where the cafeteria was.

She bought a cup of coffee and stared out the window. Thinking about her future brought up so many mixed emotions.

Parker was right. She would be proud to be Mrs. Gabriel Fierro, regardless of what he looked like when the bandages came off. But what if Gabe couldn't work as a firefighter again? That's all he'd ever wanted to do. She realized his parents would be more than happy to lend a hand, but Gabe would hate that. Would he be depressed? Would that carry over to their home life? What if he started drinking?

They'd have to figure something out.

As she was staring out the window, deep in thought, someone set a hand on her shoulder. She spun around and was shocked to see her boss, Adam. "What are you doing here?"

"I was wondering how you were. I heard some strange things were going on. And you haven't been yourself."

"You didn't answer my question. What are *you* doing here?"

He was silent for a moment, then he said, "Look, I could make up something, like that I was visiting a friend, but I saw you on your way into the hospital, so I followed you."

"Followed me? Is that the normal thing for a boss to do when his employees are a little upset?"

"You're not just an employee, Misty. You know that."

"And you're not just a boss. You're becoming a stalker."

"Don't say that!" he practically shouted.

Jesus. If her boss was actually stalking her, she had no idea what to do. Filing a sexual harassment suit might make things worse. Maybe she should just quit. *But the insurance…*

She had to get out of there. "I, um…I need to get back upstairs. I said I'd only be gone a minute."

She took off running, praying that her legs wouldn't betray her when she needed them.

※

Two weeks later, Antonio drove Gabe home from the hospital. "No one would blame you if you went to Brazil for plastic surgery, Son."

"I know, but that's just the excuse, right? I'll be home, growing up all over again, in phoenix form until I reach maturity." Now that the bandages that covered his eyes had been removed, he was able to catch his father's smirk.

"Of course. But you need at least seventy-five days for that. A few plastic surgeries and recovery time should work out to be at least that long. And because you got hurt on the job, long-term disability should kick in. You'll have plenty of time off. You can even get paternity leave when the time comes. Unless you need the money."

"I'm not worried about money. I'm more worried about Misty. How is she going to take having a bird as a husband? She's still living with you, right?"

"She'll be fine, Son. Gabriella has had some long talks with her, and Kristine came over the other day to tell her what to expect. As you know, she had to incinerate Jayce with her dragon fire. She said it was the hardest thing she ever had to do."

"Misty's not going to watch, is she?" he asked, horrified.

"No. I don't think that would serve any purpose. If she insists, well…one day, she'll go to work, and you'll be human in the morning. When she gets home, you'll be a phoenix."

"Whoa. I don't think that's a good idea. She'll be furious if she feels tricked or lied to. I know I would."

His father inhaled deeply. "I know. But she won't be

mad at you. You'll be a baby bird. She can get mad at me if she wants to."

"Damn. Why did this have to happen now? She'll be showing in a while, and everyone will think I've flown the coop."

"Pun intended?"

"Whatever."

Antonio found his deeded parking space on the street in front of their South End home and parallel parked expertly.

Gabe was thinking about cramming something large into a small spot, and his dirty mind immediately thought of Misty. He wished he could make love to her one more time before he turned into a phoenix, but with the risk of infection and much of his body still in pain, it wouldn't be possible.

It was time to get out of the car. He hated to be dependent on anyone, especially his parents at this age, but he needed a hand. His dad jogged around the car, opened the passenger-side door, helped Gabe swivel his body to face the sidewalk, and hefted him to his feet. He swallowed the pain that sudden movement caused.

He was only a few steps from the stoop, and the door opened wide. His mother stood there, grinning. "Welcome home, darling."

"Thanks, Mom."

Her smile faded as she watched him struggle up the steps. "Oh, honey. Are you in pain?"

"Only when I move," he said, deadpan.

"I filled your pain med prescription. You won't need all of it—especially after you…well, you know."

"Yup," he said. At last, he was inside and hobbling toward the couch.

"The doctor wanted to keep him a while longer," Antonio said. "Like we'd let that happen."

"Well, one thing's for sure. They won't be getting any more insurance money from me. I'm ready to get this show on the road. Where's Misty?"

"At work." Gabriella smiled. "There's one silver lining. We found out her MS improves a bit during pregnancy—as if Mother Nature knows the mother and baby need a little help during that time."

Suddenly, a whirlwind sprang up in the middle of the living room. When it disappeared, a woman in a white toga with long white hair stood in its place.

"Did I hear my name?"

Gabriella's jaw dropped. Gabe hadn't met the deity, but Antonio had told all of his sons about her and then swore them to secrecy. Apparently, they'd all kept their vow and hadn't even told their mother.

Antonio bowed slightly. "It's good to see you again, Gaia. May I introduce you to my wife, Gabriella, and my son Gabriel."

She smirked. "Ran out of names, did you? Or were you just not very creative?"

"He's named after my wife. We thought she deserved a namesake after birthing four boys."

"And yet you didn't stop there," the Goddess said.

Gabriella straightened her spine. "Now, wait a minute. I love all my sons and wouldn't give any of them back."

"Good. Because you're stuck with them." Gaia strolled around the living room with her hands clasped behind her back. "Nice place. How do you plan to set your son on fire without burning down your house and possibly all the adjacent buildings on the block? It's bad enough that my beautiful planet suffers from wildfires."

"Yes, Goddess," Antonio said. "We're firefighters, so we did come up with a safe plan. My son Jayce owns a fishing boat. We thought we'd use that to tow a rowboat and sail far enough out to sea that the fire wouldn't be spotted from the shore. Our daughter-in-law is a dragon and can quickly cremate him with a blast of her dragon fire. The phoenix on board will be able to fly to the other boat not far away."

Mother Nature folded her arms. "And what about the dragon on board?"

"She'll fly to the other boat too. As soon as Gabe has reincarnated, of course. She may have to guide him toward the boat and not toward shore. Then everyone will shift back, except Gabriel."

"Oh, right. And if you're spotted, by satellite or something, a five-foot-ten dragon won't stand out at all," she said sarcastically.

"We can alter that plan a bit, if Gabe comes right to us, and because she's fireproof, she can stay onboard until the boat is ready to sink. Then shift back and jump into the water, and our boat will be able to get close enough to fish her out and return to shore as humans—and one bird in a cage."

"A cage!" Gabe practically shouted.

"For your own protection, darling," Gabriella said. "Reincarnated phoenixes have an instinct to fly home. If you try to fly to the South End from so far away, you'll probably become exhausted and perish in the sea."

"Oh." He relaxed slightly. "Got it."

Mother Nature ceased her pacing and nodded. "It sounds possible. Just don't do it now."

"Why not now, Goddess?" Antonio asked.

"Mercury is retrograde. I know, I know... You probably think astrology is bullshit. Well, it's not. I created just about everything but didn't want perfection. What fun is that? So I tossed a little planetary trouble into the mix."

"Um, Gaia, pardon my ignorance, but what is Mercury retrograde?" Gabriella asked.

Gabe was happy to hear his mother using a more respectful tone. His father had said the Goddess was easily offended—and powerful.

"Retrograde is when the speed of Earth catches up and goes somewhat faster than that of another planet, making the other planet appear to be moving backward. In this case, Earth has caught up with Mercury and is moving faster, making Mercury appear to be moving backward."

"Oh, like when you're on a train, pulling out of the station, and the train beside you appears to be moving backward, even though the other train is just sitting there."

"Yes. That's what a retrograde planet is. A planet appearing to move backward. The sun and moon never go retrograde, by the way. Do you know how boring it is to watch the planets go 'round and 'round, 'round and 'round, 'round and 'round, endlessly?" The Goddess shrugged. "I thought it would be entertaining to watch an optical illusion once in a while. How did I know a retrograde planet would put mortals in such a tizzy? I used to get insanely bored until humans became so...so... imperfect. And during Mercury's retrograde phase, they become even more imperfect. Laughably so, depending upon how they handle it."

Antonio smiled. "I think I know what you're saying. As firefighters, my son and I have seen plenty of stupid things humans do."

She smiled slightly in return. "Okay, then. Let's remember that all kinds of communication gets screwed up during Mercury retrograde, and let's not make some idiotic mistake."

"Let's not? Like, 'let *us* not'? Are you going to help us, Goddess?" Antonio asked.

"Oh, hell no. I was just trying to be nice. I could rephrase that to 'let *you* not make any idiotic mistakes,' but I haven't heard that phrasing in decades."

"Understood," Antonio said. "When do you recommend is a good time to do this?"

Gaia tipped her face up and closed her eyes for a moment. "At least a week from now on a Wednesday."

Gabriella's expression clouded. "You mean to tell me my son has to suffer in unnecessary pain for another week?"

Mother Nature focused on Gabriella. "It's up to them. If they take their chances, their careful plan might fall apart. Your son might fly off before the others can catch him. Your dragon daughter-in-law might fall into the ocean and drown... You know. The usual screwups."

"It will give me a chance to spend some more time with Misty," Gabe offered. "I don't mind a little pain, especially if I can help prepare her for what's to come."

The Goddess walked over to him. He'd be nervous, except that she had a sincere-looking smile on her face.

"You know, young phoenix, you're a good man. I

don't say that to many mortals. But you seem to need to hear it." She patted him on the head and disappeared.

Gabriella let out a long breath in a whoosh. "Well, that was interesting."

Antonio lifted his index finger to his lips. "Sometimes she listens afterward," he whispered.

"I'm too busy to eavesdrop today." Mother Nature's voice reverberated from everywhere and nowhere. "Tell no one about my visit, and you won't be tobogganing down Mount Everest."

"My goodness." Gabriella found her way to the couch and sat down hard.

Chapter 17

HURRYING HOME FROM WORK AFTER HEARING HE WAS DIS-
charged, Misty couldn't wait to see her Gabe. Parker had
shipped out, so she was feeling adrift. She had visited
Gabe at the hospital every day, but now he was home.
At last.

She didn't mention what had happened with her boss
to either Gabe or Parker, because she didn't want to
upset them. Adam hadn't bothered her in the last two
weeks anyhow, so she was glad she'd said nothing. In
fact, he was ignoring her. Saying hello to all her coworkers but not even looking at her. He must have taken her
"stalker" comment to heart.

She burst through the door of the South End brownstone and raced through the empty living room. She
found Gabriella in the kitchen.

"Hi. Where is he?"

Gabriella chuckled. "Can't wait to see him?"

"No. I can't."

"He's in the rec room downstairs with his father."

As she threw open the door and began running down
the stairs, Gabriella called after her, "He's still in pain.
Don't jump on him!"

That's exactly what she wanted to do. Jump into his
arms and cover him with kisses. *No, that wouldn't be
good for his sterile environment either. Damn.*

He was struggling to his feet, but he looked like he

was smiling as soon as he saw her. Or was he wincing in pain? "Hi, future wife."

Thank goodness. He seemed to be okay. A lot of bandages still covered parts of his head and face as well as his hands. She stopped short and blew him a kiss. "Hi, future husband. I hope I can kiss you for real soon."

"That's my cue to leave," Antonio said.

They both chuckled as Gabe's father climbed the stairs.

"I'm glad you mentioned the whole kissing thing," Gabe said. "I want to be able to kiss you when we're pronounced husband and wife. We have a decision to make."

"Sure. What?"

"Have a seat." He dropped back down on the couch and extended his arm along the back. It looked like he was waiting for her to cuddle up next to him.

"Don't you need to be sterile? Shouldn't I not touch you?"

"Infection won't be a problem as soon as I'm reincarnated."

"When will that be?"

"That's what we need to discuss."

"Okay…" She sat on the couch, but not too close.

"Here are the choices. We can get married now, and then the timeline doesn't look like we *had to* get married—just that we had a preemie. And before you worry about my commitment, I'm just using the term *had to* because other people will. I do *want to* marry you, Misty."

"Promise?"

"I promise. There are other good reasons not to wait. We could get you on my insurance right away. You wouldn't have to work full-time unless you really want to. For me, there's less time worrying about things like infection, pain, and scarring. I'll have plenty of time to heal before the baby comes, if we get married before I… well, you know."

"Go up in flames?"

"Yeah." He smiled. "I guess you're getting used to the idea."

"It's weird, but I understand what has to happen and why. Okay. So what's the other choice?"

"We could wait seventy-five days or so, and you could plan exactly the kind of wedding you want. I know those things take time."

"I don't care about a big wedding. I also don't care what people think as far as the timeline is concerned. What do you want to do?"

"I'm all for doing this as soon as possible."

"Really?"

"Yeah. If you really don't care about planning a large wedding—"

She scooted closer to the spot next to him. "I really don't. All I care about is that the groom is willing and that the groom is you. I also like the idea of minimizing your pain."

"I'm glad we can finally talk about this. It was too risky at the hospital. They'd have transferred me to the psych ward if they overheard us."

She chuckled. "I know. Your parents were very helpful as far as telling me what to expect and answering all the questions I had. They were also extremely clear about my never allowing any conversations regarding paranormal life to be overheard."

"Good. The timing kind of sucks, I know, but I can't wait to marry you." He moved a little closer. "I want to make love on our wedding night. It may require some creative positions."

"I don't want to cause you any pain—especially the first evening we're married."

"If that's the case, it would mean putting off our wedding night for seventy-five days while I grow up in bird form all over again. It's only the second-degree burns that hurt. The third-degree burns involve nerves, and there's no feeling at all. Plus, I'll be wearing these compression bandages."

"I'll do whatever you need me to do."

"Good. I'm very glad to hear that. I want to make love to you, Misty. It's all I can think about. I love you, deeply. I want to show you how much." He leaned in and focused on her lips.

She tipped her face up, allowing him to take the lead. She had no idea how much pain a simple kiss might cause.

He puckered his lips carefully. The skin around them was already white and puckered from the burns. She imagined stretching it too far would cause even more pain. Yet he moved toward her and touched her lips with his. After a slight hesitation, he kissed her again, a little longer and harder. She wanted to cup the back of his head, but she didn't know if that would hurt him or not.

At last, he leaned back and sucked in a deep breath.

"Did that hurt?"

"Not enough to keep me from doing it again."

"Oh, Gabe. You don't need to do anything to make me happy. Just the fact that you're alive makes me happy."

He smiled. "Now that we've decided to do this quickly, there's one other thing I want to discuss."

"Anything. What is it?"

"I want you to consider quitting your job. I don't want to worry about you while I can't do anything to help you."

"But I need health insurance, just in case anything happens with the baby. I doubt I'll be added to yours immediately, especially if you're not working."

"You'll have mine as soon as we're legally married."

Misty thought that over. She imagined she'd be bored, but avoiding Adam or having to put up with his cold shoulder was becoming increasingly tedious. "Okay."

"Okay?" He sounded surprised. His eyebrows would have lifted if he'd had any.

"Yes. If it will give you peace of mind, I'll quit. I need to give two weeks' notice, though. I'd like to have a good reference from my first job in case I want to go back to work somewhere else sometime."

He seemed to be thinking it over. She wasn't at all sure he was going to agree to that. "I don't trust that slimy boss of yours. He'll probably try to talk you out of it."

"He can try, but he won't succeed, Gabe."

At last, he nodded. "Okay. A two-week notice isn't too much to ask. I respect your decision to do things right."

―――∿∿∿―――

Before the bank opened, Misty approached her boss in his office.

"Adam, can I talk to you?" It seemed odd to be asking him for a private audience instead of the other way around.

"At last," he muttered under his breath. Then with a cheery smile, he rose. "Of course. Come in."

The weather had been warming up, hinting that spring was finally coming. Misty had worn a light jacket with a deep pocket, and she had her letter of resignation in there. Pulling it out, she set it on his desk and took off her coat. She sat in the chair across from his desk and protectively folded her coat over her tiny baby. She wasn't even showing yet, but she couldn't help already responding to the maternal instinct.

Adam sat in his swivel chair across from her and pointed to the envelope. "What's this?"

"It's my two-week notice. I'll be leaving as of April fifteenth."

"*What?*"

His reaction startled her. "I—I'm resigning."

"Oh, no, you're not," he said through clenched teeth.

"Huh? You can't stop me. Plans change. People leave. It happens all the time."

He shot to his feet and began pacing. "Did your firefighter put you up to this? Because from what I understand, he's in no shape to support you anymore."

She leaned back and gaped at him. "What do you know about it?"

"I heard about a firefighter in a gas explosion. It was on the news. I—I recognized him."

"How the hell could you recognize him? He went straight to the operating room, then the ICU. He was so bandaged up after that, *I* didn't recognize him."

"They showed another picture. An old one."

She folded her arms. "I don't believe you."

"Fine. Don't. But don't throw your life away on a

disfigured firefighter who might not even be able to return to the job. They only get partial pensions if they quit before thirty-two years, you know."

"No, I didn't know that. Tell me how you knew."

He shrugged one shoulder. "I listen. Clients tell me all kinds of things when they need a loan."

"Well, don't worry about us. We'll be fine."

"I doubt it."

She shot to her feet. "What's that supposed to mean?"

"Nothing!" He backed away. "I've just seen this before. Love is blind. And apparently in your case, also deaf and dumb."

"That's it. I don't have to take your abuse."

He laughed. "Abuse? I'm just telling you the truth. Look, you're a beautiful girl. You deserve better." Under his breath, he mumbled, "And I saw you first."

Misty was becoming increasingly concerned. Suddenly, she didn't feel safe. She backed away toward the door, but before she grabbed the handle, he advanced on her and reached it first. She must have looked like a deer in headlights.

"Just think about what I've said. Okay?"

"Oh, you can count on it."

"Good." He opened the door for her.

She stumbled as she practically ran to the back room. *What should I do? Is he dangerous?* She wished she could talk to Gabe right now. He'd probably tell her to get out of there.

Her coworker Betsy followed her to the break room.

"Are you all right? You look like you've seen a ghost."

No, just a weasel who wishes my fiancé were a

ghost… "I'm okay, Betsy." Oh, hell. She had to talk to someone. "No. You know what? I'm not okay."

Betsy took her arm and led her over to the small table and chairs where they ate their lunches. "Tell me. I promise whatever it is, I can keep it to myself."

Misty let out a deep breath. Then she proceeded to spill her guts. She didn't tell her everything. Just the highlights. But that was enough.

Betsy's eyes rounded as she listened.

Finally, Adam burst in. "That's it. I heard what you said, and I won't have you spreading lies to my employees. Miss Carlisle, you're fired."

―――

Gabe heard the door slam upstairs. He needed to stand and walk around anyway. His body was stiff from sitting in the man cave.

Before he reached the basement stairs, Misty opened the door at the top. "Gabe? Are you down there?"

"Yes. Give me a minute. I'll be right up."

"No, I'll come to you." She jogged down the stairs and greeted him with a gentle peck on his lips.

"Was that you who slammed the door?"

Her cheeks turned pink. "I'm sorry. I was just so angry."

"About what?"

"I got fired."

"What? I thought you were giving your two-week notice."

"Yeah. I did that, but…well…things went south." She flopped onto the couch. "Sit down. I'll tell you all about it."

"I've been sitting all morning. I need to stand. Go ahead and tell me what happened."

Misty stood up and wrung her hands as she paced. She proceeded to tell Gabe about Adam's bizarre behavior. All the way from the car ride, which she still suspected was a ruse, to their argument that morning.

He was stunned. "Why didn't you tell me this was going on?"

"I didn't want you to worry. God, Gabe. You had enough on your plate. First, you learned you were going to be a father, something you never wanted—"

"I want it now," he reminded her.

"I know." She placed her hands on his chest. "That's such a relief and a joy…you can't imagine."

"I'm sorry I put you through that, before I realized our baby was a blessing in disguise."

"It's all in the past now."

"Yeah, but what's not in the past is your boss firing you. You did nothing to deserve it."

"I kind of did. I probably shouldn't have confided in a coworker."

"That chickenshit would have continued if he thought he could get away with it. By your telling a coworker, he knew he wasn't going to get away with it anymore."

"I should have just reported him for harassment."

"The asshole sounds totally unstable, and you were scared. I don't blame you for not knowing what to do. Shit. I wish I had been there."

"And done what? Beat him up? He was jealous of you. That might have made it worse. He'd have an excuse to put you behind bars."

He sighed. "I don't know. It sounds like you wouldn't

have been in danger if I were with you. He'd never have tried anything if I were healthy."

"Even healthy, you can't be with me every minute of every day."

Gabe realized soon he wouldn't be able to protect her at all. "It's probably a good thing he fired you. I'll feel a lot better in my alternate form, if I can actually see you. Meanwhile…" He pulled from his pocket the ring that he had been waiting to give her. "Maybe showing the world you're mine will help."

She stepped back and gasped as she eyed the beautiful diamond solitaire.

"I wish I'd been able to go shopping with you and let you pick it out instead of ordering it online, but I was unable to leave the house. If you don't like it—"

"No! I love it! It's perfect."

She grasped his shoulders. They weren't bandaged and didn't seem to be causing him any pain. Leaning in, she touched her lips to his.

"I think I've healed enough to give you a proper kiss," he said.

He slanted his lips and deepened the kiss. Their tongues were happily reunited as they swirled together. When after several moments they broke the kiss, he said, "I love you, Misty. More than I thought I could ever love anyone."

She looked down and smiled shyly. "Can you put it on my finger?"

"Oh." He hadn't realized he hadn't given the ring to her yet. "Yeah."

"Can you? I don't want you to hurt yourself."

"My hands are doing well. Actually, all of me is

doing pretty well." He slipped the ring on her finger. It fit perfectly. "It won't be long before we can make this official. We should probably discuss the kind of wedding you want."

"I haven't changed my mind. Nothing big. Just family."

"I thought you said nothing big," he teased.

"Ha. Your family *is* my family. I wouldn't want to leave any of them out. And if Parker can't be here in person, I'd like him to attend by Skype."

"I'd like that too. He should be my best man."

"Not one of your brothers?"

He laughed. "Too many choices. How would I pick between them?"

"I see what you mean."

"Jayce offered to take us out on his boat for the, um, other thing. Maybe we could find a nice beach nearby for the ceremony."

She beamed. "Get married on the beach? I love that idea. When?"

"We have to figure that out."

"Some of that depends on Parker."

"And it would need to be a day when all my brothers are off duty, so we'll have to coordinate their schedules. Thankfully, they're usually free at roughly the same times. Do you want Julie and your other girlfriends to come? We'll have to take their availability into consideration."

"Just Julie."

"Yeah, she'd probably appreciate it after we tore up her house."

Misty groaned.

What could have been extremely complicated logistics worked out fairly easily, to Misty's relief. They were able to reach Parker on Skype early in the morning while it was nighttime over in Afghanistan. He only had a couple more days at the base before his first mission. Then he'd be unreachable. Julie said she'd take the day off.

The Fierro boys were on the same shift all over the city, but they each double-checked their schedules and had the following two days off. It was a short window, but all they needed was fifteen minutes and a preacher.

Misty had gone shopping for a special dress and found something that fit perfectly, right off the rack. A simple white gown with the sweetheart neckline she loved, and silk, like gossamer, made up the décolletage and sleeves. It was exactly what she would have picked out had she oodles of time. She didn't even need to buy Gabe a ring, since he couldn't wear it when he shrank to the size of a bird and his fingers were talons.

Saturday, the whole family headed to the North Shore. Dante drove Misty and Julie in his Beemer so Gabe wouldn't see her in her dress beforehand. Antonio drove his wife and two youngest sons, Noah and Luca. Jayce and Kristine sailed there on his boat. Gabe met up with Miguel and Sandra, so the whole gang was able to arrive in three cars. A veritable feat.

Coming from Ireland, Ryan and Chloe said they'd meet Jayce and Kristine at the Cape Ann Marina where Jayce had his boat docked for the day. Then they'd "pop over" together. Gabe took his laptop so he could bring Parker in via Skype.

All the family members agreed to stay overnight in a nearby hotel, except Ryan and Chloe. Ryan was still supposed to be dead, and though people this far from Boston might not recognize him, there had been a very public funeral, and his picture was in all the papers and on the news. He couldn't tempt fate.

Gabe and Misty would have their wedding night and the following morning together. All the phoenixes and one dragon would tow a dinghy out to sea with Jayce's fishing boat.

Antonio wanted them to wait a week, but Parker's schedule required they move faster than that. No one knew how long his mission would last. Marines could be sent to some very dangerous places and be expected to stay for long periods.

Misty sat in the back of Dante's car, enjoying the banter between him and her maid of honor seated up front.

"So, those toy parties you do, Julie. How did you get into that?" he asked with a wide grin.

"Oh, you know. I just sort of fell into it."

"Ha! Do you ever do any product testing?"

"Oh boy," Misty interrupted. "You don't know who you're teasing, Dante. If you push her, even a little bit, she'll give you a demonstration."

Julie burst out laughing. "Hey, it sounds like a great idea to me." Her eyes sparkled with mischief as she glanced over at Gabe's handsome brother.

Dante's voice shot up. "Wow! I lucked out. So, what did you bring?"

"Now?" Julie groaned. "I don't have my goodies with me."

"Damn. Oh well. I might have driven us right off

the road. Can't get distracted, since I'm transporting the bride."

"Yeah, Gabe wouldn't like that," Julie said.

"Are you kidding? He'd kill me. So, without distracting me with demos, what kind of toys do you sell at these parties?"

"Oh, the usual. Vibrators, flavored lube, nipple clamps, blindfolds… You know, the kind of things that come in fifty shades."

Dante gulped. "That stuff is *usual* now? Boy, I must be dating the wrong girls. Maybe I should venture out to the suburbs more often."

Julie giggled. Actually giggled! Misty hadn't seen her friend act like a girly girl, ever! Was there a romance brewing before her eyes? Probably not. Dante was a notorious flirt.

At last, they arrived at gorgeous Crane Beach. They timed it so she'd be the last to arrive and they'd have Gabe facing out to sea until they told him to turn around for his first look. She was surprised to realize her nerves were tingling. *Is that the MS, or am I just nervous?* Since her mouth was dry and her pulse was racing, she decided it was a case of nerves.

Dante jumped out and opened the back door for her. She ducked so she wouldn't knock her short veil askew. The only real problem she'd had with her outfit was what to wear for shoes. A satin heel would be destroyed by the sand. So even though it was April and chilly despite the bright morning sun, she wore strappy gold sandals. If anyone gave her crap about wearing all white, she could point to her feet. Not that anyone would do that…except maybe her brother. No. Even as much as he enjoyed inappropriate teasing, he wouldn't do it on her wedding day.

Standing still for a moment to be sure her legs weren't going to give out on her, she took a deep breath of fresh ocean air. The see-through material covering her chest and arms kept the chill away surprisingly well. *So far, so good.*

Antonio met her at the wooden walkway that led from the parking lot to the beach. He smiled and crooked his arm. "Ready?"

"Yup." That was about all she could say around the lump in her throat. *I'm getting married. To Gabe!* Her childhood dream was coming true.

She didn't know how Gabe would feel about his own appearance. She hoped he wouldn't be self-conscious about the hair and eyebrows that hadn't grown back and the many scars he still bore. She didn't care what he looked like. Only that he was there—willingly.

Dante hurried down the walkway to join the rest of his family. Julie lined up in front of Misty and her soon-to-be father-in-law. She didn't realize how tightly she was clutching Antonio's arm until he laid his hand over hers and whispered, "Relax. You'll be fine."

She nodded dumbly. He escorted her to about six feet behind the groom. Gabe's bandages had been removed from his head and face. He was wearing a black tux and white gloves instead of compression bandages on his hands. Luca was off to one side, waiting with camera poised.

Antonio asked again, "Ready?"

She took a deep breath. "Yes."

He stepped back and said, "Gabe. You can turn around now."

When her groom took his first look at her in her wedding dress, his jaw dropped. She hoped it was because he liked what he saw and not that he realized what he was about to do. She'd have to wait and see if he took off in a panic.

Luca was taking pictures from different angles, and she hoped he got the huge smile that lit up Gabe's whole face. She couldn't believe how handsome he was despite the obvious remnants of his accident.

She was grinning too.

"You look gorgeous," he said.

"And you look positively dashing."

His gaze dropped to the sand, but he was still smiling.

She had been so focused on Gabe, she hadn't even noticed the stranger among all her future in-laws. He carried a folder and stepped out of the crowd.

"Shall we begin?" the officiant asked.

"Wait a minute. We need to loop in the best man," Gabe said.

"I've got him right here," Noah said, holding up the tablet.

There was her brother's smiling face. He was wearing his camo uniform.

"Sorry about my appearance. I forgot to pack my good suit," he joked.

"You look great," Gabe said. "I'm just glad you're here. Well, there, but here too."

Parker chuckled. "Come on, bro. Marry my sister already."

She couldn't have been more grateful for his change in attitude.

"Okay, okay. Reverend, we're ready," Gabe said.

"Dearly beloved…"

The preacher began with Genesis—and he could have been talking directly to Gabe. "Then the Lord God said, 'It is not good that the man should be alone; I will make him a helper fit for him.'"

Was she fit for him? She had plenty of faults and a degenerative disease, too. Could she really be all that he needed her to be? Misty couldn't concentrate on what the preacher was saying.

She refocused her attention when he was reading from Corinthians. At least, that's where she thought the part about "Love is patient and kind" came from. Had she been patient and kind? She hoped so. Had Gabe? Not always, but then the preacher got to the part about forgiveness. That sort of implied that people would mess up occasionally. *Okay, so neither of us are perfect.*

But they both nailed the next part the preacher read. "It does not rejoice at wrongdoing, but rejoices with the truth."

He had always been truthful with her. Even when he was in conflict, he was honest about it. Could she believe his declarations of love now? *Absolutely.* She relaxed enough to enjoy the rest of the sermon and say the appropriate words in the appropriate places.

"Do you, Misty Mary Carlisle, take Gabriel to be your wedded husband? Do you promise to love, comfort, honor, and keep him? For better or worse, for richer or poorer, in sickness and in health, and forsaking all others, be faithful only to him so long as you both shall live?"

"I do."

"And do you, Gabriel Peter Fierro, take Misty to be

your wedded wife? Do you promise to love, comfort, honor, and keep her? For better or worse, for richer or poorer, in sickness and in health, and forsaking all others, be faithful only to her so long as you both shall live?"

"I do."

Misty couldn't help breathing a sigh of relief. She didn't know what the future would bring, but at least they were in it together.

Chapter 18

After the ceremony, the family got together for a luncheon at a local restaurant. It resembled one of their Sunday dinners, with a lot of teasing banter but sincere congratulations, and then they went their separate ways. No first dances. No wedding cake. Just the way Gabe would have planned it if he'd had a choice.

"You know, Gabe," Misty said back in their hotel room, "you don't have to go through with this. Not on my account."

He was startled. "Go through with what? Our marriage? Do you regret it already?"

"No!" She stumbled on her way over to him, and he grabbed her, then guided her to the bed.

"Are you okay? Are your legs tingling or numb?"

"No. There was a bump in the rug."

He looked down at the old oriental carpet. Sure enough, it tented up in the very spot she'd tripped. He fixed it by pulling one corner.

"I meant you don't have to go through with the whole transformation thing," she continued. "I don't care if you have scars or even if your hair never grows back."

He laughed, partly with relief. Now that the wedding was over, he was happy they did it. Sitting beside her, he took her hand gently. "I love you, Misty. I know you just promised to take me in sickness and in health, but if I don't have to be scarred and in residual pain, why would I choose to be?"

She sighed. "I understand." After gazing into his eyes for a moment, she whispered, "I'm just going to miss you. That's all. Are you sure it takes two whole months?"

"At least. About one month as a bird equals ten years as a human. I should actually wait about ten weeks. If I come back earlier, I'll look even younger. Ryan got away with it, because he moved far away with Chloe. They look about the same age."

"How long did he wait?"

"Only a few days past two months. He looks twenty-five at the most, instead of thirty-three."

"But you're only twenty-six now."

"I'll be turning twenty-seven in May. May fifth."

"Oh! While you're in bird form? But how can we celebrate your birthday?"

He smirked. "Just give me some special bird food. Maybe some pumpkin seeds already hulled. It will be just like cake to me."

She rested her head on his shoulder. "I guess so."

"I'm sure you'll agree with the family's decision after I return. Instead of worrying about whether I'm fully healed and able to do the job, I'll be in top shape. All pain and scars gone."

She sat up straight again. "Whoa! Two things. First, won't that be suspicious? I hear it takes months and sometimes years to fully heal from third-degree burns. And second, do you have to be a firefighter? I know you said it was all you wanted, but—"

"But what? If you could dance again, wouldn't you?"

"Of course I would. There's no question about it. Okay. I get it. I think."

"Misty, there's nothing to think about. My mother has always been able to handle her husband and sons being firefighters because she knows if the worst happens, we'll reincarnate, lay low at home for a while, and come back healthy. It's only a couple of months. After that, we'll have a lifetime together."

She smiled and nodded. "I do love you, Gabe. I want you to be happy."

"And I will be. I'll watch our baby grow inside you, and I'll be back in human form long before the birth. Do you have any important appointments lined up that I'll miss?"

"Yeah. The ultrasound. Do you want to know the sex of the baby?"

A slow smile spread across his face. "The only sex I want right now has nothing to do with the baby." *Other than how it got here in the first place.*

"I guess our wedding night is starting early." She grinned.

"It will if you want it to."

"Yes. Gabe, I want you so much. You have no idea." She rose and turned her back to him. "Would you mind unzipping my dress?"

"Ha. Mind? Not even a little bit." He stood behind her and slowly lowered her zipper, taking the time to kiss a path down her spine.

She shivered.

"Are you cold, hon?"

"No." She turned enough so he could see her smile. "That was the first time you used an endearment for my name."

"Is it? Well, it won't be the last…although it might be the last for a while," he said sadly. *What a terrible boyfriend I was. I'm lucky she wants me at all.*

When he reached the bottom of her dress, he let it fall and pool around her feet. "Let me help you." He moved around to face her and held her hand as she stepped out of the silky fabric. She was wearing a white lace corset under it all. He swallowed hard. "You've really seemed to be a little steadier on your feet lately."

"I am. I was hoping MS was a misdiagnosis, but the doctor said it's more likely the pregnancy. MS improves temporarily during that time."

"Well, we'll have to keep you barefoot and pregnant," he said, hoping to lighten the mood.

She placed a hand on her luscious hip. "I don't think so. Maybe your mom could handle seven kids, but I don't even want to try."

He chuckled. "I don't blame you." He reached for her waist and drew her to him. Leaning down, he captured her lips and gave her a long, languorous kiss. The first in too long.

"Did that hurt?" she asked.

"Who cares?"

"I care."

"Well, don't worry. If something hurts, I'll stop. Trust me." He fiddled with the corset. "How do I get you out of this contraption?"

She laughed and said, "It laces up in back."

"Who got you into it?"

"Your mom."

It was a good thing she was living with his parents. *If Dante had laced her up…* He had to stop thinking that way. He knew he didn't have anything to worry about. Misty was his.

He loosened the laces. "Do I leave the laces in place like on sneakers? Or should I take them all the way out of the holes?"

She giggled. "You can just leave them loose. I'll wiggle out of it."

His mouth watered as he watched her shimmy out of the corset and whip off the final item...white lace panties.

When she was finally gloriously naked, he paused to appreciate the gift he had just unwrapped. "You're so beautiful," he said lamely. He wished he had a more poetic way with words.

"Thanks. I can help you out of your clothes too."

"Oh no. You'll take too long." He kicked off his shoes at the same time as he whipped his tie over his head. In about thirty seconds, he was undressed. His face, neck, and hands were where the worst of the scars were, and she had already seen them, so he wasn't as self-conscious as he thought he might be.

She touched the brand on his ribs. "What is this?"

He worried what she'd think of him if he told her the truth. He had heated up Buddy's dog tag and branded himself with it when he was fifteen. It was supposed to be a reminder to stay out of relationships.

"It was there before the fire."

"I know. I saw it the night we...well, the night of my birthday."

He glanced down. It had served its purpose, and he was ready to get rid of that too. "It was supposed to be a brand. Just something stupid I did as a teenager."

Her eyes rounded, and she touched it gently. "You did this to yourself? Didn't it hurt like the dickens?"

He smirked. "That's a cute way of saying it hurt like a mother... But yeah. It hurt a lot."

"It must have." She touched it again. "Will it go away too?"

"I'll be good as new. I think. I never asked my brothers if they had any scars before their reincarnations. You know what?" He walked her backward toward the bed.

She grinned. "What?"

"I think it's time to stop talking."

The backs of her legs hit the mattress, and she fell backward. While she giggled, he lay down beside her and stretched out. Tipping up her chin, he said, "I love you, honey. I may not be the most romantic guy, but don't ever doubt that I feel it."

"I won't," she whispered.

He bent to kiss her, and she responded instantly. He hoped he'd be able to give her a wonderful wedding night. Maybe not the all-night-long loving they gave each other on her birthday, but enough to hold her for a couple of months.

"I...uh...I brought something that will help me." He rose, and she sat up.

Rummaging in his small duffel bag, he removed a long white box. He handed it to her and said, "It's not a romantic wedding gift, but like I said, it's more to help me out here."

She took the box. There was a cellophane window displaying some kind of long-handled tube with a ball on the end. It was too big to be what she thought it was.

"I'm sorry if you already bought one of these from Julie at your toy party, but I've heard this is the best."

"Is this a *Bob*?"

"A what?"

"A battery-operated boyfriend."

He laughed. "No. It's more of a *Him*. A Hitachi intimate massager." He took it from her, unwrapped the cord, and plugged it in. "No need to worry about batteries dying. I even brought an extension cord if we need one." He pressed the button on the handle, and the thing whirred to life. Handing it back to her, he said, "Now I can go all night long."

"Is this whole thing supposed to fit in me?"

Gabe burst out laughing. When he was able to calm down to a chuckle, he said, "No. It just takes the place of my hands and mouth. It gives you the kind of pleasure you can't get with just my cock in you." He cracked up laughing again.

She giggled. "Oh. Then I can't wait to try it."

After a surprisingly fulfilling and romantic wedding night, the morning Gabe hadn't been looking forward to finally dawned. He and Misty dressed in jeans and sweaters and walked to the marina hand in hand. Most of his brothers and his father were already on Jayce's boat.

His mother and sister-in-law Kristine were chatting on the dock next to the dinghy. It was tied to the fishing boat with a thick towing line. They looked up when the couple approached. There were no cheery greetings. He was grateful for that, because his and Misty's moods were decidedly somber.

His mother strolled over to them. She stood on her toes, and Gabe leaned down enough to kiss her on the cheek and accept her warm hug. When he straightened his posture and watched Gabriella put her arm around his bride, he noticed tears in Misty's eyes.

"Hey, none of that now. I'm not dying. Well, not permanently."

Misty bit her lip and nodded. He could tell she was trying hard not to let the tears fall.

Gabriella rubbed her back and whispered comforting words.

Gabe imagined his mother was trying to bolster herself as well. He had to get going before he changed his mind.

"I take it I'm rowing?" he called up to Jayce.

His brother chuckled. "Nope. We'll tow you. Just sit back and relax. Take care of my precious cargo, though."

Gabe looked into the empty rowboat. "What cargo?"

Kristine raised her hand. "That would be me. You and I are in the disposable boat."

He smiled. Interesting way to put it. There had been times in his life when he felt, well, not disposable, but certainly replaceable. Being the middle of seven boisterous boys could result in feeling a little lost at times. Especially since he had always been the quiet one.

He was getting his time in the spotlight now, and he didn't really care for it.

He grasped Misty's arms and gave her a quick kiss on the lips. "Take care of yourself and our baby, hon. I love you."

"I will. I love you too."

After a nod to his mother, he sprinted to the dinghy, then hopped inside. He held out his hand to Kristine, helping her into the little rowboat.

When she was seated, he called up to Jayce, "Let's go, Captain."

Gabe watched the shore recede and then gradually disappear behind them. His mother and Misty stood together at the end of the dock the entire time.

It seemed like they'd been sailing for hours, but in order to put enough distance between the fishing boat and the shore so a fire wouldn't be spotted, they'd have to be well out to sea. At last, Jayce eased up on the throttle, and they slowed down.

"You know what's going to happen, right?" Kristine said.

"Yeah. You're going to go all dragon on my ass."

She giggled. "Pretty much. Listen, I did this for Jayce before I was really prepared for it. I just had to trust that what others were telling me to do was for his good. It was one of the hardest things I've ever done."

"You're not doubting it now, are you?"

"Oh, hell no. I have no problem frying your ass." She winked.

He laughed.

"No. I just wanted to know if you've ever witnessed it. Have you? A phoenix rising from its own ashes, I mean."

"No. When Ryan went through it, he was on the job in a high-rise fire. Jayce, well, from what I heard, he was locked in a cage?"

"That's right. He was already unconscious in a smoke-filled basement, so it wasn't like I had to look into his eyes or anything. This time, you're right here. To be honest, I'm a little nervous."

"Well, don't be. I'm ready and willing."

"I know. But just the same, I think it would be a little easier if you face away from everyone."

"Oh. You're thinking it might be hard on my brothers to watch me go from parboiled to crispy?"

One side of her mouth quirked up in a half smile. "Yeah. I imagine they'd rather not witness the gory details."

"Hmmm…I never thought of them having a problem with it."

She placed a hand over his. "I thought you might not. Gabe, you don't even realize what an integral part of this family you are."

He laughed. "You're right. I don't."

Her expression became serious. "Well, you are. Jayce tells me you're the one everyone turns to if they need a favor and would rather skip the exhaustive details. When you guys came to New York to help me, the rest wanted to know who I was, why I needed help, the whole nine yards. You just said, 'Where do I need to be and when?'"

Gabe smiled and nodded, remembering the time all his brothers banded together to help a stranger, despite their father's direct order to not get involved.

"Well, it's that kind of thing they all know about you. If they need to fly and know they'll have to duck in somewhere private to change, they just ask you to leave your window open. You do it and even put out some extra clothes. No questions asked."

He nodded. He hadn't even realized the boundless-ness of his own trust, but it sounded as if everyone else knew he'd be there for them. All they had to do was ask. "Okay, so for their sakes, I'll face away from Jayce's boat."

"And from me," Kristine added.

"Okay. When?"

"Now," she said.

The larger boat cut its engine, and the air suddenly seemed very still, as if something momentous was about to take place and even nature knew enough to be quiet.

He turned away and heard rustling behind him. Then Luca whined from the main boat, "C'mon, Jayce. I've never seen a real live dragon transform before."

"Yeah, and you won't if the only dragon you ever know is my wife. Now shut your damn eyes while she gets naked."

Gabe heard everyone chuckle. The bright noon sun didn't cast many shadows, but Gabe couldn't help catching the shadow of giant wings appearing on the water just in front of him.

Then searing heat hit him. It was different from the heat of the sun over their heads. The air around him didn't relieve the heat but fed it and added to it. He had promised himself not to cry out in pain. Oddly enough, he didn't think he could. A sort of paralysis overcame him.

Soon, he couldn't keep his eyes open, and he allowed himself to drift off into a deep sleep.

"What the hell?" Antonio Fierro yelled.

Gabe woke to gasps and shocked expressions. His little boat was on fire, and he figured he must be rising from the ashes. At least, he should have been. He turned to see Kristine through the smoke, still bathing him in fire despite the look of panic in her eyes.

He tried to rise, but something was definitely wrong. Extending his wings seemed much more difficult. They were heavy, and when he turned his head enough to look at what everyone else was gaping at, he realized his wings were huge—and webbed! Where were his feathers?

He couldn't simply sit there with the charred boat crumbling beneath them. He tried the giant wings and rose into the air. Kristine flew up next to him. He couldn't steer well. His tail wasn't doing its job. She pushed him with her nose toward the fishing boat, and his brothers scattered.

Then she hovered over him and clasped his shoulders in her talons, pushing him down onto the deck. He pulled in his wings, determined to land under his own power, but his tiny bird legs couldn't hold his weight, and he pitched onto his side.

Jayce and Antonio rushed over to him. The others just gave them room. Smoke was still rising off him, and the unmistakable smell of cinders filled the air. When Gabe tried to speak, he croaked.

Kristine transformed behind the cabin and reappeared wearing a black sweat suit. She rushed to his side.

"What happened?" Jayce asked.

"I have no idea," she said. "I'm—I'm stunned."

Antonio's expression looked like fear mixed with concern. "Son? Do you feel all right? Are you in pain?"

Again, he tried to speak and could only croak.

Kristine snapped her fingers. "I think I know who to ask. I'll be right back." She disappeared before everyone's eyes.

Jayce didn't seem concerned that his wife was there one moment and gone the next.

Dante blinked at the empty space. "Where's Kristine?"

"Probably speaking with her boss," Jayce answered.

"Ah." Antonio nodded.

"The chief?" Dante asked. "I don't understand."

A moment later, Kristine and a vaguely familiar female Gabe had met a few months earlier—the one they called Gaia or Mother Nature—peered over him. Her white hair was long and loose, and she was dressed in a white toga.

The woman jammed her hands on her hips. "Well, this is a fine mess."

Kristine wrung her hands. "Gaia, what's going on?"

"Didn't I tell you to wait *until after* Mercury went direct again? It hasn't finished its retrograde rotation. You humans really don't listen." She crossed her arms and tapped her foot.

"I apologize, Goddess," Antonio said. "I remember your saying that. I'm afraid we got sidetracked with wedding plans and scheduled events when everyone could attend…"

"What wedding?" she asked.

"Gabe's." Antonio pointed to his son, helplessly lying on his side. His big dragon wings were spread akimbo on the deck with his tiny bird legs and tail somewhere beneath him.

Thank heavens Misty isn't here to see this.

Mother Nature sighed. "One of you dragon-phoenix couples asked me if I could give you children. At the time, I said, 'Absolutely not.' I didn't want to create a new mutation called a dragnix—or phoegon. Well, a few moments ago, I was remembering that conversation, and *blam*. It looks like I made one accidentally." She covered her eyes and shook her head. "Damn. When will I learn to ignore what you humans say you want?"

His brothers crept closer and took curious peeks at him. They also took a closer look at Mother Nature— and backed off pretty quickly when she gave them the hairy eyeball.

Luca pointed to Gabe's bottom half. "Yeah. I see his red and yellow phoenix tail feathers and his bird legs, but the upper half of him is all dragon."

Hearing that, Gabe began to panic. He'd go back to his human form if he could. He'd gladly live with scars and discolored skin, instead of this...this...abomination he had become. But he was afraid to shift, since he didn't know what would happen with his top half. Would the bottom half of him be a human baby? Wouldn't that be a hell of a thing to diaper?

He waited, hoping one or the other form would take over. One of them had to be dominant. Right? Gaia just strolled around him on the deck, as if studying her new creation. He didn't fully become one paranormal being or the other. He flopped on the deck, trying to right himself.

Antonio pleaded with Mother Nature. "There has to be something we can do. What if we were to set him on fire again?"

"Nothing would happen, I'm afraid. Dragons are fireproof, and the phoenix half would just return from the ashes as the bottom half of a bird, like you see him now."

Antonio dropped to his knees on the deck and patted

Gabe's big dragon head. "My poor son. I'm so sorry. I wish there was something we could do."

"Well, for starters," Mother Nature snapped, "you can stop asking me for the impossible. If dragons and phoenixes were supposed to procreate, they would be doing so."

"But phoenixes and humans can," Noah pointed out quietly.

"And dragons and humans can't," she replied harshly. "Can you imagine all the immature dragons walking the earth, setting my beautiful planet on fire every time they got frustrated or angry?"

She tossed her hands in the air. "I've had it with you stupid humans, just destroying things every time something doesn't go your way. Did you know humans are the only animals who destroy their homes? And only those dragons with a responsible dragon parent, who can teach them to control themselves, get to procreate. I knew what I was doing all those millennia ago."

"I'm sure you did, ma'am, but—"

Mother Nature rose a few feet off the deck and glared at him. "Do not call me ma'am! This is why I don't reveal myself to modern humans. I'm *Goddess* to you, son number…number…" She dropped her hands to her sides as she landed on the deck again. "Oh, hell. I can't keep you all straight."

Antonio chuckled. "Neither can I."

"That probably didn't help with the mix-up," she grumbled. "Look, I'll straighten it out. Give me a minute to think."

The mysterious goddess disappeared. A rumble of thunder was heard overhead, and a bolt of lightning hit the water.

"Oh boy," Kristine muttered. "She's pissed."

A moment later, it began to rain. Gabe felt himself shrinking. The long, webbed wings gave way to shorter, feathered ones. His peripheral vision changed. He could see from his eyes on either side of his head, not from one direction facing forward.

"Oh, thank the Goddess!" Kristine cried.

Gabe was able to right himself onto his birdlike feet and happily hopped around the wet deck. He spread his phoenix wings and turned enough to admire his colorful tail. *I'll never complain about the color of our feathers again.*

Everyone let out sighs of relief. Jayce retrieved the cage and opened the wire door. Gabe hopped right in. He was never so happy to fit into a bird cage in his life.

Antonio faced skyward. "Thank you, Gaia!" he called out.

"Yeah, yeah." A female voice reverberated from everywhere and nowhere. "Now don't bother me for at least a century. Okay?"

"Yes, Goddess," Antonio said like a man who had learned the words "yes, dear" were sometimes the only acceptable answer.

Chapter 19

MISTY WATCHED FROM THE SHORE UNTIL THE BOATS BLENDED into the horizon. At last, Gabriella put an arm around her shoulder and said, "He's gone."

Her eyes must have looked like saucers, because Gabriella backed up quickly and took her hands. "No, no. I don't mean it like that. He's not dead. He'll be back...in a few weeks. I promise."

Misty nodded. "I know. I'm just going to miss him so badly."

Gabriella tugged her in the direction of the family car. "I know, honey. I know. I've been through this with Ryan and Jayce. One of the hardest things is to watch their loved ones suffer as if they're never going to see them again. But you know you will! Kristine didn't know what was happening, and poor Chloe! Well, I hate what that girl went through, thinking Ryan had died in her arms." She shook her head sadly. "Now let's go out to lunch or something."

"I can't eat right now." Misty was tempted to stay right where she was and wait for the boat to return. She had to see for herself that Gabe was alive. It seemed impossible that they'd incinerate him to ash and he'd somehow survive.

"Okay. I guess you've lost your appetite. Then let's go shopping. You still need clothes, and it would be nice for me to try things on without Antonio hemming and hawing and wishing he could be anywhere else."

Misty smiled weakly. "I guess that's what they mean when they say, 'When the going gets tough, the tough go shopping.'"

Gabriella grinned. "That's my girl." As their feet crunched on the sand, she continued chatting, probably trying to distract her new daughter-in-law. "Now I could use a couple of pairs of pants, and you know what I think you can use?"

"What?"

"Maternity clothes!"

"Oh! Yeah. I haven't bought any yet."

"Well, let's not wait until your pants don't fit." Gabriella chuckled and opened the old Buick's car door for her. Then she flipped the lock on the driver's side and climbed in. "Do you know if there is a mall around here?"

"I know where there's one in Saugus near my grand-parents'—I mean, my uncle's house. It's right on Route 1. Probably half an hour from here."

"Okay, get me to Route 1," Gabriella said in a chipper voice.

Misty appreciated what her brand-new mother-in-law was trying to do. Hopefully, she was right, and some retail therapy would be just what she needed. She guided Gabriella to the mall with no trouble, except the usual maddening Route 1 traffic.

When they arrived, Gabriella went straight to the information desk and asked, "Is there a maternity store in the mall? I'm sure there are maternity sections in some of the larger stores, but I think it would be fun to go to a boutique that specializes in all things maternity."

The young blonde behind the counter smiled and said,

"Yes, there is a Destination Motherhood store. It's on the second floor on the left as you get off the escalator."

Suddenly, this pregnancy took on a whole new meaning. *Motherhood*, Misty thought. She hadn't quite pictured herself holding a child's hand and being called Mommy. It felt strange but good. She just wished she could go through this "expectant" stage with Gabe.

"I'm sure I'll have plenty of advice, since I've been through it so many times," Gabriella said as they rode the escalator. "But I'll try to contain myself. Feel free to tell me to butt out if I'm overwhelming you. I know it can get confusing when there's too much input. Your doctor will probably be the one you listen to, and I understand that, so don't worry about hurting my feelings. Plus, everyone has their own parenting style."

Misty was nowhere near needing parenting advice. "All that can wait. The only style I'm interested in right now is clothing." They entered the store, and she was immediately struck by how few choices there seemed to be for the moms and how many there were for the little mini-mes. The saleswoman came over and asked if she could help her find her size.

Misty told her she was a six, and the saleswoman brought her over to a rack with only four sizes. Extra small, small, medium, and large. They seemed to have the psychology of the pregnant woman down pat. "Now, you look more like a four to me, but we'll try the small first. What would you say your style is?" she asked.

"Trying to look like I haven't given up."

Gabriella laughed. "You always look wonderfully well put-together. I'd say your style is classic with a pop of bright color."

Misty realized she was right. "I never really thought of my style as having a name. I just know what I like and don't like. I like things that don't go out of style. Nothing too fussy like lace or ruffles. No crazy prints, but I like to look feminine, and I hate material that doesn't breathe."

"Yup, that's classic. Do you mind ironing?" the saleswoman asked.

"Not if I really love the garment. Then it's worth it."

Gabriella sighed. "I used to dress nicely, but then I had seven kids!" She laughed. "My clothes had to be practical. Thank God for spandex."

Misty had to choke back the urge to cry out, *Deliver me from spandex!*

Thankfully, the saleswoman wasn't listening or ignored Gabriella. She pulled a pair of beige linen pants from the small rack and handed them to Misty. They had that elastic panel over the tummy, and everything became real again. Then the saleswoman brought over two blouses, one a bright red, and the other a sapphire blue. After a second look, she realized they were a little boxier and longer than regular blouses, more like tunics.

Misty took the blue one and said, "I like this."

The woman smiled. "You have good taste. That's a silk-cotton blend. Very classic, it breathes, and it's easy care. You can hand-wash it."

Gabriella raised her eyebrows but said nothing. *Good*, Misty thought. I guess she really can keep her opinions to herself.

"I'd like to try these on."

The saleswoman seemed a little too delighted. Misty realized she hadn't checked the price. She glanced at the tag and almost swallowed her tongue. "Oh. I didn't realize these were so expensive. I'm afraid I can't afford such good taste."

"Please don't worry about it," Gabriella said. "It's my treat. We needed to get you a wedding gift, anyway. Call it your trousseau."

"I can't let you do that."

"Don't you know shopping is more fun if someone else is paying for it?"

Misty smiled at that. "I'll have to win a shopping spree. I'm used to going to department stores that cater to young women my age. They know we don't spend a lot, but we like to look as if we did." The blouse fabric felt silky smooth as it slipped between her fingers, but was it worth almost two hundred dollars?

"That's what I usually do too, but this is special. This is your first maternity outfit. And since you're my first daughter-in-law to need one, I'd be thrilled to buy it for you."

Misty doubted she'd be thrilled when she saw the price, but she couldn't argue with her in front of the saleswoman. "Okay, if you'll just show me to the fitting room."

All three of them traipsed into the back. The saleswoman stood next to Gabriella, and it looked as if she wasn't going to leave. Misty stepped inside the changing room and put on the outfit.

She hated it. It fit her shoulders perfectly, but she wasn't used to seeing herself in anything that didn't hug her body. She realized she had to buy looser-fitting items, but she didn't want to look dowdy.

Turning and looking in the mirror again definitely didn't help. *Ugh. I look awful. I'll probably be wearing muumuus soon*. She felt tears brimming in her eyes. By the time Gabe turned back, she'd be wearing clothing like this all the time. How would he look at her then? Would she see the same hunger in his eyes?

"How does it fit?" the saleslady asked brightly.

Misty barely got the word "Fine" past her lips without choking on it.

"Is everything all right? Do you need any help?" the saleswoman asked.

"No," Misty said, a little too quickly. "I'm...fine."

She heard Gabriella asking the saleswoman to give them a minute.

She didn't know whether to be grateful or worried. She just wanted to get out of there. This wasn't where she belonged. She was only twenty-three. She wasn't ready to be a mommy. She wasn't even ready to give up the idea of owning a stellar wardrobe. *Spandex, here I come*.

Gabriella knocked. "Can I come in?"

Misty unlocked the door.

Gabriella stood back and took her in. "The clothes look beautiful on you, so that can't be causing the tears in your eyes."

Misty's posture deflated. She swallowed hard. "I...I don't think I can put into words what I'm feeling. I just don't want to be here right now. I'm sorry."

"Oh, honey. Don't be sorry. You've had an awful lot to deal with lately. I kind of wondered when it was going to lead to some waterworks. I'm surprised you've held up so well until now."

"Can we go to a fabric store?" Misty asked.

Gabriella looked surprised. "You like to sew?"

"Um, I wouldn't say I like it, but sometimes it's necessary. Like when I want something special and can't find it at a store. Special dance costumes, mostly. Not that I'll be sewing sequins all over my maternity wear."

Gabriella gave her a weak smile. "Let's get out of here. I have the feeling that what you want and need isn't in any store."

When Gabe arrived home in his bird cage, Misty rushed over to him. He hopped toward her and chirped. To his surprise, she threw her arms around the cage and hugged it.

With his paranormal hearing, he overheard his father whisper to his mother, "And you worried about that boy finding true love… I think you can put your fears to rest."

Out of his right eye, he saw his mother's soft smile as she rested her head on his father's chest, and he finally understood why she wanted to see all of her sons happily married. That soft expression on her face warmed his heart. She really did love his father dearly and only wanted the same for her sons.

"Can we let him out of the cage?" Misty asked.

"Not just yet," Antonio cautioned. "If we go downstairs to the rec room and close the door behind us, we could let him out to stretch his wings."

"Let's do that." Misty smiled and lifted the cage carefully. "Does he understand me?"

Gabe chirped again. He wished he were a songbird and could make a pretty set of sounds instead of the loud squawk of his species. At least as a little bird, his sound was less harsh.

"I think he just answered you," Gabriella said. "Why

don't you all go downstairs, and I'll prepare a snack to bring down in a few minutes."

"That sounds good," Antonio said.

Gabe hoped his mother wouldn't forget to give him some food too. He'd had a very stressful day already. Getting out of the cage for a while would be welcome, and he was grateful Misty had suggested it. He was surprised at how much of his former life he remembered. He'd thought maybe the amnesia of human infancy would be part of starting over.

As soon as they'd reached the basement level of the home and Misty had set his cage on the coffee table, she opened the cage door, and he hopped out happily. If he flew up onto her shoulder, he didn't think he'd scare her... *Only one way to find out.*

He flapped his little wings and flitted up to her face. She didn't shrink from him or turn away. Landing on her shoulder, she remained still. At last, she let out a deep breath, and he realized she'd been holding it.

"Kristine said she and Jayce had come up with a couple of ways to communicate. Do you still have the Ouija board?" Misty asked.

"Oh boy. We did until Luca saw it. He had a fit, saying something about demons using it to control kids. Sounded like a bunch of urban myth nonsense to me, but we let him throw it out anyway."

"It's not nonsense," Luca said as he came out of the adjacent bedroom. "Some of my friends at Northeastern had an incident in their dorm—"

The Fierro elder held up his hand. "Don't repeat that story, Luca. Misty just wants to talk to Gabe. Not a bunch of poltergeists that may or may not exist."

"Fine." Luca stood with his feet apart and folded his arms.

It was the first time Gabe had seen his youngest brother resemble a man instead of the little kid he'd always been. He probably hadn't noticed Luca growing up with all the other drama in his own life.

"So, how else did Kristine recommend communicating?" Antonio asked.

"She said they came up with a code. If Jayce turned his head to the right and looked at her with his left eye, it meant no. But if he turned it the other way and looked at her with his right eye, it meant yes." Misty was gently patting Gabe's feathers with her finger, and he didn't want to move. The love she communicated came through with every stroke.

"Okay. Let's try that," Luca said. "Hey, Gabe. Are the Red Sox going to win this year?"

Antonio laughed. "I think that qualifies as an unfair question."

Luca shrugged. "Fine. You try."

Antonio looked at Gabe head-on. "Are you happy to be home?"

"Ha. Another trick question," Luca said. "He'd probably rather be at his own apartment in bed with his bride."

Misty's face heated. Gabe was so close, he could feel it. Maybe she could ask a fair question if he gave her the space to make eye contact. So he left her shoulder and flitted down onto the coffee table.

She sat down and faced him head-on. "Do you want to use that system to talk, Gabe?"

He turned his head left, so he could look at her with his right eye.

"That means yes. Correct?"

He faced her square on and then turned in the same direction to confirm his answer.

She grinned. "I think that will work. We just need to ask yes or no questions that he can answer without a bunch of explanations."

Antonio laughed. "That's Gabe's preferred way of communicating anyway."

The door upstairs opened, and his mother called out, "Stay downstairs, Gabe. Antonio, can you give me a hand, please?"

"Luca, can you give your mother a hand please?"

Luca rolled his eyes but walked up the stairs to take a tray from Gabriella. When he returned, Gabe was delighted to see a whole pile of shredded meat in one corner. As soon as Luca set it down, he perched on the raised edge of the tray and pecked at his treat.

"He must be starving," Misty said.

Antonio laughed. "Gabe is always starving. Didn't you notice his hollow leg?"

Misty's gaze dropped to her lap. He imagined she was remembering the times he couldn't eat at all, because of their tumultuous relationship. Damn. He had put her through an emotional roller coaster. If only he could communicate how much he loved her now.

Wait. He could. He picked up a strip of beef in his beak and flew to her leg. Then he placed the food in her lap.

"Awww," she said.

Antonio smiled. "There's no mistaking that meaning."

"Give me a break," Luca muttered as he returned to his bedroom. "I have to memorize the ten codes."

Misty gazed after him for a few seconds. "Is he still studying to be a cop?"

Antonio snorted. "Unfortunately. I can't imagine how I raised a cop after six firefighters. Oh well. There's a black sheep in every family."

Gabriella was on her way down the stairs and had apparently overheard his comment. "Antonio Fierro. Don't you dare call any of our sons a black sheep."

"Okay. If he's going to be a cop, I'll call him the blue sheep. Is that better?"

Gabriella let out a deep breath of resignation.

Gabe faced his father and turned his right eye toward him.

Antonio laughed. "See? Gabe agrees with me."

------—~~~———

Over the next few weeks, Misty and Gabe perfected their communication to the point where it was almost not awkward at all. *Almost*. When he disagreed with something she said or wanted to do, he'd flap his wings and squawk. Repeatedly, if he really felt strongly about it.

One day, the doorbell rang, and Misty was home alone with Gabe. When no one else was around, they shut him in his cage with the explanation that only another phoenix could go after him, if he "escaped." Misty thought it was ridiculous but went along with it.

She finally realized the wisdom of that policy when she opened the door and Adam was on the other side.

"Adam! What are you doing here?"

"Uh, are you able to talk? Outside?"

Gabe squawked his head off and was beating the

cage with his feathers so hard, she was afraid he'd hurt himself.

"Uh, no. You can say whatever you have to say right here."

He peered around her at the bird in the large cage. It was situated between the living room and dining room so Gabe could see and participate—sort of—in most family discussions.

"I wanted to apologize for firing you. I realize I may have overreacted…and…and I want you back."

Gabe was making so much noise, she wasn't sure she heard Adam right. "Huh?"

"You know. Back at work. At the bank. I miss your… people skills."

Well, that part could be true. The guy has no people skills at all. "You have plenty of tellers who are friendly and nice to the customers. You don't need me."

Gabe was starting to calm down. Until Adam reached for her hand, and then he went nuts, squawking and flying around as much as the cage allowed.

"I'm sorry, Adam. I'm not coming back to work. I don't know if you noticed, but I'm almost five months pregnant." She smoothed the sundress over her belly, revealing the infant growing there.

"Oh. Well, you can have maternity leave, you know. Then you'll be able to keep your insurance benefits and—"

Before Gabe reacted to that, she held up one hand. "Stop, Adam. Just stop. I'm not coming back." She flipped her hand over so he could see her rings. "I'm married now, and I have insurance through the fire department."

"But—"

"No. Your apology is accepted, but our business is concluded." She shut the door and locked it. Spinning toward Gabe's cage, she said, "You didn't have to make such a ruckus. I won't be going back to work for him now or in the future."

Gabe quieted but still seemed tense. She approached the cage slowly.

"I love you, you know. I wouldn't do anything to hurt you. Not now or ever." He seemed to relax and smooth his ruffled feathers. "That doesn't mean you can tell me what to do. It just means I'll do my best to communicate with you about all major decisions before making any. That's what any married couple should do."

He bobbed his head in agreement. Then he tipped his head, meaning he had a question.

Oh, goody. We get to play twenty questions or however many I have to ask before I hit on the right one. What could he want to know?

"Are you wondering how he found me here?"

He bobbed his head.

Oh, good. Got it in one. "I had to give him a forwarding address so he'd know where to send my last check."

He righted his head in the neutral position, neither looking right nor left. She interpreted that as his being satisfied with her answer.

"Do you want me to read to you for a while?"

He looked at her with his left eye.

"So, that's a no. Okay. Do you mind if I read to myself?"

He also gave her a no. So she picked up the novel she doubted he'd be interested in and put her feet up. She was just getting into it when Antonio and Gabriella returned home.

"Who was that at the door a few minutes ago?" Antonio asked. "We were still parking the car when he left."

"Just my old boss. He wanted me to come back to work."

"After firing you?" Gabriella asked.

"Yeah. He apologized, saying he'd overreacted."

"So, are you going back to work?" Antonio glanced over toward Gabe—probably asking more for his benefit than hers. He didn't know they'd already "discussed" the matter.

"I'm not." She almost felt the need to defend her refusal since just sitting around on their couch and reading made her feel like a lazy, good-for-nothing squatter anyway.

He simply nodded. Gabriella let out a deep breath as if she'd been holding it.

"Are you interested in taking a walk? It's a beautiful day out there."

"Sure." Misty needed some air to clear her head and was grateful for the opportunity to talk with Gabriella alone. Her new mother-in-law had become a good friend. She was always sunny and positive but would listen whenever Misty was down in the dumps.

She found that taking walks around the neighborhood was helpful too. Getting some sunshine and letting the warmth sink into her skin helped Misty's hormonal moods immensely. "I'll just visit the little girls' room and be right with you."

As soon as they were both ready, they set off.

"So, how did you feel about your old boss's visit?" Gabriella didn't waste any time, and Misty was fine with that. She wanted to talk but wouldn't really know how to bring it up.

"I was okay, but Gabe… He went nuts! He acted like he was trying to beat his way out of the cage."

"Oh, well, he's a bird of prey. He must have felt a threat was near."

"*A bird of prey*," she said, shocked.

"If you were thinking he'd eat birdseed and tweet happily from a tree branch, well, you must have been thinking of a chickadee. He's no chickadee, dearest.

"But one thing is good," Gabriella continued. "He's happy to be with you and delighted to see the baby growing. When he was a smaller bird, any time you were taking a nap, he hopped onto your thigh and laid his head on your baby bump. He may have been listening to the heartbeat…or just expressing his love."

Misty smiled, knowing her baby's father would protect them both. As a bird or a man.

"Are you going to find out the sex of the baby soon?"

"We agreed to keep the baby's sex a surprise. He'll be back long before the birth. If we change our minds, we'll do it together." Meanwhile, Misty periodically wondered if she was carrying a little Gabe or a little Misty. They hadn't discussed names yet, but that's how she thought of their child in the meantime.

They were passing by the fire station where Gabe had worked. Of course, no one at the fire station knew Gabe was at home, least of all in bird form. They thought he had gone to Brazil to a plastic surgeon who specialized in skin transplants and some cutting-edge methods to restore the healing and self-image of severe burn victims in record time.

The captain recognized Gabriella and waved as he walked toward them. A moment later, his eyes lit up as he recognized Misty. "You're Gabe's wife, aren't you?"

"Yes. Misty Fierro," she said and extended her hand when he extended his. They shook hands, and he grinned.

"I was there when he proposed to you. He must have said the right words, because here you are, out walking with your mother-in-law."

"And I'm going to be a grandma," Gabriella said.

"I'm sure you're happy about that."

"Beyond thrilled," she said.

"Is Gabe home yet?"

"Not yet." Gabriella explained that because of Misty's pregnancy, she'd decided to stay in Boston. If anything came up, Gabe wouldn't be in any shape to help her, and Misty spoke neither Portuguese nor Spanish. So Gabriella and Antonio were looking after her.

"Double congratulations, then. Boy, when that man decides to do something, he does it up right. Tell him we miss him. He's one of my best firefighters. Well, don't tell him that. We don't want him to get a swelled head." The captain laughed.

Misty thought about making some kind of joke about the surgery and how his head might be swollen from that but decided against it. Sure, it would be going along with the fiction, but it wouldn't sound very respectful. She'd leave the joking to Antonio.

"I hope you found someone to cover his shifts," she finally said.

"Oh, sure. We took on a probie. He's a little wild behind the wheel, but he just needs practice. Believe me, he's getting plenty."

"Oh? Has it been busier than normal?" Gabriella asked.

"Yeah. It usually slows down when the students leave for the summer. Not this year. We're as busy as ever."

"Really? With fires?" Misty asked.

"Drug overdoses mostly," the captain said.

"I'm sorry to hear that," Gabriella said. "Is the problem getting worse?"

"It seems so. Hopefully, the state will put a little more funding into rehab and prevention. When we get the call, we do what we can to save the person's life, but most of the time, as soon as they're able, they go looking for their next fix."

Misty was truly struck by this. "I wish there was something more that could be done."

The captain set a fatherly hand on her shoulder. "Just raise your children right. A lot of addicts never had a chance. It doesn't matter if they're from affluent homes or the slums. If they're neglected and allowed to run wild, they're going to get into trouble. You can impress on them the dangers of drugs at an early age."

Gabriella looked like she wanted to say something, but she stayed quiet until they'd said their goodbyes.

Continuing their walk, Misty said, "What is it? You looked uncomfortable back there."

"Not at all, but he brought up something I've been meaning to talk with you about. I know it's none of my business, but I hope you'll consider being a stay-at-home mom. At least until the child goes to school."

Misty opened her mouth to respond, but something caught her attention. A man in a hoodie, who didn't look right wearing one. *Is that Adam?* The figure faded back into an alley, and by the time they pulled up even with it, he was gone.

When she was able to focus on what Gabriella had said, she mumbled, "I'll need to talk to Gabe about it."

Her mother-in-law nodded and seemed satisfied with her answer. Misty wondered if she should mention the guy she'd seen. Finally, she decided not to. She was probably being paranoid.

Chapter 20

A COUPLE OF WEEKS LATER, GABRIELLA HAD CAUGHT A RARE summer cold, and Misty had to avoid her. She missed walking with her and having someone to comment to when she saw a beautiful rosebush exploding into bloom or recognized one of the firefighters on Engine 22 as they cruised by.

"Aren't you going for your walk?" Antonio asked as he entered the living room one day.

She looked up from her book. Gabe had been sitting next to her but hopped a few feet away in case she wanted to push herself up off the couch. "I'd really like to, but…" She didn't know how to follow that up. *I think I might have a stalker? I'd feel safer with another person around?* Suddenly, she felt silly. "You know what? I do want to walk. I could really use the exercise."

Antonio grinned. "Yeah, wow. You look like you've put on a few pounds, girl! That's quite the spare tire you've got there."

"Oh, thanks," she said, deadpan. Planting her hands on the sofa, she heaved herself to her feet. "I would ask you to go with me, but not after that crack."

Antonio laughed. "Good. I'm tired. And you don't need an escort in the middle of a beautiful Saturday afternoon."

She realized he was right. It had been two weeks since she'd seen Adam—even if the guy in the hoodie, lurking, was him, she hadn't seen anything else suspicious. She figured he'd gotten the hint.

"Okay. In that case, I'll be back in a few." She turned to blow a kiss to Gabe, but he flew up onto her shoulder.

"Oh, you want to come too?"

He bobbed his head.

"No can do, Son," Antonio said. "You know the rules."

Misty felt bad for him. She got the exercise she needed, but did he? "Is that only because of the tail feathers getting attention from passersby?"

"Yes. Getting *unwanted* attention," Antonio stressed.

"Can't he do something to cover them up?"

Antonio smirked. "I'd say no, but you're not stupid. The boys have found ways... Jayce does 'the chimney sweep,' he calls it. I think he got that from Ryan. And... Never mind. I shouldn't be giving anyone ideas." He tipped his head toward Gabe. "Remember, it's only temporary. I'm going downstairs to watch the BU vs. BC game."

"Have fun," Misty called out as she moved toward the front door.

As soon as Antonio had shut the door to the man cave, she returned to Gabe. "I have an idea," she said excitedly.

He cocked his head.

"How would you like to go for a walk with me? You must be dying to get outside in this beautiful weather."

He swiftly turned his right eye toward her.

"I thought so. Listen. Your mom keeps a big tin of cocoa in the pantry. Could you still fly if I coat your tail feathers in cocoa?"

He squawked as he bobbed his head, which she took as an excited yes.

"Awesome. Let's hope your mom is still lying down upstairs and we can have the kitchen to ourselves for a few minutes."

Gabe sailed into the kitchen and returned, bobbing his head as if to say the coast was clear.

Misty giggled, feeling like a naughty girl about to get away with some forbidden fun. What could go wrong? *Famous last words...*

Misty quickly coated the butcher-block counter with a generous amount of cocoa, and after Gabe landed nearby, she took a handful of powder and smoothed it down his tail feathers, hoping that would work.

"Should I add some water to make it muddy? Would that help it stick better?"

Gabe showed her his left eye for no, so she just smoothed the chocolate powder down his tail feathers again. He made a cooing sound that she'd never heard before. He must've enjoyed it. At least she hoped so.

She cleaned up the mess and let him perch on her finger as she walked out the front door, locking it behind her.

"Go, honey. Fly. Be free." Gabe took off and soared several feet above her, circling as she walked. She glanced upward a few times to see that he was still there. He obviously wanted to stay close by. It warmed her heart.

A familiar face was coming toward her. *Adam? Again? Really?*

"Misty! I was just coming to see you."

Suddenly, Gabe was dive-bombing her visitor. Even though he was an *unwanted* visitor, she didn't want anything to happen to him...or Gabe. "No! Stop, Ga—"

Adam ducked. Gabe veered away from his face and instead circled around, beating the back of his head with his wings as he swooped by. Some of the chocolate was dislodged, and a bit of bright color showed through.

"Jesus, Misty! Call off your bird."

"Please, stop!" Misty cried. "Let me handle this."

Gabe flew up to perch on a wire overhead.

"What the hell is that thing? An attack bird?"

Misty smiled slyly. Crossing her arms, she said, "Yes. It's my Amazon attack bird."

"And you named it Gay?"

"Yeah. She's usually quite happy. I guess she thought I was in danger. Am I? In danger, I mean?"

"Christ, no. I was just coming to tell you I'm seeing Terri now. I won't be bothering you again."

Misty remembered Terri saying that he wasn't a bad guy and she would go out with him if he asked her. Plus, as a single mother, Terri could use the kind of financial help Adam seemed happy to provide.

"I'm glad to hear that. Terri is a sweetheart. I hope you two hit it off, and I wish you both the best."

Adam glanced up at the bird a couple of times. "Well, I'll be on my way now. If that's the kind of thing they have in the Amazon rain forest, I guess I don't mind people cutting it down."

As he walked away, Gabe swooped over him and crapped on his head.

"Jesus!" He shot a glare at Misty. "Get your damn bird under control."

Misty giggled. "In some cultures, getting hit with bird poop is considered good luck."

"Well, in that case, good luck to you too."

~

The last few weeks of Gabe's confinement were without incident. They had set July 4 as his return date.
Independence Day. Completely fitting, he thought. The
entire family was gathered to celebrate the holiday. Two
holidays, actually. The Fourth of July, and New Gabe
Day, as his mother was calling it.

Misty had been excitedly chattering with Gabriella
and helping her prepare food all morning. She was wearing an adorable pink high-waisted sundress that she had
made, telling him sewing would keep her out of trouble.
He suspected she wanted something special for the
occasion—and having a hobby was never a bad thing.

He was excited too. It was all he could do to wait
until everyone had arrived and Gabriella announced
everything was ready.

Misty ran upstairs to their bedroom. She laid out some
clothes for him and said she'd wait downstairs with everyone else. Blowing him a kiss, she closed the bedroom
door behind her, and he heard her footsteps running down
the stairs. She hadn't fallen in months. He hoped, for her
sake, the reprieve from her MS symptoms would last.

He couldn't wait another second. He concentrated on
his human form and felt himself growing and shifting.
At last, he glanced down and saw his feet and legs and,
well, the stiffy, courtesy of Misty and her adorableness.
He looked in the mirror over his dresser and saw his
flawless face. No scars. No discoloring. Just the same
old face he was used to. Breathing a sigh of relief, he
grinned and put on the jeans she had chosen for him.

Before he pulled the fire department T-shirt over
his head, he checked the spot on his ribs where he'd
branded himself with Buddy's dog tag. It was as smooth

as the skin he was born with. He wasn't sad to see it had disappeared. The reason for it being there wasn't to remember his dog. It was to punish himself. It seemed as if he had finally conquered the need to do that.

Now.. how to make an appropriate entrance?

He wished he had a dozen roses to give Misty, but it was pretty hard arranging something like that without the ability to speak. Then he remembered something from his younger years that he'd hidden away. The piece had always carried sad memories, but he couldn't get rid of it. It was another reminder that he shouldn't get involved with a woman. Or in this case a girl who distracted him from his responsibilities.

He fished a small box out of the back of his closet, opened it, and was happy to see the necklace hadn't tarnished even a dozen years later. It was a tiny gold heart on a thin gold chain. He had been planning to give it to the girl who'd taken his virginity. But when his dog died, he pushed her away rather than let her see him cry. She thought it was because she wasn't good enough in bed. Then she set about to prove she was—with half the football team.

It would look beautiful on Misty's long, slender neck. He'd almost given the little necklace to her after her parents were killed. He understood what an inconsolable loss felt like.

Now, thinking about her wearing it gave him a warm feeling inside. He gazed at the heart and saw it in a whole new light. Misty was the one who had made it possible for him to get over his loss. She'd given him the kind of unconditional love he didn't think existed. She deserved the token of his affection and so much more.

He tucked it in his pocket and jogged down the stairs. When he rounded the corner to the living room, he was greeted with loud hoots and applause from his entire boisterous family. The whole gang was there. Ryan and Chloe, Jayce and Kristine, Miguel and Sandra, Dante, Noah, Luca, his parents, and, of course, his beautiful wife, Misty. Her name fit as he gazed at her beautiful blue eyes, filling with moisture.

She wasn't the only misty-eyed one in the bunch. His mother and sisters-in-law all looked like they had happy tears about to spill.

Misty led the long procession of kisses and hugs, handshakes, and pats on the back. As soon as his mother had stopped kissing him on both cheeks, twice, Gabe stepped back and found Misty in the crowd. As he walked over to her, he drew the necklace out of his pocket and opened the clasp.

He held up the little heart so she could see it and then reached around her slim, tan neck and fastened it. No words were needed.

The flood she had been holding back finally let go, but she was smiling as she was sobbing, so he knew they were happy tears. She slipped her arms around his neck and hugged him for a very long time. Which was just fine with him, because he never wanted to let her go either.

At last, Gabriella announced, "Let's go into the dining room and eat some of the feast that Misty and I slaved over all morning."

"There's one last thing before we do that," Antonio said.

Everyone halted. Antonio pulled an envelope out of his pocket and crossed to the happy couple. "We never gave you two a wedding present."

"We don't need presents," Gabe said. "I have my gift." He looked lovingly at Misty.

She cuddled up to him and laid her head on his shoulder. "Me too."

"I'm glad you feel that way, because you're not getting a bunch of presents. Just one."

Chuckles and laughter followed, but Gabe wasn't the least bit embarrassed. One gift. That's how he wanted it.

"Everyone contributed to it," Gabriella said as his father handed Gabe the envelope.

Opening it, he found a hotel brochure and two plane tickets to Venice, dated the following day. "Wow! This is great, everybody, but shouldn't I be getting back to work? It's been ten weeks."

"So what's another week?" Antonio smiled. "Don't worry, Son. It's been cleared with the chief."

"A week in Venice?" Misty asked, wide-eyed.

"*Divertiti, bella*," Gabriella said and kissed her daughter-in-law on both cheeks.

"What does that mean?" Misty asked.

Gabe translated for her. "Enjoy yourself, sweetheart."

She smiled at Gabriella. "Thank you. We will. Thanks, all of you!"

Gabe handed the envelope to his brother. "Hey, Jayce. Hold this for me." As soon as Gabe had his hands free, he dipped Misty and followed her down for a long, deep kiss.

Jayce laughed harder than the rest. "Ah, newlyweds."

————

"A honeymoon in Venice. I still can't believe we're here," Misty said breathlessly. Gabe was taking her picture from the bridge over one of the canals.

"Believe it, babe. You deserve it."

"Me? What did I do?"

He laughed, draped an arm over her shoulder, and started walking toward the more populated area. "You waited for me."

She smiled up at him. "Is that all? That was easy. I had nowhere else to go."

He laughed. "And there's also the part where you're going to be the mother of my child."

She slowed. "About that… We need to talk."

He halted and stared at her.

"Oh! I didn't mean to alarm you. I just know there might be challenges with my MS, and we haven't even discussed it."

He took in a deep breath and let it out. "True, but what do we need to discuss? I figure there's not much we can do about it. If a problem comes up, we'll just cross that bridge when we come to it." As if illustrating his point, they stepped off the bridge and headed down one of the many cobblestone streets built on pylons centuries ago.

"I don't know what to expect. Maybe there's no way to know, but we should probably have some kind of a plan. We slept on the plane most of the way over here to minimize jet lag. But now that we're here, I just want to come up with some contingency plans."

"I'm going to need to do this on a full stomach. Let's find a sidewalk café."

They proceeded farther toward the main square and came upon a café by the canal. "Is this okay?" Misty asked.

Gabe glanced up and down the street. "Perfect. Not a pigeon in sight."

As they found a table, she asked, "You don't like pigeons?"

"Not swarms of them. If you have food in St. Mark's Square, they'll surround you. Some may even sit on your head. We should buy you a hat, just in case."

"I'll bet Adam wished he had a hat that day."

Gabe burst out laughing. A smiling waiter came over to them and took their orders for two chocolate gelatos. As soon as he left, a woman with long, flowing white hair pulled a chair over and joined them. She removed a large floppy hat and laid it on the table, taking up most of it.

"That's what I like to see," she said. "Humans in love, laughing, and enjoying my beautiful day. It makes my job worthwhile."

Gabe's eyes widened. Misty wondered who the heck this nervy, weird woman was and why Gabe seemed so shocked to see her.

At last, he found his voice. "Ah, Misty, allow me to introduce you to Gaia. I think she already knows who you are."

"Oh? Are you a Fierro family friend?" Misty asked as she extended her arm, offering to shake hands with the strange woman.

Gaia gazed at Misty's hand and hesitated a moment before she gave one firm shake. Then she leaned back in her chair. "I'm afraid I don't have a lot of time, but I need to talk to you two alone—and preferably before you talk to each other about the little matter you brought up on the bridge."

"You heard that?" Misty asked incredulously.

The woman rolled her eyes as if to say *"Obviously,"*

then snapped her fingers. The waiter heading their way froze. In fact, everyone in the café appeared frozen in place. Conversation had ceased. Even the breeze died down to nothing. It was the strangest thing Misty had ever seen, and lately, she'd seen some pretty strange things.

"Hey. I wanted that." Gabe pointed to the gelatos on the waiter's tray.

The woman narrowed her eyes, and suddenly, Gabe was gone.

Misty jerked to attention. "What? Where's my husband?"

A second later, Gabe reappeared, covered in snow-flakes and shivering. "That's o-k-k-k-kay. I c-can wait," he said, teeth chattering.

"Now." Gaia stretched her arms over her head as if getting ready to work. "As I said, I don't have a lot of time, and what I'm about to ask you will require some consideration. I'll have to return for your answer later."

What could this insane woman want? Misty just nodded dumbly.

"Gabe didn't give you my title, only my name," she continued. "I'm Mother Nature. I made you, him"—she waved at the canal and the sky—"everyone and all this. Now, I need a favor, and after all I've done for the world, I think you should consider taking the job I'm going to offer you."

"Oh!" Misty pushed past the fear and disbelief and felt compelled to address the words *job* and *offer* imme-diately. "I'm sorry, Gaia. I'm not looking for a job. I'll have my hands full with our baby very soon." She pointed to her expanding belly.

"Yes. I know. I made that possible too." The woman

smirked. "Here's the thing. My original muses need help. They're overwhelmed with all the changes that have occurred in the modern world. I've been recruiting modern women who can be trusted with some pretty cool powers to help them out. I try to find those who have the needed skills they lack."

"Wh-what skills do I have?" Misty asked. "I never went beyond high school, and I only worked in a bank briefly. I used to dance—"

Gaia waved away her comment. "I have a muse of dance. Terpsichore. She's very busy with all these crazy new moves she calls hip-hop, popping and locking, breakdancing, and they're coming up with more all the time. She says it should be named 'break-your-neck dancing.' It's all she can do to keep these fools from bodily harm as they defy my laws of gravity."

"Oookaaay," Misty said.

"Goddess, what my wife and I would like to know is what you're expecting of her?" Gabe said.

"Expecting? Just the best you can do. And I'm offering a lot—not money. Something only I can pull off. I want my muses to willingly accept the job I feel they're suited for. I want you to be the modern muse of parenting. You know the saying, 'It takes a village to raise a child'?"

"Yeah," Misty murmured, still in shock.

"I've been saying that for centuries. People still don't get the hint. My humans used to be nomads, and they traveled together in bands for safety. Even when they settled in one spot, they looked out for each other—and one another's children."

"You want her to babysit?" Gabe asked.

Gaia blew out a breath of frustration. "No, dragnix.

And if I were you, I wouldn't test my patience with stupid questions."

Gabe made a gesture of zippering his mouth.

The goddess turned her attention back to Misty. "It's a huge compliment, girlie. And because I know you'll be caring for your own child, I'm willing to help in a big way—but only if you accept."

Misty chewed her lip. "I still don't know what I'd be doing."

"Here, let me show you." Mother Nature drew a large circle in the air, and an image came into view. A young girl, maybe a teenager, was trying to get a baby to stop crying. She tried to give him a bottle, but he turned his head, refusing it. She checked his diaper, which was dry. She tried rocking him and was getting increasingly frustrated when he only settled for a second and started to cry again.

At last, she held the baby up in front of her and angrily yelled, "What do you want?" Then she began to shake him.

"No! Stop!" Misty cried. "Don't shake that baby!"

One side of Mother Nature's lip curved up. The girl glanced around and finally carried the baby down the hall and put him in his bed. Shutting the door, she walked a few steps away and let herself have a good cry too.

A few moments later, the baby stopped crying. The young mother tiptoed back to the child's room and looked in on him. He was asleep. She quietly shut the door and leaned against the wall, relief washing over her.

When the picture faded, Misty gazed at Gaia. "What just happened?" Remembering who she was talking to, she took a respectful tone. "What are you trying to tell me, Goddess?"

"Your instincts are good," she said. "You're going to make an excellent mother. The thing is, there are a lot of parents out there, hundreds of thousands, perhaps millions, who are frustrated, overwhelmed, and isolated! There's no village to help them. Not only that, but some don't have the faintest idea what they're doing.

"I just need you to be a friend when they need one most. A calm whisper in their ears. Do you remember how that girl stopped shaking the baby, put him to bed, and then faced her own frustration?"

Misty nodded.

"You did that. You told her not to shake the baby. And she stopped."

"She heard me?"

"She did. In her own mind, though. It just sounded like her own voice of reason…that little inner voice that people learn to listen to if they have any smarts at all."

"Are you saying that little voice inside my head is a muse?"

"Not always. But often enough."

"So when I knew a dance move was beyond my ability and stopped myself from attempting it, knowing I could get hurt…"

Gaia shrugged. "It might have been your own good sense, or it might have been Terpsichore. You can ask her if you become her colleague."

Misty remained in stunned silence for a few moments as she put together the disjointed pieces of this "job offer." It seemed as if with Gaia's help, Misty would be able to save babies from some of the horrific headlines she'd seen in the news. If all she had to do was see a picture and yell at it, it would probably be okay. In fact, if she were successful, it would be extremely gratifying.

Gaia had said something about powers. Was that the only power she was referring to—being able to talk to people through a bubble in the air?

"Not at all." Gaia startled her out of her reverie, apparently answering her unspoken question. "There are a number of powers that all my muses have. And there would be a gift for accepting the job. Some muses have had the nerve to call it a bribe. I prefer to call it a sign-on and retention bonus."

Gabe chewed his lip. "Goddess, with all due respect, if Misty is helping thousands of parents to take care of their children, how will she take care of ours?"

Mother Nature folded her arms and looked annoyed. "Do you think I would saddle her with a job that would overwhelm her and make her just one more of the many parents she's trying to help?"

Gabe shrugged.

Mother Nature heaved a sigh. "Look, it's not very complicated. She'll be trained by another muse before she's expected to do anything. Here are some of the particulars that might help you understand. First, a muse is a minor goddess who can manipulate time a bit. Second, she can travel in the blink of an eye. She won't miss a trick at home."

"So, travel is involved?" Misty asked.

"Only if you wish to be close enough to intervene, although your involvement will be limited. You would have to stand outside the scene in a spot called the ether. It's neither here nor there, just sort of a cool fog between physical and spiritual worlds. And you can take your baby with you, if necessary. Neither of you can be seen, because popping out of thin air in front of a human wouldn't cause any suspicion at all." Mother Nature rolled her eyes and snorted at her own sarcasm.

"Would it help if you tell her there are a couple of muses she knows already?" Gabe asked.

Gaia tilted her head. "Probably. Why don't you tell her?"

Misty gazed at Gabe. He said, "Jayce's wife, Kristine. And Ryan's wife, Chloe. They're both modern muses now. Kristine is the muse of wireless communication, like cell phones and walkie-talkies and stuff. And Chloe is the modern muse of fire safety."

"She would take care of telling parents when their children are playing with matches. We try to avoid overlap," Gaia added.

"Two of my sisters-in-law are muses? And you didn't tell me, Gabe?"

"I didn't know if I could. It's drummed into our heads that humans can't handle any knowledge of a paranormal world. We're not supposed to tell anyone mortal about paranormal beings, powers, or any of it."

Misty glanced at Mother Nature. "But it's okay if he tells me everything now, isn't it? I mean, you're here offering to make me…a what? Minor goddess? Would I be paranormal?"

Gaia smirked. "Well, modern muses aren't exactly normal, are they?"

Misty sighed. Then it suddenly occurred to her that as a paranormal being, she might have the enhanced health and recuperative powers she had heard about. She sat bolt upright. "If I become a modern muse, would I still have MS?"

Gaia looked at the sky and muttered, "At last, she gets it."

Misty turned excitedly toward Gabe and grabbed his hands. "Do you know what this means? I can be healthy again. We don't have to worry about how to take care of our baby and me too if you're at work for a few nights."

"I wouldn't rush it, honey. In fact, Gaia already said you're going to need to think about it."

Misty practically bounced in her seat. "What's to think about? I can be cured!"

Mother Nature rose. "Well, I have to turn my attention to an earthquake that just hit Asia, so I'd suggest you talk to your sisters-in-law and see what they think of my offer. I'll drop by later."

With that, the all-powerful goddess disappeared, and the noise and activity of the busy café resumed.

"Oh! She forgot her hat!"

"Keep it," the goddess's voice answered.

"Did you hear that?" Misty asked Gabe.

"Hear what?"

She sighed. That must have been a demonstration of the "inner voice" she was told about. If she accepted the job, she could be that voice for others. Misty plopped Mother Nature's floppy hat onto her head. "That was…something."

The waiter set the little bowls of gelato in front of them. "Enjoy." His complete unawareness of everyone's temporary inanimate state, including his own, blew Misty's mind.

She picked up her spoon. She'd half expected her

gelato to be melted by now, but apparently interrupting the law of physics extended to food too.

Gabe lifted her free hand and kissed her fingers. "So, what do you want to do?"

"Right now?" She shrugged. "I want to eat this gelato." She dug into it with her spoon and enjoyed the cold, chocolate taste as it melted on her tongue.

Chapter 21

BACK IN THEIR HOTEL ROOM THAT NIGHT, GABE NEEDED A moment to reflect. He excused himself and retreated to the impressive green marble bathroom. If he turned on the shower, she would probably join him, so he simply sat on the edge of the tub for a few minutes.

All afternoon, Misty had been nothing but excited about the prospect of becoming a muse. There were certain advantages to him too, if he were honest.

Not having to worry about her health was a biggie. Even the inevitable—death—would no longer be a problem! No wonder his older brothers were so damn happy. Well, two out of the three. As far as he knew, Sandra was still very human. And until recently, his own mother was in the dark when it came to Gaia's existence. So his father and Miguel were still willing to risk loss in order to love.

So was he. Misty didn't have to do this, and he needed to make sure she knew it.

A knock at the door made him smile. He was tempted to be a smart-ass and ask *Who is it?*

"Can I come in?" Misty asked through the door.

"Sure."

As soon as she stepped in, he perused her naked body. Even six months pregnant, she was beautiful. Her hair had grown longer and shinier than ever. It was almost to her waist. Her breasts were noticeably fuller, getting ready to nurse their child.

"Would you like to join me in the shower?" Gabe asked.

"Maybe in a minute. First, I want to apologize."

Surprised, Gabe asked, "For what?"

She sat next to him on the tub and took his hand in hers. Her beautiful blue eyes conveyed a touch of sadness. "I've been so excited about this whole muse thing, I didn't even consider how you would feel about it. I want to know what you think."

Gabe slipped his arm around her shoulder. "Actually, I was just mulling the whole thing over in my mind. The only thing I've decided for certain is that you don't have to take this on if you don't want to. Don't worry about me worrying about you. We'll cope no matter what. I know it's tempting, but if you have any misgivings at all, I want you to investigate them before making a final decision."

"Thank you." She laid her head on his shoulder. "I was getting a little carried away earlier. I think I ought to talk to Kristine or Chloe. Do you have their phone numbers?"

"No need," Kristine's voice announced. "Gaia said you might want to talk."

Misty's gaze ricocheted all over the bathroom as she covered her breasts and mons with her hands. "Where are you? Can you see me?"

"I'm in the ether, facing the other way."

Sure you are… Gabe almost snickered. Thank goodness he was still dressed.

"Give me a minute to throw on a robe, okay?" Misty dashed to the bedroom, and Gabe followed her. She wrapped herself in her red satin robe and tied it above her belly. Even though it was opaque, it was sexy as hell, clinging to her curves and leaving little to the imagination.

"Ready," she called out.

Kristine appeared near their window, looking out at the view. She turned around and smiled. "Beautiful room you have here. I was hoping you'd have a view of the Grand Canal, and I see that you do."

Still barefoot, Misty crossed the painted tile floor. "Yes. It's a terrific view. Be sure to tell everyone thank you for us when you get back." As soon as she reached her sister-in-law, they hugged.

Kristine backed up, still holding Misty's shoulders. Glancing down, she said, "Your baby's growing by leaps and bounds. Is it seven months already?"

"Six." There was a bench near the window, and Misty sat on it, patting the space next to her. "Have a seat, Kristine."

"I can't stay. I have dinner in the oven. I set the timer so I can hear it. There's about fifteen minutes before the lasagna is done."

Gabe wandered over and took the seat next to Misty. "Mmm, lasagna. I know what I'll be ordering when we go out tonight."

Misty laughed. "All he thinks about is his stomach."

He patted her expanding belly. "And yours."

Kristine grinned. "You two are the perfect pair. I'm so glad you got together."

Gabe took Misty's hand and kissed it. "We are too."

"So, what would you like to know about being a muse?"

Misty shrugged. "I don't even know the questions to ask. I guess first I want to know if you like it? If you're good at it? If you wish you'd never accepted the job? That sort of thing."

Kristine laughed. "First"—she used her fingers to

count off her answers to Misty's questions—"I like it very much. Second, I think I'm pretty good at it. And third, I'd do it again."

"That's encouraging," Misty responded. "How long did it take you to learn what to do?"

Kristine tipped her head in thought. "I'm not sure. My training was only about a week or so. But I still have questions—or just need encouragement, and I can talk to my trainer whenever something comes up."

"Who's your trainer?"

Kristine chuckled. "I have one of the original muses— Melpomene. The muse of tragedy. Not the most cheery individual, not that it matters much. All she taught me was how to use my powers. The rest is up to me."

"And you're the muse of wireless communication?" Gabe asked.

"Pretty much. Mother Nature noticed I was pretty comfortable using my own cell phone and the fire departments' radios. But sometimes I get a distress call involving a device I'm not familiar with, like a ham radio or satellite."

"What do you do then?" Misty asked.

Kristine shrugged. "I do my best. It's not up to me to fix devices that don't work, but sometimes I have to tell the more clueless individuals how to use them."

"But how do you tell a ham radio operator how to use his radio if you don't know yourself?"

"That's when I produce a manual and whisper into the person's ear something like 'RTFM.'"

Gabe laughed. Misty looked confused, so he translated. "RTFM means 'read the fucking manual.'"

She giggled. "Oh. So, it sounds like you can have

a bit of fun, as long as there's no life-and-death stuff involved, right?"

Kristine's expression saddened, and she placed a hand on Misty's shoulder. "I don't envy you the job you're being offered. Forgive me for saying it this way, but you're young. You may not realize that you can't always save people—especially from themselves. But by being there, you might be able to make a difference. In other words, you won't win them all. That's my only concern about you taking this job."

Gabe hadn't even thought of that. He was used to life-and-death situations. Misty wasn't.

"But Mother Nature thought I could do the job. She must be right, right?"

"I don't doubt you can do the job," Kristine said. "In fact, I think you'd be really good at it. I just wanted to be honest and let you know you might not always succeed."

Gabe's concern grew as he took in Misty's face. "If seeing children abused is going to make you too depressed, I want you to say so." She gazed at him with her bright blue eyes. She looked so innocent, and he would hate to see that wide-eyed innocence die.

"Of course that would make me sad, but if I could make a difference with just one child... Well, I can't imagine anything more fulfilling. I mean, I'm sure raising our own children will be fulfilling enough, but to know my influence is helping others, perhaps hundreds or thousands of others...it seems worth a little sadness." She glanced between Gabe and Kristine a couple of times. "How do you do it? You're both firefighters. You both see terrible things. How do you cope?"

"There's really no one answer to that."

"I guess it's an individual thing." Gabe put his arm around her shoulder. "For me, it's knowing I'm doing something worthwhile that not everyone can do. Now that I have you and little whosie-whatsit here," he said, tapping her on the stomach, "I have even more reason for doing what I do and not letting it get to me."

"But that's just it. How do you not let it get to you?"

Kristine stepped in, thank goodness. "Some of the guys blow off steam in different ways. On the job, they have each other for support. Off the job, they have hobbies or sports or any number of distractions. Vacations are important too."

Gabe realized Misty's support system might need some beefing up. She couldn't just come home from a job taking care of the world's children and return to taking care of her own children without having someone to talk to about it.

"How long does Misty have to decide? Did Mother Nature give you a deadline?" Kristine asked.

"Not that we know of. Does she usually do that?" Gabe asked.

Kristine smirked. "She's not the most patient person, by her own admission, but she's pretty understanding. I imagine she knows it's important to think long and hard about this."

"Yes," Misty said. "It's a good thing she gave us time to reflect on it. I would have jumped at the chance to be cured. I think she even knew that, so she told me to think it over and talk to you or Chloe. Do you think Chloe would have any other advice I should listen to?"

Suddenly, Chloe appeared. "I think Kristine

covered it fairly well. So, do you have any questions for me in particular?"

"Ah, Sister." Kristine hugged Chloe. "I'm glad you're here. I need to get home before my lasagna burns. Maybe you can take over for me?"

"Only if you're talkin' about takin' over the advisin' and not the cookin'. It's always a pleasure to see you, but I understand if you've got to leave."

Chloe whispered something in Kristine's ear. Misty probably didn't hear it, but Gabe did. Chloe reminded Kristine that she could fiddle with time a bit and pop back home before the lasagna burned even if she stayed long enough for that to happen. *Wow, that must be a cool power to have.*

Misty rose. "Thank you for coming, Kristine. And thanks for answering all my questions. I might have more in the future. I hope that's all right."

Kristine laughed. "I don't doubt it. You can talk to me anytime."

"Or me," Chloe said.

Gabe rose and hugged one sister-in-law goodbye and the other hello. Then he stood next to Misty with an arm around what was once her waist.

Chloe sighed as she surveyed Misty's expanding middle. "Ah, children. It's not meant to be for Ryan and I. Although at one time I wished it."

Gabe gave her the hairy eyeball. "Ah. So *you're* the one."

She reared back. "I'm the one what?"

How could he tell her that Mother Nature turned him into a dragnix because of a conversation with one of his brother's wives? He waved away the question.

"Never mind. I'm sure you'll hear all about it at the next family gathering."

"Hmmm... I don't know what you're referrin' to, but if you don't care to talk about it—"

"I don't. Believe me, I don't."

Chloe shrugged. "Whatever floats your boat."

He eyed her curiously. It happened on a boat. Was her expression a coincidence, or was she there watching and now playing dumb?

Learning about the ether, he realized a muse could be anywhere and he'd never know it. That was sort of their job. Chloe was the muse of fire safety. His family was pulling a risky move with fire when they had Kristine bathe him in dragon fire, intending to reduce him to ashes.

"You really don't know?"

Chloe shook her head.

Gabe inhaled deeply. "Fine. I'll tell you. But don't laugh. Apparently, one of my older brothers and his wife wanted Gaia to make it possible for a dragon and phoenix to reproduce."

"That would have been us, yes."

"Well, let me just assure you, it was a terrible idea. I came back as one during my reincarnation. For a few minutes, only the top half of me was visible on the little boat, because that half of me was fireproof—like a dragon. When I looked down, I had scales and an enormous wingspan. My bottom half was indeed a pile of ashes."

"Like a phoenix in fire," she supplied. "Oh no. What happened? How did you rise from the ashes?"

"It wasn't graceful."

"Oh dear." Her hand covered her mouth, like she was trying to hide a smile. When she got herself under control, she said, "I never meant for it to happen like that. I just hoped she could make it possible for a dragon and phoenix to have offspring—not with any powers or anythin'. Just a normal child." Then her smile threatened to return. "No wonder she got so angry and refused."

"Yeah, well. I doubt it will ever happen again."

"Good thing. Ryan and I are actually quite happy without children. If we had little ones running around the edge of a cliff every time they went outside, I'd be beside meself with worry."

"And that's where I'd come in," Misty said.

"What would ye do in that case?" Chloe asked.

"I'd yell, 'Hey, parents! Build a fucking fence!'"

Chloe laughed. "See? You're a natural!"

Gabe enveloped Misty in his arms and kissed the top of her head. "Not that it hasn't been nice seeing you, Chloe, but we *are* on our honeymoon."

"Sure'n I'll be off, then. Have a grand time!" And with that, Chloe disappeared.

Gabe placed his finger under Misty's chin and tipped up her face. "I love you, no matter what. You know that, right?"

She smiled. "Yes. I know."

"Then let's get this honeymoon off the ground." He swept her off her feet and carried her to the bed.

He threw back the covers and laid her in the middle of the queen size bed. Standing next to it, he studied her curiously for a moment, then crawled in beside her.

"What?"

"Nothing."

"Oh, no. You don't get to do that with me. You can be the strong, silent type with the rest of the world, but not with me."

He smirked. "Okay. I just wondered how making love at this stage of your pregnancy might affect the baby."

She laughed. "Everything I've read says it doesn't matter. At my last checkup, I asked the doctor how long we'd be able to have sex, and she said that if no problems present themselves during the pregnancy, there's no reason not to enjoy sexual intercourse throughout the entire nine months. That's almost a direct quote."

"Really?"

"Yeah. Some people who have no reason to limit themselves but do anyway are missing out. After all, how great it is to not worry about pregnancy and stopping to put on a condom. And the vaginal hormonal lubrication of pregnancy makes for a nice, slick ride."

He laughed.

"What?"

"You have a way with words."

"Oh. Well, she also said it's good for couples to have intercourse during pregnancy because it prepares the pelvic floor muscles for delivery, it can help with any body image issues by making me feel sexy, which you do, and it's nice to have this closeness *now*, since once the baby arrives, it's a lot more difficult to find the time and energy to devote to each other."

"She's not wrong about that." He eyed her hungrily.

As if reading his mind, she added, "I feel great. In other words, go for it."

He did. He practically pounced on her. While devouring her mouth, his hands caressed her everywhere. They kneaded and squeezed her breasts, creating incredible sensations. Then he moved down to suck them, and his fingers played with the curls at the apex of her thighs.

Sliding a finger over and through her folds, he sank one digit into her opening and finger-fucked her. *Wow*. That got her even hotter.

By the time he stroked her clit, she was ready to explode. Arching almost off the bed, she came apart, screaming in ecstasy. He didn't stop when she thought he might but kept up his sweet assault on her senses.

After her third climax, she grabbed his hand and yanked it away. "Stop...I can't...no more..."

He chuckled and leaned back with the most self-satisfied look on his face.

"Oh, you think you're done? Not yet, hot shot." Misty winked. "But I need your help."

"What can I do for you, m'lady?"

"Well, since I'm boneless and can't move, why don't you straddle my face and let me suck you while you watch."

"Jesus."

She didn't have to ask twice. He levered himself up and straddled her instantly. His engorged shaft waited impatiently for her mouth.

She took him in as far as she could without gagging and applied suction as he withdrew. He tossed back his head and moaned. They repeated the move over and over until he withdrew sharply and hissed, "No more. I'll come."

"You can if you want to."

He let out a deep breath in a whoosh. "I want to come *with* you. How do you want me?"

"Every which way."

He chuckled. "How about if you lie on your side?"

Surprised, she faced away from him. They'd never done it that way, but why not? When she got bigger, it might be a handy position to know.

He entered her from behind, and *wow*. It felt incredible. He began his rhythm as he played with her breasts.

"Oh, that feels nice."

"Yeah. You know what's even nicer?"

"What?" she asked breathlessly.

He slid his hand over her hip and reached her sweet spot. Still sensitized, she jumped the moment he touched it. "Oh God."

"Oh yeah." He curled tightly around her and sped up his thrusts. When he was furiously pounding into her, he came with a thunderous roar.

Her orgasm hit hard, transporting her out of her body. She lost awareness of her surroundings. It seemed as if Gabe was the only anchor she had to the earth, and she wasn't sure he wasn't floating in space too.

Several minutes later, they lay limp and exhausted. Gabe nuzzled her neck and whispered words of love in her ear.

She knew why people tried to describe certain things they felt passionate about as "better than sex." There was nothing like this feeling. And there was nothing better than sex with the man you loved most in the universe.

Epilogue

"PUSH, MISTY!" GABE COACHED.

"You push!" she cried out.

"I wish I could." He'd take over for her if it were possible. Anything to spare her the pain of the last few hours. After all, she was giving birth to his child. They still didn't know the sex of the baby. No one did except her OB-GYN doctor, and she had agreed to keep it to herself.

"Come on, honey. You're almost there," Gabriella said.

Gabe was grateful that his mother was acting as the midwife, although they had a professional on standby in the living room. She had given birth to all seven of her kids right there in the kitchen on a rented hospital bed. *If she could do it...*

Why did we wait until after the birth for Misty to become a muse? He was tempted to summon Mother Nature and ask her to change his wife that instant. He figured everything—birth included—would be easier on a minor goddess than a human. *Oh, yeah. Misty wanted the whole human experience. Something about a bonding story with other mothers.*

She panted a few times and then gave it one last concerted effort, gritting her teeth and practically howling. A dark, hairy dome peeked out from her opening.

"I see it!" he cried.

She looked surprised but encouraged. She took one more deep breath and bore down with all her might. Out popped his son, into his waiting arms.

"It's a boy!" he shouted.

She was panting too hard to speak, but the grin on her face and tears in her eyes said it all. Gabe cleared the baby's face with the edge of a waiting warm cloth and stared in awe.

"Give him to me," his mother demanded.

Knowing that tone of voice, he handed over his son. She grabbed him by the feet, and as he hung upside down, she tapped his back. He took a deep breath and let out a healthy howl.

"That's it, little man," Gabriella cooed. "You're a Fierro, all right." She laid the baby in Misty's arms and kissed him on the forehead. "Let me take over down there," she said to Gabe. "You just enjoy your son. What's his name, by the way?"

He happily traded places with his mother and let her handle the afterbirth. "Tony, after Dad. We decided to Americanize his name with the common nickname. It won't get confusing that way. But we'll tell Dad he's named after the Red Sox legend Tony Conigliaro so he doesn't get all puffed up."

Gabriella laughed. "He'd love it either way."

The goddess they'd come to know better over the past few months materialized. Gaia's long white hair was tied up in a bun, and she wore a white lab coat over her white toga.

"I knew you could do it. I made women for this," she said to Misty proudly.

Gabe didn't want to point out that some women didn't

make it, and he couldn't help worrying about his wife until it was all over. But as Mother Nature produced a clean blanket and helped Gabe cut the cord and wrap up his little boy, all was forgiven.

They'd decided that Misty could handle the job of muse of parenting if she was allowed to see some of the wonderful moments as well as the challenging. She'd read everything she could get her hands on to prepare her for just about any situation. She was ready and raring to go after maternity leave. Fortunately, Gaia was okay with a maternity leave before the job even started.

It had been decided that Bliss Cameron would be her mentor and trainer. She was another modern muse, married to a firefighter. Kristine would be there if she needed backup. She would have trained her full-time, but she was often busy, enjoying her job with the Boston Fire Department.

And so was Gabe. He'd been able to return to Engine 22 and pick up where he'd left off, but soon, he was transferring to the marine unit. Having a brief experience with the panic that comes from being trapped on a burning boat, he could imagine what humans felt like.

The harbor was close to the financial district. Ironically, he'd be closer to Misty's old bank after all. That didn't mean he'd be popping in to use the account he opened there. Thank goodness for online banking.

And thank goodness for strong vaults on timers, poor impulse control, and the unconditional love of a special woman he'd known most of his life. They looked forward to enjoying their love and family for the rest of it.

Keep reading for an excerpt from

NEVER DARE A
DRAGON

Available now from Sourcebooks Casablanca

"PRIDE OF MIDTOWN. NEVER MISSED A PERFORMANCE?"

Someone with a deep, sexy voice was reading the FDNY patch on Kristine Scott's dress uniform. She swiveled enough to see a dark-haired, devastatingly handsome Boston firefighter—a lieutenant, from the insignia on his uniform. He was admiring not only the patch but also *her*. She was tall, five-foot-ten, but he was taller.

The after-funeral crowd noise obliterated anything but close conversation in the firehouse, and yet she didn't mind his proximity. Not one bit.

"Yeah. I guess you wouldn't know what our motto means, being from Boston and all." She picked up a canapé from a long folding table.

He smiled—and, oh God, he had dimples.

"Enlighten me," he said.

She chewed and swallowed the little cracker before launching into her explanation. "We're located in Manhattan, close to Broadway but in an affordable neighborhood, so a lot of actors live in the area."

"Affordable? In Manhattan? Even a mere Bostonian like me knows that's like finding a unicorn in Central Park."

She chuckled. *Damn. So sexy, except for that hideous Boston accent.* "I work in the second-oldest fire station in the country. The area is known as Hell's Kitchen. Maybe you've heard of it?"

"Shit. Only as a horrible place where hundreds of thousands of immigrants died of nasty diseases."

"Yeah, that was a long time ago. We're becoming gentrified and fairly disease-free these days."

He looked her up and down. "Now there's a relief."

"And what is that supposed to mean, Boston?"

"Oh, nothing." He heaved a deep sigh. "You live in Manhattan, and I live in Charlestown—the part of Boston where Old Ironsides is docked. You don't care about that. The point is…it would never work." His sad smile spoke of resignation.

"Oh? Were you thinking of asking me out?"

That devastating grin of his returned. "Is there any chance you'd consider moving to Boston?"

"Ha! Nope," she said, trying to sound casual. Not that she'd date a firefighter *anywhere*.

"Then we have an insurmountable problem. I can't leave Boston because of family obligations. And you can't—or won't—leave New York. I guess we might as well break up now."

She hoped her disappointment didn't show, but she had a sinking feeling she didn't hide it well enough.

As if he'd just come up with a solution, he snapped his fingers. "I know. Since we can't date anyway, why don't we tell each other all of our annoying habits right off the bat? That way we won't worry about what might have been."

She couldn't help letting out a loud laugh. Probably

inappropriate after a funeral, and several nearby fire-fighters turned toward them. *Oops*. "Sorry," she mumbled.

"I'll start," her potential ex said. "I forget to floss about ninety percent of the time."

Playing along, she crossed her arms. "Ugh. That's disgusting. Don't you know that's the only way to brush between your teeth?"

He simply showed off his pearly whites and said, "Your turn."

"Okay... I wear granny panties."

"No way!" He cringed and recoiled. "Haven't you ever heard of that not-so-secret store? If we were dating, which we're not, I'd get you a gift certificate."

"Ah. There's another thing that would annoy me. I want to be accepted exactly the way I am."

He let out a snort. "You're not wrong, but a little sexy something for your man to uncover goes a long way."

"Hey. I'm a firefighter. You don't want to floss your teeth? I don't want to floss my butt—I'll leave that to the girls who slide down a different kind of pole."

He laughed "I guess it might be inconvenient on the job."

She shrugged one shoulder. "You think? Well... It's your turn again."

"Okay. When I'm home, I can be a slob. I leave my clothes in a disorganized pile," he said.

"That's ridiculous! You must have to keep your area at the fire station neat. Why not at home?"

He smirked. "Because I can. Your turn."

One of the nearby firefighters interrupted before she had a chance to respond.

"Hey, Jayce. If you're flirting, that's the worst I've ever seen."

He laughed and slung his arm around the other firefighter's shoulder. "This is my brother Gabe, who should be minding his own business."

"I was about to say the same thing as Gabe," another firefighter chimed in.

"And that's my brother Noah. Same goes for you, buddy."

The family resemblance was hard to miss. Tall, dark, and good-looking, every one of them. But there was something special about the one they called "Jayce." His brown eyes were darker—almost black, and full of mischief—and he had killer dimples. Suddenly she realized she and he hadn't even introduced themselves.

"So, is Jayce short for Jason?"

"Nope. My given name is J-a-y-c-e. And who have I had the pleasure of breaking up with?"

"My name is Kristine. Kristine Scott. They call me Scotty."

"Hey, Fierro!" a firefighter called to the group.

"Yeah?" the three men answered at once.

"Your dad and the chief are looking for you."

"Wait," Kristine said. "The firefighter we memorialized today was named Fierro. Are you related?"

"Yeah. He was my younger brother," Jayce said. "A probie."

"Holy fuck," she muttered. "I've been joking and laughing with the deceased's brother?"

"Guess so," Jayce answered matter-of-factly.

"How can you be so callous?" The words were out before she could think about them. *Oh well. Since we're being totally honest…* "It's a good thing we're breaking up before we even get started. That kind of insensitivity just blows." She found a hole in the crowd and stomped off before he could object.

He called after her. "Hey, pride of Midtown."

She stopped and turned around.

He sidled up next to her. "Do you know which is the oldest fire station in the country?"

She shook her head.

"You've been standing in it for the last fifteen minutes."

"How do you know I've been here for fifteen minutes?"

"I noticed you the minute you walked in." He grinned. "Can I get your phone number?"

Still miffed, she answered, "Yeah… It's 911."

He winked and then strode off, leaving her without the satisfaction of a dramatic exit.

How infuriating! But she couldn't help admiring his gorgeous ass as he walked away.

Leaving the firehouse, Kristine shivered in the January wind and made her way to her car in the Prudential parking garage. On the way there, she ran the gamut of emotions. Her outrage gave way to sympathy. She tried to give Jayce the benefit of the doubt. Some people coped with grief through denial. Maybe that was what he was doing. However, she had a feeling that wasn't all of it. He was too charming. Too polished. He seemed totally comfortable in his own skin. Usually that would be a turn-on. But today of all days?

Something was off about that whole funeral. The only one who seemed truly devastated was the firefighter's fiancée. She tried to be brave, but tears shimmered in the corners of her eyes. Occasionally her head dropped and her whole body shook as if she were literally racked with sobs, but no sound came out. She was a firefighter too—probably doing her best to be brave. *Just another reason to stick to my vow of not dating firefighters.*

And it wasn't just Jayce who was acting like it was a normal Tuesday and not the solemn day they were burying his brother. All the brothers she met seemed to be taking it rather well. Their only complaint about Jayce's flirting was that he was doing it wrong? *What the hell?* Of course, she wasn't inside the church during the service. Thousands of firefighters from all over the country attended, so only family members and those closest to them were allowed inside. Maybe they got their tears out there.

Still…smiling and joking? If that had happened at the 9/11 funerals, somebody would have been pounded into Ground Zero… Her mind was definitely boggled.

"Scotty! Wait," a familiar voice called.

She stuck her fist on her hip and waited for Donovan, the guy she had carpooled with. *Damn.*

"Jesus, Scott, were you about to take off without me?"

"Sorry," she mumbled. "I thought you could get a ride from any of the other hundred FDNY attendees."

"Well, it would have been nice if you'd told me that you were leaving."

She chewed her lip and popped the passenger side door open with her key fob. When they were both seated inside the tiny rented sports car, he scrutinized her.

"What's wrong?"

There was no hiding emotions from guys you lived with almost as much as your family.

"It's nothing." The universal code for *I don't want to talk about it*.

"Bullshit. Did the funeral hit you that hard? Enough to make you want to get the hell out of town without even telling me? Did you run into someone you knew?"

"No. Nothing like that."

"Then what?"

She backed out of the parking space, turning the rented Corvette toward the exit without explaining herself.

"Are you on your period?"

She stomped on the brakes. "You are never, ever, ever allowed to ask a woman that—ever!"

He leaned away with his hands up. "Okay, okay. Don't shoot."

She resumed her exit from the parking garage with a bit more speed than was prudent. Donovan glanced over at her a couple of times but didn't say another word.

———

Jayce and his brothers found their father and mother among the crowd. The chief was nowhere in sight.

"What did you want, Dad?"

"Me? Nothing. Why?"

"Miguel said you and the chief were looking for us."

The brother in question spoke from behind them. "I was saving your ass. Do you even know how inappropriate your flirting with a girl at your brother's funeral is?"

Their tiny mother stepped forward. "You were flirting with someone, Jayce?"

He heaved a sigh. "Yeah. I'm sorry. There was this

drop-dead-gorgeous redhead, or strawberry blonde, kinda golden-red—whatever—with the most incredible turquoise eyes... We got to talking."

"And laughing," Miguel added.

Jayce shot him an angry look designed to shut him up.

Mrs. Fierro placed a soothing hand on Jayce's arm. "Well, I'm not upset about it at all. I want all my boys happy, and that means settled down with a good woman." She glanced around at her fidgeting sons, except Miguel—the only married man in the bunch, naturally.

Mr. Fierro pulled Jayce closer so he could whisper, even though all of his supernatural sons could hear him. Obviously he didn't want their human mother to overhear. "You know I want to retire in the Caribbean, and your mama refuses to leave until you're all married off. Flirting is fine, but remember where you are. We're all aware that Ryan is alive, but no one else knows that, including Chloe."

Jayce glanced over to where his brother's fiancée, in her dress uniform, leaned against her own big brother, Rory. He seemed to be propping her up. Most firefighters had seen some horrors, but few had had to watch helplessly as the person they loved most burned to death in front of them.

"Whatever you do, don't let it slip to that poor girl," Antonio Fierro continued. "She's devastated, and we can't let her know Ryan has reincarnated. She'd never recognize him in his new form, and, well, you know what would happen..."

"Got it. Message received," Jayce whispered back. He stepped away and said, "I think I'll go to the restroom and see if I can muster up a few tears." Just thinking about what that cute NY firefighter said to him was enough to dampen his mood.

Mrs. Fierro smiled at her son as he kissed her on the cheek and excused himself. She had a not-so-hidden agenda, and all of her remaining sons knew it well. But the chances of finding a lover who could stand the shock of what he really was seemed slim to none. Some girls might like to know that if the worst happened, a blazing bird would rise from its own ashes—and several weeks later their lover would return to human form. But telling the truth about their supernatural natures could have devastating consequences. Ryan had learned that with his first fiancée, Melanie. The only reason she hadn't screamed it to the world was her fear of being locked up and labeled crazy.

The brothers had to avoid telling a potential mate until they were a hundred percent certain the love they shared was strong enough to survive such a revelation. Miguel had gotten lucky. Sandra adored him, and she always would. And as much as his mother teased his father, she'd throw herself on a sword for him. The Fierro men treated their women like the rare treasures they were.

Jayce bypassed the restroom and stepped outside. Some of his fellow firefighters were smoking. Knowing how many fires were started by unattended cigarettes, he thought the habit weird, but the stress of the job was too much for some to manage without a vice. He knew doctors and nurses who smoked too.

"Jayce!" His buddy Mike strolled over to him. "I know I said it before, but I'm really sorry about Ryan. He was a good man and, from what I've heard, a great firefighter. No one could have survived that backdraft."

"I know."

Yet somehow Chloe managed to survive. She had said she was thrown clear of the blast, but with two floors of a high-rise completely engulfed in flames, her escape was a miracle. Jayce didn't believe in miracles.

She said she had been knocked out and really didn't know how she had made it out alive. The theory was that she was thrown into the stairwell and had fallen onto a safe floor. When Ryan could tell his side of the story, they'd find out what really happened.

Even with a mystery like that to puzzle over, Jayce's mind kept returning to the beautiful, redheaded, granny-panty-wearing FDNY firefighter. He doubted he'd ever see Kristine again. If he did, she'd probably still think he was some kind of cold, heartless monster.

Mike squeezed Jayce's shoulder and wandered back to the butt can, where he crushed out his cigarette. When he returned he said, "There's a great buffet in there. Want to get a bite to eat?"

Jayce sighed. "I don't think I can."

Mike nodded. "I understand, man."

He really didn't. The firefighter brotherhood was good for understanding a lot of things, but only his biological brothers could possibly know what he was feeling right now. Fortunately there were a lot of them, so support was never far away.

As if conjured, Luca, the youngest Fierro brother, stepped outside. "Hey, Jayce. The captain is about to make a speech."

"Shit. Another speech?"

"I guess he didn't want to be outdone by the chief."

Luca and Jayce returned to the fire station where

Ryan and their father had worked. It was time for the brothers to brush up on their acting skills.

Acting. Everything reminded him of Kristine, even after only a ten-minute conversation. *What the hell is wrong with me?*

———

Two days later, Kristine was back to work at her fire station in Hell's Kitchen, back to studying for the lieutenant's exam. Her life seemed on track, but something was missing.

Her mind had returned over and over again to that bright smile and those dark eyes glinting with naughtiness. She kept telling herself to forget about the handsome Boston lieutenant. When he had mentioned her transferring to Boston, she had thought about it for all of one heartbeat. Then she remembered everything she would be giving up in New York.

If she went to Boston, she'd have to go through the fire academy all over again and start at the bottom rung as a probie. During their early days on the job, a firefighter was on probation, therefore the term "probie" became common slang, like "rookie" for a brand-new cop. The technical term was FFOP—Firefighter on Probation. That was no better. Either way, it seemed like a slap in the face after all she'd been through. And with only a few months left to finish her degree in fire science, she had a better chance for a promotion to captain or chief someday. Not to mention that her mother depended upon her half of the rent.

Years ago, Hell's Kitchen had been a tough neighborhood. Mother and daughter were dragons—not as vulnerable as humans, so they felt safe enough there. Then in the early '90s, the middle class began moving in and gentrifying the area. Kristine and her mother had lived there all that time and had watched their rent go up, up, up. With no father to help or pay child support, her mother had had to work two jobs—while pursuing an acting career. Kristine vowed she would never forget that. It still took two salaries to live there, but only one of them would be her mother's. Amy Scott had finally landed her dream job. She taught at a nearby acting school.

Even though Kristine had grown up among actors, artists, and writers, she hadn't inherited the need to express herself publicly. Despite being paranormally gifted, she had been a sheltered kid—and that was fine with her. As a little dragon, she'd never felt like she fit in. She was happiest when reading in her room overlooking Ninth Avenue.

She knew she wasn't supposed to talk about shapeshifting or demonstrate what she could do, ever. When she grew up, she realized there was something special she could do with her powers other than just protect herself. Because she was fireproof, she would make an ideal firefighter. She could protect her community.

She loved the job. Only a handful of women worked for the FDNY, and half of them were on ambulances. She was one of the few with the strength and fortitude to do the heavy lifting required of a firefighter on the front lines.

She had proven herself to be the equal of any man in her battalion. They respected her and depended upon her to have their backs. And as much as she cared about her fellow firefighters, she could never see herself falling in love with one of them. She would worry constantly, knowing what he was up against as a mere mortal.

One ordinary Thursday, her battalion was gathered around the long kitchen table, eating lunch and watching *Judge Judy* on the wall-mounted TV, when the tones rang out. They all rushed to their turnout gear, suited up, and jumped into their usual roles.

Kristine rode next to Donovan on the ladder truck. When the truck pulled up to the high-rise office building, smoke was pouring out of two large broken windows on the fourth floor. A police cruiser was already there, getting people to clear the area for the fire apparatus. So far nothing seemed unusual.

Kristine and Donovan followed the captain into the building to locate the seat of the fire. Alarms were blaring, and people were filing down the stairs. When the firefighters came to the fourth floor, they located the office they had seen from the outside. The captain pounded on the door and yelled, identifying them as the fire department.

When there was no response, the captain instructed Kristine and Donovan to take off the door with the ax and halligan bar. Two other firefighters from the engine company rushed up behind them hauling the hose. One of them broke into the firebox on the wall. As soon as the door was breached, flames shot out from the hole.

They had the right place.

When they got the door open, the captain barked out, "Scotty, stay with me. Donovan, go above and see if anyone is still up there."

"Yes sir," he said and dashed to the stairs.

The captain didn't need to tell Kristine to step aside.

When the pressurized water hit the fire, steam filled the hallway. The guy carrying the hose entered slowly, bathing the place in water. Between the smoke and steam, firefighters had to go in blind and look for survivors or people who weren't that lucky.

"Scotty, stay beside me."

Kristine followed the captain's orders, even though she knew he was in more danger than she was. He kept one gloved hand on the wall to avoid becoming lost. She placed a hand on his shoulder and walked a few feet to his right. Even a dragon could barely see through this.

Her foot hit something dense but soft. Squatting down, she felt a leg. "I've got someone," she said. Hauling the person up by the arms, she tossed his torso over her shoulder and made her way back to the door.

She heard the captain shouting into the radio that she was coming down and to have EMS ready. Something felt off about the body she was carrying. She had to adjust its position to account for an uneven distribution of weight.

When she finally made it to the street level, the EMTs were there to meet her, but as she emerged, their eyes bugged out of their heads.

"You're covered in blood!" the female EMT exclaimed.

She glanced down and saw that it was true. She squatted down, braced the victim's back with her hand, and gently laid the headless body onto the sidewalk. Startled, she jumped backward and gasped.

The cop who had been redirecting traffic ran over. "What the hell?"

The chief strode over and set his hands on his hips.

"As soon as we put the fire out, you can have your crime scene."

"Jesus," muttered the male EMT. "The coroner won't have any problem identifying cause of death."

The captain's voice crackled over the radio, alerting the chief that he was coming out with another body.

"You don't have to go back in there, Scotty. You've got to be pretty shaken up right now."

"No, sir. I'm fine. I'd like to go back in there and help where I'm needed."

The chief smiled and nodded.

On her way back in, she passed the captain, carrying a second body in the same condition. She didn't take the time to find out if he knew what was going on; she just rushed up the stairs faster.

I wonder where the heads are.

When she reached the fourth floor, the steam met her as soon as she opened the fire door. She rushed through it and worried about her mortal coworkers, who could be standing in boiling water.

If she had to shift, her thick scales would protect her, and her alternate form's wings wouldn't show because her turnout gear covered her up to the neck. She only had to worry about her snout protruding and interfering with her breathing apparatus. Fortunately, she wasn't huge like the dragons of Hollywood. She was five-foot-ten as a human or dragon.

The fire was almost out, and she could see that the walls of the room were still intact, as was the ceiling. Apparently they had stopped this fire from traveling very far. The building's sprinklers may have helped slightly. She suspected that the fire was meant to cover the crime scene—and that the location of the bodies would prove to be where the fire was set...deliberately.

Even in New York, this was unusual. Not that fires weren't accidents—faulty wiring, an unattended cigarette, deep-fried turkeys—oh yeah, plenty of accidents. They had their fair share of arson too, but it was usually to defraud an insurance company. Not to cover up decapitations.

As the smoke and steam cleared, she glanced around the room, casually looking for a couple of male heads. The other two firefighters seemed blissfully unaware of the unusual circumstances. Just thinking about it, bile rose to her throat. She didn't envy the cops their jobs, especially after something like this.

She couldn't help wondering if this sort of stuff happened in Boston too. It probably did, but maybe on a smaller scale.

Boston again. When would she stop thinking about what it would be like to be a firefighter in Boston, working with a particular sexy firefighter she couldn't seem to get off her mind?

About the Author

Ashlyn Chase describes herself as an Almond Joy bar: a little nutty, a little flaky, but basically sweet, wanting only to give her readers a satisfying experience.

She holds a degree in behavioral sciences, worked as a psychiatric RN for fifteen years, and spent a few more years working for the American Red Cross. She credits her sense of humor to her former careers, since comedy helped preserve whatever was left of her sanity. She is a multi-published, award-winning author of humorous erotic and paranormal romances, represented by the Seymour Agency.

Ashlyn lives in beautiful New Hampshire with her true-life hero husband who looks like Hugh Jackman with a salt-and-pepper dye job, and they're owned by a spoiled brat cat.

Ashlyn loves to hear from readers! Visit ashlynchase .com to sign up for her newsletter. She's also on Facebook (AuthorAshlynChase), Twitter (@GoddessAsh), Yahoo groups (ashlynsnewbestfriends), and ask her to sign your ebook at authorgraph.com.

I DREAM OF DRAGONS

Tempers flare and sparks fly in this dragon-shifter
series from award-winning author Ashlyn Chase

When Rory Arish and his two fiery dragon siblings are run
out of their ancestral Irish home, it seems their luck has run
out—until they arrive in Boston and find a paranormal-
friendly apartment building. There's only one problem: a
stubborn woman claims the apartment is hers.

Amber McNally needs this apartment. And not even
a fire-breathing dragon with Irish charm and scorching
good looks is going to scare her away. Holing up in their
respective corners, who will be the first to blink...or give
in to their off-the-charts chemistry and decide to make this
unorthodox living arrangement a little more permanent?

"This story has it all, laughter, tears, magic, and
sizzling heat."

—*Night Owl Reviews*, 5 Stars, Top Pick!

For more Ashlyn Chase, visit:

sourcebooks.com

MY WILD IRISH DRAGON

One job opening, two shifters = Sparks fly

Dragon shifter Chloe Arish is hell-bent on becoming a Boston firefighter. She knows she has to work every bit as hard as a man—harder if she wants their respect. Born into a legendary Boston firefighting family, phoenix shifter Ryan Fierro can't possibly let someone best him on the job. He'd never hear the end of it. When a feisty new recruit seems determined to do just that, Ryan plots to kick her out—until their sizzling chemistry turns explosive...

NEVER DARE A DRAGON

Dragon and phoenix shifters collide with fiery results
in the third Boston Dragons book

Lieutenant Jayce Fierro belongs to a legendary Boston
firefighting family of phoenix shifters. Hiding his true form
makes relationships impossible, so when he hits it off with
a fellow shifter and firefighter, he's thrilled. Less thrilling?
Finding out she lives in New York—three hours away.

Dragon shifter and firefighter for the NYC Fire
Department Kristine Scott can't stop thinking about Jayce.
She's determined to control the heat between them, but
when Kristine lands herself in a blaze of trouble, Jayce will do
whatever it takes to help…and prove he's worth the distance.

"A great addition to Chase's stellar library."

—RT Book Reviews, 4 Stars for *My Wild Irish Dragon*

For more Ashlyn Chase, visit:
sourcebooks.com